IPOs
for Everyone

The 12 Secrets
of Investing in IPOs

Linda R. Killian
Kathleen Shelton Smith
William K. Smith

John Wiley & Sons, Inc.

New York • Chichester • Weinheim • Brisbane • Singapore • Toronto

Published by John Wiley & Sons, Inc.

Published simultaneously in Canada.

This publication is designed to provide accurate and authoritative information in
regard to the subject matter covered. It is sold with the understanding that the
publisher is not engaged in rendering professional services. If professional advice or
other expert assistance is required, the services of a competent professional person
should be sought.

Library of Congress Cataloging-in-Publication Data:

Killian, Linda R.
    IPOs for everyone : the 12 secrets of investing in IPOs / Linda R. Killian,
  Kathleen S. Smith, and William K. Smith.
      p.   cm.
    Includes index.
    ISBN 0-471-39915-9 (alk. paper)
      1. Going public (Securities).   2. Investments.   I. Smith, Kathleen S.
  II. Smith, William K. (William Kevin), 1951–.   III. Title.

  HG4028.S7 K54 2001
  332.63'22—dc21

                                                                00-053174

Printed in the United States of America.

10 9 8 7 6 5 4 3 2 1

IPOs for Everyone is dedicated to individual investors who deserve the knowledge, tools, and access to the most exciting and challenging companies in the stock market—Initial Public Offerings.

Foreword

I first became intrigued by initial public offerings twenty years ago while working on my doctorate at the University of Chicago. Beginning as an assistant professor at the University of Pennsylvania's Wharton School and continuing at the University of Florida, where I am the Cordell Professor of Finance, I have tried to understand what makes the IPO market tick.

A long, long time ago, back in the 1980s, IPOs were esoteric securities that few people knew about. With the exception of an occasional highly touted offering by a young company with a name such as Apple Computer or Microsoft, one had to search through the back pages of the *Wall Street Journal* to find out anything at all about them. In the 1980s, the average price jump from the offer price to the closing market price on the first day was only 7 percent. In all of the 1980s, only seven out of more than two thousand IPOs doubled in price on their first day. Apple and Microsoft were not among the handful that doubled.

In the 1990s, the IPO market began to change. More than four thousand companies went public. The average first-day return tripled, to 21 percent. CNBC and CNNfn gave instant coverage to IPOs. New business magazines such as *Red Herring* and *The Industry Standard* devoted enormous coverage to IPOs. And in the late 1990s, the Internet bubble changed the IPO market dramatically. Web sites sprang up providing instant information on IPOs. In 1999 alone, 117 IPOs doubled in price on the first day. But with all of this attention, it became harder and harder for an individual to invest in IPOs.

Throughout the 1980s and early 1990s, Linda Killian, Kathy Smith, and Bill Smith toiled away on Wall Street, active participants in the IPO market. Then, in 1991, they formed Renaissance Capital to provide independent research on IPOs. Renaissance Capital was unique because it was not subject to the restrictive regulations or the conflicts of interest faced by sell-side analysts (those working for the investment banking firms that were selling IPOs). Renaissance Capital quickly developed a reputation for quality, independent analysis, and it attracted as clients many institutions that bought IPOs. The financial press picked up on the fact that these were knowledgeable, savvy IPO professionals. If there was a story on IPOs, one of the three of them, Linda Killian, Kathy Smith, or Bill Smith, was sure to be quoted.

I first came into contact with the folks at Renaissance Capital after they and I were quoted in the same *Wall Street Journal* article several times. I gave them a call one day, and after talking with them, it became clear that we shared a fascination with the IPO market. As practitioners, they were concerned with how to avoid the clunkers and identify the IPOs with upside potential. In contrast, my academic work tends to look for the "big picture" patterns, rather than trying to focus on the deal du jour. But sometimes, to understand how the forest grows, you've got to look at the trees in more detail. When I visited their Greenwich, Connecticut, offices and perused their research reports, I was duly impressed. Since then, I've gotten to know the folks at Renaissance well and have used their work as the basis for my own academic publications.

IPOs for Everyone is written by real pros. It explains how investment bankers price the issues and how they decide who gets shares and who doesn't. It offers tips on how to increase your chances of getting shares. *IPOs for Everyone* covers Internet and non-Internet IPOs and offerings by foreign companies, a sector of the market that is becoming increasingly important as the globalization of capital markets continues. It is a complete coverage of today's IPO market by the people who have been there and done that.

This book discloses what to look for when buying IPOs, by people who put their money where their mouths are. In late 1997, Renaissance

Capital started its IPO+ Fund, offering an opportunity for individuals to invest in IPOs via a professionally managed fund. To date, the upswings have been more frequent than the downswings. After reading this book, you'll understand why investing in IPOs is not for the fainthearted. Most importantly, you'll know how to move the odds in your favor.

JAY R. RITTER
University of Florida

Acknowledgments

Colleagues and friends have been generous with their time to help make *IPOs for Everyone* the best it could be. We would like to thank all of the Renaissance Capital research analysts who contributed anecdotes and comments. Valuable input from Paul Bard, Robert Finnerty, Ken Fleming, Melanie Hase, Peony Kao, Mary Lupo, and Randall Roth made *IPOs for Everyone* come to life. Thanks also to Renaissance staffers Linda Cummins, Deborah Iobbi, and Barbara Soldano for their support and encouragement. Spouse Timothy Thompson faithfully commented on the manuscript. Warren Greene and G. Peter O'Brien, two of the IPO+ Fund's board members, were patient reviewers of the text. Our agent, Rafe Sagalyn, guided us to our talented and enthusiastic editorial and marketing team at John Wiley & Sons—Joan O'Neil, Debby Englander, and Meredith McGinniss. Professor Jay Ritter provided us with insight and valuable historical statistics. Thanks to all.

LINDA R. KILLIAN
KATHLEEN SHELTON SMITH
WILLIAM K. SMITH

Contents

Exhibits

Introduction

Initial public offerings (IPOs) were long the well-kept secret of Wall Street insiders. But in March 1996 individual investors suddenly woke up to the power of IPOs.

That spring we were on vacation, flying at 30,000 feet over the Rocky Mountains to go skiing in Canada, when we got an urgent call from a *Wall Street Journal* reporter who had somehow tracked us down. The reporter said, "Yahoo!, the search engine, just announced that it is going to go public. Do you think it's going to be a hot deal?"

Hmmm. Now, the Yahoo! deal was weeks away. It had just filed with the Securities and Exchange Commission (SEC). But here was a reporter calling us on the airphone at 30,000 feet with all of the other passengers staring. "Yessss!" we shouted. "It's a hot deal! Yahoo!"

Yahoo! went on to be a legend among IPOs. It priced at $13 and swiftly rocketed to $33, up 154 percent, nearly surpassing previous records set by Home Shopping Network and Secure Computing. These 100 percent-plus returns have since been surpassed by the IPOs of VA Linux, Redhat, Brocade Communications, theglobe, and others. Before Yahoo!, there had been other much ballyhooed IPOs, like the Boston Chicken restaurant chain and Planet Hollywood, the once cool celebrity restaurant group. But the Yahoo! IPO galvanized the attention of individual investors because it was the first mainstream Internet company to go public. And it was an IPO known by a whole new breed of individual investors—online traders.

IPO stocks are different from other equities. An initial public offering is the process of taking public a company that had previously been private. At the time of the offering, the shares are given out to investors

I

who have told their broker that they wanted to buy in at the offering price. Most times, there is more demand for shares than there are shares to give out. An imbalance produces the Yahoo!-like returns. After the initial public offering, the new IPO trades freely on one of the securities exchanges, available for purchase by the public. This is called "aftermarket trading."

After Yahoo!, investor interest in IPOs erupted like a long dormant volcano. You couldn't read the morning newspaper, watch television, or listen to the radio without being bombarded with stories about IPOs.

Today's IPO market is like the opening of the American West over 150 years ago—the transcontinental railroad, the Gold Rush, and the availability of land made the opportunities seem limitless. If you look back through the history of the United States, you will see time and again how revolutionary technologies captured the excitement of the U.S. and European investing public. The building of canals in the early 1800s, the debuts of railroads in the 1830s and the telegraph in the 1840s, and the introduction of the Kodak camera in 1888 created excitement among U.S. and European investors that equals the interest in IPOs today. Investing in new technologies through IPOs is a way you can catch the future and monetize it in your portfolio.

The forces driving the IPO market of the twenty-first century are revolutions in technology, in the Internet, and in medicine. These advances are radically changing the ways we communicate, conduct business, and stay alive. Moreover, global economic and political reforms are opening up markets in South America, Asia, and Europe to new companies. And, as with the development of the American West, the first areas to be developed may not turn out to be the long-term winners. It wasn't the forty-niners sieving muddy water in the Sacramento Hills who made the big bucks in the Gold Rush. It was the immigrant Levi Strauss who made work pants out of denim and sold them to the forty-niners.

Investing in IPOs is very different from investing in familiar, large-capitalization favorites like IBM, Gillette, or Kellogg. With IPOs, you feel as if you are putting your money to work in building exciting new enterprises. And that's because you are. If you are fortunate enough to get IPO shares on the offering, your investment is going directly to a growing company.

IPOs are different from established companies in several significant ways. First, there is a lack of knowledge about the company and its management. Although an IPO must publish information about the company, its finances, and its management prior to the IPO, few investors avail themselves of the material, and even fewer study it fully. By law, underwriters are prevented from providing research prior to an IPO. So, investors have little to guide them, except their own opinions.

Second, a relatively small number of shares, typically under 10 million, hit the market all at once. On that first frantic day of trading, an IPO will have huge volume as day traders flip out of the stock, institutional investors lucky to get IPO shares fill out positions, and other investors wade in for the first time. Unlike a seasoned stock, an IPO does not come with a handy stock chart or a technical analysis to help determine trading patterns. Contrast that with the hundreds of millions of outstanding shares of IBM or Kodak. Finally, the IPO process is a mystery to most investors.

This book is designed to help you understand how to invest successfully in IPOs. Our credo is that knowledge, particularly specialized knowledge, gives you an edge. We'll give you that knowledge by sharing with you the "secrets" that we have learned over the years and by taking you behind the scenes of Wall Street's IPO powerhouses.

When we started Renaissance Capital in 1991, the stage was being set for a new IPO market that was different in terms of both the companies and the players. Renaissance Capital was the first research firm to focus on IPOs. Historically, IPOs have tended to be emerging growth companies. That was certainly true in the early 1980s, when many personal computer (PC) companies and biotechnology companies were launched. When the small-capitalization technology sector imploded in 1983 due to an oversupply of risky, little PC companies, financing for venture capital dried up. The venture capital companies, which gather funds from institutional and high-net-worth investors and use the money to buy interests in attractive private companies, had to rebuild their coffers and find new emerging growth companies to germinate. These new investments were focused on telecommunications, medical breakthroughs in less invasive surgery and genomics, and new consumer concepts.

New types of issuers were also considering the public equity markets. Big U.S. companies that had gone private in the 1980s through leveraged buyouts were now mean and lean through cutting costs. They were ready to shed their high-priced debt and to focus on growth strategies. European companies and governments eyed the U.S. capital markets. The Cold War was over, and Great Britain and other countries had elected no-nonsense free market leaders who wanted to privatize government assets.

And so were unleashed powerful waves of new emerging growth companies and established older corporations seeking equity capital in the U.S. IPO market. They encompassed every sector of the U.S. economy. IPOs were just as likely to be biotechnology companies as makers of ice cream. There was Eskimo Pie, a maker of ice cream desserts. There was St. John's Knits, the maker of upscale women's knitwear. Celestial Seasonings, the purveyor of herbal teas, was another notable IPO. Ladies' shoe seller Nine West, Dr. Pepper, and General Nutrition were all IPOs from the "Class of 1992."

European and Asian IPOs lent more diversity to the mix. Industrie Natuzzi, the Italian manufacturer of affordable leather furniture, debuted with much success. Ek Chor China, the Chinese bicycle manufacturer, was one of the first IPOs to come out of Asia.

We quickly realized that the IPO market had changed. It was far less risky than it had been in the past, and it was far more diverse. There were big companies and little companies. And the IPO market truly represented a broad swath of the global economy. Driving all of this IPO activity were entrepreneurs trying to raise capital to grow, government liberalizations in Asia and Europe, new concepts in retailing, and changes in telecommunications.

As the IPO activity continued, new investors began looking at the IPO market. For years, the IPO market had been the playing field of emerging-growth portfolio managers and knowledgeable Wall Street insiders. Now, a large-capitalization manager could buy the leading provider of next-day parcel deliveries by purchasing United Parcel Service (UPS), and an international manager could participate by buying Portugal Telecom or Industrie Natuzzi. As shown in Exhibit I.1, "The 10 Biggest U.S. IPOs," companies like AT&T Wireless have raised billions of dollars.

As you will discover in *IPOs for Everyone*, the Internet frenzy was

Exhibit I.1 The 10 Biggest U.S. IPOs

Company	Description	Date	Offer Proceeds (billions)
AT&T Wireless Group	Tracking stock of AT&T's wireless division	4/26/00	$10.6
United Parcel Service	World's largest package delivery company	11/9/99	5.5
Conoco	DuPont spin-off of its oil and gas subsidiary	10/21/98	4.4
Goldman Sachs Group	Global investment banking firm	5/3/99	3.6
Charter Communications	Fourth largest U.S. cable television operator	11/8/99	3.2
Lucent Technologies	AT&T spin-off of its telecom equipment business	4/2/96	3.0
MetLife	Provider of insurance and financial services	4/4/00	2.9
Infinity Broadcasting	CBS spin-off of its radio broadcasting arm	12/9/98	2.9
Fox Entertainment Group	Fourth largest U.S. television network and film producer	11/10/98	2.8
Pepsi Bottling Group	Pepsi spin-off of its bottling operations	3/30/99	2.3

Source: Renaissance Capital, Greenwich, CT (IPOhome.com).

another chapter in what is a predictable and repeating IPO cycle. Although there are many aspects to IPOs that some investors find problematic—the sometimes-bloated valuations, for example—normal day-to-day activity in the IPO market is spurred by entrepreneurs trying to turn their ideas into reality.

The IPO market in the early 1990s presented an enormous opportunity for us (the authors). Each of us had spent many years toiling in the canyons of Wall Street doing investment research, portfolio management, investment banking, and helping young companies raise money by doing IPOs. We met in graduate business school at the Wharton School in Philadelphia. Two of us, Bill and Kathy, are married; and Linda married another Wharton classmate.

Having worked on Wall Street for many years, we knew that the IPO market was a clubby place ripe for some fresh faces. We also knew that no one was providing investment research on IPOs. The reason? Federal securities laws prevent Wall Street firms involved in the offering from issuing research on companies that are going public for a period of time before and after the IPO. And so, IPO Intelligence, our research service, was born.

IPO Intelligence was designed to give institutional investors like mutual funds a thorough, independent take on each IPO that came to market. Our analysts pore through each prospectus to figure out what the company does, what firms it competes with, whether management is capable, and whether its business model is sound. We rank every deal according to four criteria: (1) fundamentals, (2) management, (3) valuation, and (4) stock momentum. We will share with you later our system for ranking IPOs.

Institutional investors want an independent view on Wall Street's IPOs because the underwriters are invariably positive, and IPO Intelligence quickly became the gold standard. Our research on IPOs is so highly valued by Wall Street pros that one portfolio manager suggested to us that we charge more money and restrict the research service to a small group of elite investors, a comment that sums up Wall Street's attitude toward IPOs in the 1970s, 1980s, and 1990s. IPOs were a secret guarded by Wall Street pros. Smart institutional investors knew that when companies went public, the lead manager (the banker in charge of the deal) would price the IPO lower than what might possibly be charged. This is done because many IPOs are new companies lacking long track records or because the company is issuing a large number of shares and needs to entice investors with a good price. The IPO "discount" has averaged about 7 percent to 25 percent over time. (A good friend of ours, Professor Jay Ritter of the University of Florida, has studies of IPOs going back into the 1960s that support this.) So, institutional investors know that over a relatively short period of time they will make 15 percent or more. The Street calls this "free money."

So Wall Street was very happy that the rest of the world mistakenly regarded the IPO market as a risky and esoteric dark outpost of the equity market. The Street and we enjoyed seeing the IPO market called a "sucker's game" because we knew it wasn't. Despite the fact that IPOs have made up 25 percent to 30 percent of all new equity capital raised in the United States since the early 1970s, they remained an insider's secret. Wall Street has a joke that IPO doesn't stand for *initial public offering*, it really stands for *immense profit opportunity* for *important people only*. It was a great time to be an IPO insider.

But things changed. In 1995, *Forbes* magazine ran its biannual IPO issue, which had traditionally excoriated IPOs as being dumb investments. But this time, *Forbes* reluctantly conceded that the IPO market produced above-average returns. And in 1996, the much heralded Yahoo! offering pointed the investing public's attention to the strong performance of IPOs. Since then, the IPO market has been a place of awe-inspiring one-day returns.

In 1998, five IPOs pierced the 200 percent barrier for one-day returns. But in 1999, 48 IPOs exploded through 200 percent on their first day of trading, with 8 producing returns of over 400 percent. Suddenly IPOs were on the front pages of newpapers and highlighted on television and radio. The investing public was in full cry, wondering how they could get in on the action. The insiders' secret was pushed center stage.

IPOs are an important part of the equity market. Not only do they make up nearly a third of all equity capital raised, but they represent the area of the most growth and activity in the United States and around the globe. Gillette doesn't raise equity capital, because it is not growing rapidly. However, Sycamore Networks, the fiber-optic telecommunications equipment vendor, and Amazon.com, the dot com that sells books and other products, are in the most dynamic parts of our economy.

Venture capital is also fueling the IPO market. In 1999, private money going into venture capital funds was $47 billion and for the first time dwarfed all other types of private equity investments. Venture capital investments in entrepreneurial companies are expected to reach $65 billion annually, ensuring many IPOs for the future.

For investors who want to be at the center of current economic activity, IPOs are the place to be. IPOs are a special segment of the broader equity market. They have distinct characteristics. Still, an investor must be forewarned that IPOs are a high-risk/high-return type of investment. IPOs shouldn't make up a large portion of a personal portfolio. But for many investors they are a way to diversify and to add value to a more traditional mix of stocks and bonds. Owning IPOs is also a way to ensure investment in the future.

Time and again, when new market opportunities arise, small, focused companies outwit large companies. This is not intuitive. The large company has too much to lose in its installed base, its employees who are used to an old way of doing things, and its legacy systems. Big companies are too afraid of mothballing their existing business and of channel conflict. Who was first to use the Internet to sell books? Old-line Barnes & Noble? No. Amazon.com. Was white-shoed auction house Sotheby's the first to capitalize on online auctions? No again. It was eBay. The list goes on.

These small companies stimulate change by capturing a share of the market and then by becoming real players, as MCI proved in its battle against AT&T. Larger companies are slow to address change. That's why the IPO market is the place to find the future market leaders.

Successful IPO investing requires special knowledge, focus, and high tolerance of risk. The good news is that powerful U.S. and global economic forces are creating a long-term trend for an enduring IPO market.

Renaissance Capital's philosophy of investing in IPOs is to seek out companies that have superior business models, managements whose interests are closely aligned with those of the investor, reasonable valuations, and sectors where the stock market performance of similar companies is strong. We do this by sifting through the material every prospective IPO must disclose before it goes public—the preliminary prospectus.

Our analysts are trained to look objectively at each company and to come to a conclusion based on the four criteria we mentioned earlier. At the end of every workday, we gather in our conference room to discuss the IPOs. We use a team approach in which each analyst has completed his or her report, working with one of us or with a senior analyst. The rest of the group reads the report cold, just like a client would.

We recently had a debate about a small company that provides automated information technology (IT) services to corporations. Our in-house IT guru came into the meeting. "Oh yes, this is a really good way for companies to save a lot of money and time," she said. "If something goes wrong with your computer, the program walks you through a self-help program." We debated its small size now versus its aggressive forecasted revenue ramp. Though the company's revenues to date were miniscule and it would have to run hard to make its $15 million projected revenues from its current $2 million per quarter run rate, we concluded it could do it.

"Never bet against a company's forecasted ramp," said one analyst. "Companies know what's at stake if they can't make it."

"A company has to have its numbers baked," observed another analyst. "They know what the consequences are."

In the end, we concluded that it was a better company than we had thought at first, and we boosted the rating.

The main reason for writing *IPOs for Everyone* is to share with you what we have learned about IPO investing from our years of researching IPOs and managing the IPO+ Fund (IPOSX). The beauty of IPO investing is that you, the individual investor, are largely on the same ground as the institutional investor. You have access to all of the important information. Picking good IPO investments is not like deciding to buy IBM. Hundreds of research analysts follow IBM. In the case of IBM, what edge do you as an individual investor have? None. On the other hand, Wall Street is prohibited from issuing research before the IPO and for a period afterward. And when the Wall Street analyst opines on a deal, it's always positively biased—always. If you follow our strategy, you will know more about that IPO than 99 percent of the investment community—including institutional investors. You will have the know-how and the tools to form an independent opinion. By learning the secrets of IPO investing and doing your homework, you will have an edge.

We started the IPO+ Fund, the first mutual fund to invest in IPOs, to address the needs of investors who don't have the time to do the work involved in analyzing and following their direct IPO investments and of people who prefer professional money management. The IPO+ Fund invests in IPOs purchased at the time of the offering and in subsequent aftermarket trading. We set the initial investments at a low $2,500 for a regular account and $500 for an individual retirement account (IRA) to make IPO+ Fund investing accessible.

To give individual investors access to timely IPO information, news, and statistics, we started IPOhome.com. If you visit our Web site, you can see the best performing IPOs and the worst performing IPOs, and you can keep up with pending IPOs through our calendars. IPOhome has all of the tools for successful IPO investing, and it also offers a focused chat board. The Web site is highly rated by *Forbes* magazine as "The Best of the Web."

Although reading *IPOs for Everyone* doesn't guarantee you'll get shares of white hot IPOs at their offering prices, it will provide you with the tools you'll need to have a chance at getting IPO shares. In Secret 2 we provide a step-by-step plan to improve your chances of getting IPOs. You will also learn strategies for investing in the aftermarket—when the IPO trades publicly. *IPOs for Everyone* will show you other ways of benefiting from IPOs—how to gain from the technology-driven economy and how to avoid the many landmines that come with the volatile IPO territory. You will be privy to little known "secrets" of IPO investing that we have learned over the years. After reading *IPOs for Everyone*, you will know more than your broker will, and you will understand what it takes to make money in the IPO space.

In *IPOs for Everyone*, we start off with descriptions of what IPOs are and who the major players are in the IPO market. In the third chapter (Secret 3), we share with you our approach to analyzing IPOs. The fourth secret is the most technical; it is a detailed analysis on how to mine a prospectus for its secrets. We cover the attributes of a good IPO and the failings of bad IPOs in the fifth and sixth chapters, respectively.

The remainder of the book provides further analysis on topics that we believe are important for an IPO investor to understand. Secret 7 focuses on Internet and technology companies, which are usually hard for nontechies to comprehend and value. We show you an approach to getting to understand their businesses and making sense of the valuations. The diverse and growing number of non-U.S. IPOs and stock markets focused on new companies is the subject of Secret 8. Because the management of IPOs is so critical to the stock's success, we devote the entire ninth secret to that subject. In Secret 10, we cover the trading patterns of IPOs. This is an important chapter to read if you are going to invest directly in the aftermarket. The eleventh secret presents our thoughts on where the IPO market is headed for the future and why IPOs are here to stay. The last secret completes *IPOs for Everyone* with a concise list of the best resources on IPOs and IPO investing.

The premise of *IPOs for Everyone* is that every individual investor deserves to benefit from the growth of the U.S. and worldwide economies through IPOs. Individual investors are capable of making their own decisions. The advent of the Internet has leveled the once supreme advantage of large, institutional investors.

We wish you well as you begin your journey into understanding the world of IPOs, and we hope that *IPOs for Everyone* provides you with the knowledge and ammunition for catching the IPO wave.

SECRET 1

How the IPO Market Works

It should come as no surprise that New York City was home to the first hot U.S. initial public offering (IPO). In the spring of 1791, the first Bank of the United States (BUS), which was the young American government's new central bank, began plans for a stock subscription to raise $10 million. When the stock subscription—what Wall Street brokers called IPOs back then—was launched in July, it sold out in an hour.

The lucky purchasers of BUS stock were the U.S. government itself, buying $2 million worth of shares, and the powerful, London-based Barings Bank, which scooped up the rest. The shares, priced at $100 each, quickly shot up to $185 before dropping back to $130 that September. Until BUS was forced to go out of business by the federal government in 1811, its shares were a popular speculative stock for New York's stock market participants, who traded shares at the Merchants Coffee House at the corner of Wall and Water streets.

The great success of the BUS offering spurred other entrepreneurs to organize banks and raise money. Following a pattern that would be repeated many times over the next three centuries, the first companies to go public in a particular business sector are usually the strongest, and they are quickly followed by weaker and weaker fry. The Bank of New York, today a staid New York institution, became the first company to trade on the new New York Stock Exchange (NYSE) in 1792. It became a favorite of the sharp-elbowed speculators who made up the

majority of NYSE participants. The ease of raising money drew in hus-
tlers, who launched issues of the Million Bank of the State of New York,
Tammany Bank, and others. The frenzy to buy bank shares was so high
that some of the banks were able to attract shareholders even though
they had no customers, branches, or deposits. The Internet phenomenon of profitless and revenueless companies isn't so new after all!

Alexander Hamilton, who was serving then as the first Secretary of
the Treasury and who had been instrumental in the creation of the Bank
of the United States and of the Bank of New York, worried about "un-
principled Gamblers," much as Alan Greenspan would later fret about
"irrational exuberance."

Prices of the bank stocks soared. During the 1790s, over 290 companies were formed, mostly banks and insurance companies. Inundated
by the flood of issues, suddenly people realized that many of these banks
were complete frauds. Investors panicked and tried to dump their shares.
When the dust settled, only the Bank of the United States and the Bank
of New York survived.

This scenario of greed followed by fear would be repeated time after
time on Wall Street. In 1817 it was canal companies. The Erie Canal
Company was the first to offer shares to the public. At the time, canals
were a major revolution in travel and commerce, dramatically reducing
the time it took to get goods to markets and allowing more products to
be transported. The Erie Canal, which was completed in 1825, connected
New York harbor, at the mouth of the Hudson River, to what would
later become Buffalo on the shores of Lake Erie. The canal vastly reduced the cost of shipping goods from the west to the east, made New
York the major East Coast port, and spurred westward migration. These
developments captured the imaginations of investors, and they scooped
up shares.

Just like the Internet revolution almost two hundred years later, the
success of the Erie Canal created a frenzy for other canal stocks. Offerings for the Blackstone Canal in Rhode Island and the Morris Canal in
New Jersey were vastly oversubscribed, with many more investors than
there were securities to give out. Investors didn't bother to look closely
at the business, its management, or its finances. Investors gave the
Chesapeake and Ohio Canal Company $22 million to build a canal that

was never completed. Within 10 years, the stocks of most of these companies were worthless.

It is worth examining this bit of history because IPOs have always been at the cutting edge of the economy. The Internet infrastructure companies of today are the railroads of the 1840s, the mining companies that came out of the craze that marked the 1848 California Gold Rush, the telegraph companies of the 1850s, and the electric companies of the 1870s.

Every public company started life as an IPO. Companies that would later become stock market behemoths were launched during these heady times. American Express and Wells Fargo, later to become giant financial institutions, came into existence as couriers delivering stock certificates and cash to and from the increasingly busy brokerage houses. The business evolutions of both those companies help put the public's fascination with Amazon.com and eBay in perspective. Companies that are long-term winners evolve over time, changing as technology changes. As a unique sector of the equity market, IPOs are situated in terms of risk and potential return between the high-risk venture capital companies and older, established companies. Exhibit 1.1, "IPOs—A Unique Asset Class," shows this risk/return profile.

It is also worth pointing out that the first to try to exploit a new opportunity are not always the first to claim success. The now defunct Internet retailers, who were the first to try to commercialize the World Wide Web, have predecessors in history. Most of the men who sieved muddy water in the streams of Northern California never really benefited from the California Gold Rush. Rather, it was the Bavarian immigrant who began selling them work clothes made of blue denim in 1853 who created wealth that has endured. Levi Strauss, in fact, did its IPO in 1971, over a century after its founding.

The greed-and-fear cycle of the stock market, with its booms and busts, is played out with much more intensity with IPOs. The feeding frenzy over Internet stocks in 1999 was just another chapter in the normal cycle of the IPO market. Hysteria develops over IPOs because of the known investment rewards of getting in early on new technologies. Demand is strong because the supply of shares is limited. At the beginning, the investment potential seems limitless. Investors see IPOs as a

Exhibit 1.1   IPOs—A Unique Asset Class

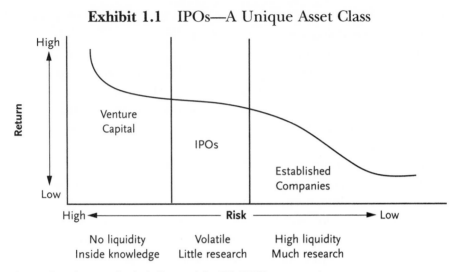

Source: Renaissance Capital, Greenwich, CT (IPOhome.com).

way to buy a ticket to the future. Weak, copycat IPOs force investors to look closely for flaws. And when they do, reality sets in. Then, just as bad money drives out good money, investors see flaws in *every* IPO and frantically dump them all.

This cycle happened with Internet retailing in 1998 and 1999. At first, companies that sold goods over the Internet were driven up to impossibly high valuations, as was the case with Amazon.com and eBay. And then Christmas of 1999 happened. Investors who owned the "e-tailing" stocks bought things from the companies and quickly realized that prices were high and fulfillment was dreadful. Investors watching television or listening to radio were barraged by commercials on no-name dot.coms. They realized they couldn't remember which ads were for what IPOs. The twin problems of poor execution and overspending with too little results caused investors to rethink their infatuation with e-tailers. And down, down, down, the stocks came. The pattern was *exactly* the same as it was for the bank stocks of the 1790s— when the dust settles, only the sound companies are viable.

This doesn't happen only to Internet retailers. In the early 1990s, the federal and state governments allowed Indian tribes to open casinos. Grand Casinos, which operated two Las Vegas-style casinos for the Ojibwe Indian tribe, was one of the first to take advantage of this new ruling in 1991. Then state governments up and down the Mississippi River relaxed gaming laws, spawning a new industry—riverboat gaming. In 1992, Casino Magic, which ran one Gulf Coast casino, went public with great fanfare. It was followed by President Riverboat Casino, which claimed to have the largest riverboat casino in the United States, operating out of Davenport, Ohio. Even tennis great Jimmy Connors was an investor. The floodgates really opened in 1993, when it seemed like anyone with a seaworthy barge, a few packs of cards, and a gambling license could go public.

Faced with an oversupply of small gaming operations, investors took a close look at what they had bought and didn't like what they saw. Mounting an IPO on the business model of having a single, small gambling barge was pretty risky. What about hurricanes? Ooops! Bad weather along the Mississippi and disaffected investors practically drove the smaller players out of business. Since 1993, the IPO market has not seen another gaming IPO from a legitimate underwriter.

IPOs are often cast by the media as the whipping boys of the stock market because of these experiences. However, speculation and frenzies over IPOs are created by people who participate in the stock market without knowing what the companies are doing, without studying them, without learning lessons from the past, and by letting greed overcome common sense.

Investors today have a much better chance of getting in on the IPO action. Years ago, the stock markets were rife with fraud. Luckily, ordinary people simply didn't have the money to buy even one share of stock. Incomes were low, and share prices were high. Information about companies was available only to groups of insiders. As recently as the mid-1930s, publicly traded companies routinely withheld critical financial and business information from shareholders. Today, the process of an IPO is more open and the Securities and Exchange Commission (SEC) is more vigilant against fraud than it was in the "bad old days."

The starting place to getting smart about IPOs is understanding the process of going public. An IPO is a privately held company that issues shares in a public stock market. In the United States that means the New York Stock Exchange (NYSE) or the Nasdaq. The NYSE is an auction market, where members of the exchange meet five days a week to buy and sell stocks that are "listed" on the exchange. To be listed, a company must meet NYSE minimum requirements for revenue, market capitalization, and profitability. Because of these standards, most IPOs are offered on the Nasdaq, which is a dealers' market. There is no established physical place where dealers gather to buy and sell over-the-counter (OTC) securities. Rather, individual dealers at brokerage houses make markets in particular stocks and post their prices electronically.

Although the U.S. equity market is the biggest stock market in the world, other stock markets are developing worldwide, specifically for emerging growth companies. Germany's Neuer Markt is one of the fastest growing. IPOs are becoming an even more important part of Wall Street as their numbers climb and the number of dollars raised grows. As seen in Exhibit 1.2, "Number of IPOs Has Boomed," and Exhibit 1.3, "Increasing Capital Raised by IPOs," these trends have been building for years.

WHAT KIND OF IPO?

IPOs come in a number of different flavors. First, there is the *plain vanilla IPO*—a company is privately held and mostly owned by management.

Exhibit 1.2 Number of IPOs Has Boomed

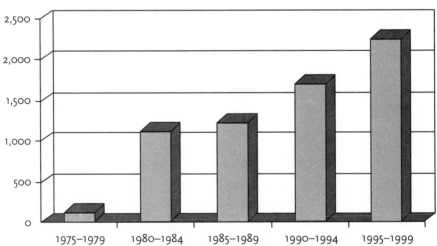

Sources: Renaissance Capital and Professor Jay Ritter, University of Florida.

Exhibit 1.3   Increasing Capital Raised by IPOs

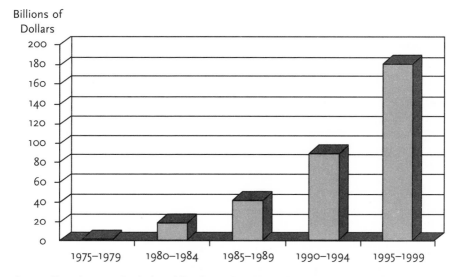

Sources: Renaissance Capital and Professor Jay Ritter, University of Florida.

The company has probably been in business for several years and is going public because management needs more money for expansion than they can raise privately. Until recently, the median IPO had been in business seven years.

Many IPOs are *venture capital–backed deals*—management has sold shares of the company to one or more groups of private investors in return for funding and advice. It used to be that a venture capital firm would let a company germinate in its portfolio for several years, get on the cusp of profitability, and then go public. Not so any more. Some IPOs are hurried through the process in months, which doesn't create the environment for a successful company. The supposed advantage to buying venture-backed IPOs is that experienced venture capitalists have vetted the company and have good contacts with major underwriters. It is regrettable that with the dramatic amounts of money flowing into venture capital coffers, decisions on funding are now more likely to be made by a stressed out, inexperienced young MBA.

Another type of IPO is a *reverse leveraged buyout* (LBO)—management uses the proceeds of the IPO to pay off the debt accumulated when the company was bought out, or LBO'd, as they say on the Street.

Reverse LBOs were common in the early 1990s as debt-ridden companies unburdened themselves of the high interest debt accumulated in the late 1980s. Reverse LBOs are examples of companies that need to recapitalize to pay off debt (to change the proportions of the underlying debt and equity on the balance sheet). During the 1980s, when interest rates were relatively high, companies like Revlon, Maybelline, and Playtex were acquired by takeover specialists who bet that they could chop expenses and refinance in a couple of years when interest rates went down. Gagging with high coupon debt, Revlon, Maybelline, and Playtex used the proceeds from the IPO to pay off the high-priced debt and to put in place lower priced debt. Reverse LBOs are generally disappointing investments to all but the creditors who are being paid off with the proceeds from the IPO.

Sometimes, a large corporation will "spin off" a noncore business to the public. A *spin-off* is created when a large company carves out a distinct, stand-alone part of its business and offers all or part of it to the public. A well-known spin-off was Lucent, which was the telecommunications equipment business of AT&T. The reason for the spin-off was that other telecommunications companies would be more likely to buy Lucent's products if it wasn't wholly owned by AT&T. By doing a spin-off, the parent company is able to shine light on what may have been a relatively small but profitable division. Sometimes the stock market's valuation of the spin-off increases the valuation of the parent, which usually retains some stock. Spin-offs have often times been excellent IPO investments. Though lacking huge first-day pops due to the large number of shares offered and the relative maturity of their business, the management of the spin-off is highly motivated to do well.

Tracking stocks have come back into favor. Unlike a spin-off, in which the parent company is actually selling a particular business to shareholders, tracking IPOs do not carry any of the actual assets of the business nor do the tracking shares have the right to vote. The tracking IPO is meant to "track," or to follow, the results of the business. A parent company may choose to issue a tracking stock if it wants to highlight the results of a particular division but retain ownership of the assets. A tracking stock IPO route may be the chosen structure also because the assets of a division are not easily separated from the parent company.

AT&T Wireless is a tracking stock, as are Sprint PCS and GM Hughes Electronic. Tracking stocks have been far less successful than spin-offs, largely due to the ownership issue. Often, tracking stocks have built-in conflicts with their parents, due to ongoing ties, the lack of asset separation, brand control, or competition.

An IPO can be a *privatization* of a government-owned company. For example, Deutsche Telekom and France Telecom were the IPOs done by the German and the French governments of their telecommunications operations. Most privatizations are non-U.S. However, if the U.S. government ever decided to sell the U.S. Postal Service, that would probably be a record IPO. When non-U.S. companies list in the United States, they do so by issuing American depository receipts (ADRs). ADRs are not the direct shares of the non-U.S. issuer but rather receipts issued by a U.S. bank and backed by the actual shares.

As the investing public has recently learned, IPOs can be *developmental stage* companies, lacking not only profits but products. Most of the developmental stage companies that investors will encounter are biotech operations with a drug or drugs that are still in advanced stages of clinical testing but close to winning government approval. The companies need additional capital for the final and most expensive stages of testing the drug before commercialization. The mapping of the human genome brought a new wave of less knowledgeable investors to this group, simply because of the huge opportunity genomics and its branches represent. These "scientifically challenged" investors are likely to dump the stocks at the first sign of disappointing results.

WHY GO PUBLIC?

A company's management decides to go public for a variety of reasons. The most obvious is *raising capital* to build its business. In the case of the Erie Canal or Motorola's ill-fated attempt to build a worldwide wireless satellite network called Iridium, the funds were used to build large, capital-intensive infrastructures. Many dot.coms, particularly retailers and business-to-business (B2B) companies, use the funds raised in the offering to publicize their brands through advertising and promotions. A private company may also go public to offer stock or options to motivate management. An IPO may be undertaken by a family-owned business to transition succession to professional managers.

There is always a certain urgency to go public. A company that is first to market in a particular sector has powerful ammunition its still-private competitors lack—cash and a publicly traded stock that can be used to grow the company by making acquisitions. Amazon.com, the first Internet bookstore, got a tremendous boost over its arch rival, Barnes and Noble, because it was the first to raise a significant amount of money. Even though barnesandnoble.com followed a year later with its IPO, barnesandnoble.com never caught up in terms of market share or publicity. Amazon.com was able to use its cash hoard to develop its business and its high stock price to acquire other e-tailers.

Sometimes companies have odd reasons for going public. When one CEO (chief executive officer) was asked why he was taking his regional bank public, he replied, "I'm getting a divorce and need the cash for the settlement." That type of candor is unusual.

The single worst reason a company goes public is to *cash out insiders.* This indicates that management and the owners have little faith in the future of their company. Insiders sometimes do it by selling stock directly in the offering. However, sometimes they cash out by paying themselves a big fat bonus right out of the proceeds of the IPO.

As one CEO summed it up in a survey conducted by the Investor Access Corporation: "Make sure you go public for the right reasons and at a realistic price."

THE BEAUTY CONTEST: PICKING AN UNDERWRITER

When a company decides to go public, management will meet with bankers from Wall Street brokerage houses to discuss how the IPO will be marketed to the public. This rite of passage is called a "beauty contest" because each of the bankers is competing for the business. (As you can see in Exhibit 1.4, "Key Dates in the Life of an IPO," this is the first step in the IPO time line.) The bankers will try to entice the management with promises of a high IPO price and ongoing research coverage. Sometimes the expertise of the underwriter's capital markets group, the people who will sell the deal to investors, wins the day. Sometimes the prospect of having a well-respected Wall Street analyst write research

Exhibit 1.4 Key Dates in the Life of an IPO

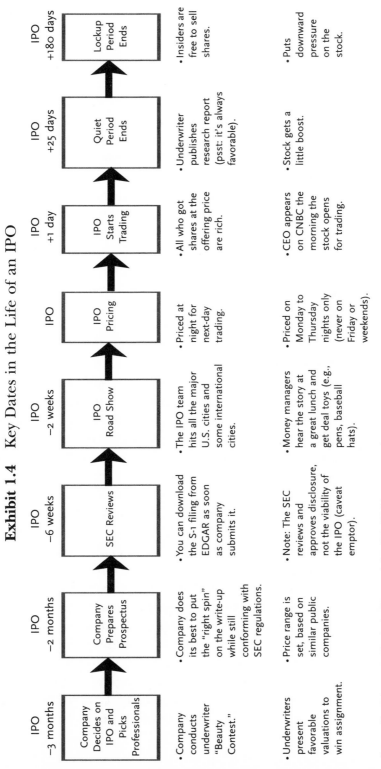

IPO −3 months	IPO −2 months	IPO −6 weeks	IPO −2 weeks	IPO Pricing	IPO +1 day	IPO +25 days	IPO +180 days
Company Decides on IPO and Picks Professionals	Company Prepares Prospectus	SEC Reviews	IPO Road Show	IPO Pricing	IPO Starts Trading	Quiet Period Ends	Lockup Period Ends
• Company conducts underwriter "Beauty Contest."	• Company does its best to put the "right spin" on the write-up while still conforming with SEC regulations.	• You can download the S-1 filing from EDGAR as soon as company submits it.	• The IPO team hits all the major U.S. cities and some international cities.	• Priced at night for next-day trading.	• All who got shares at the offering price are rich.	• Underwriter publishes research report (psst: it's always favorable).	• Insiders are free to sell shares.
• Underwriters present favorable valuations to win assignment.	• Price range is set, based on similar public companies.	• Note: The SEC reviews and approves disclosure, not the viability of the IPO (caveat emptor).	• Money managers hear the story at a great lunch and get deal toys (e.g., pens, baseball hats).	• Priced on Monday to Thursday nights only (never on Friday or weekends).	• CEO appears on CNBC the morning the stock opens for trading.	• Stock gets a little boost.	• Puts downward pressure on the stock.

Source: Renaissance Capital, Greenwich, CT (IPOhome.com).

on the company after the IPO is the deal clincher. Remember, the companies know that an essential part of the deal is that the research is always positive.

Brokerage houses develop special strengths through their research analysts or a specialized banking team that seeks potential IPOs. Large brokerage houses like Morgan Stanley Dean Witter, Goldman Sachs, Salomon Smith Barney, CS First Boston, UBS Warburg, and Merrill Lynch have deep benches. Because they have much experience taking companies public, they and other established firms usually apply certain standards of quality to the companies they are willing to underwrite. The operative word here is *usually*. Usually, the internal investment banking committees conduct due diligence (asking questions about the management and finances of the company). There are many on Wall Street who think that the Internet gold rush has led to a decline in standards.

Again, usually, the biggest, best-known underwriters get the best IPOs. Companies that are in the process of deciding who is going to do their IPO are concerned with how well the deal will be distributed, and they want to have ongoing research by the brokerage house's analyst. Every large brokerage house mans a research department with analysts who toil away issuing research and investment opinions on stocks. Brokerage houses compete for star analysts who are on the "*II*" team (an annual survey done by the industry rag, *Institutional Investor,* a magazine that ranks analysts in many industries). Mary Meeker, dubbed the "Internet Queen," is Morgan Stanley's lead Web analyst. It's every Web retailer's and B2B provider's dream to be followed by her.

It is a simple fact that underwriting IPOs is one of the most profitable businesses for Wall Street. On a $100 million technology IPO, an underwriter would gross about $8 million. The underwriters grossed over $400 million on the monster UPS offering. Faced with getting stock commissions of three to five cents a share on institutional trades and with the competitive pressure on the retail side from discount brokers, IPOs are critical to continued profitability and fat bonuses. Underwriting decisions are more influenced by what underwriters think they can sell to the public than by the quality of the company.

It used to be that when an IPO was launched, the lead manager (the underwriter running the deal) would invite other underwriters into a "syndicate" to help distribute the deal. These top managers would then bring lesser Wall Street firms in to be part of the selling group. Shares of the offering would be distributed among the firms, with the lead manager getting the most and the rest of the underwriters getting allocations according to their status. The syndicate would manage the offering, sometimes supporting the stock price in early trading.

That was the old days. Today, with profits paramount, oftentimes the lead manager keeps all of the shares or only doles out a small percentage of the deal to other underwriters. The lead manager is the underwriter on the upper-left-hand side of the list of underwriters found on the front page of the prospectus—but not always. There are times when the lead manager is lead in name only and one of the other managers is actually calling the shots. Wall Street can be a funny place. The bottom line is that the lead manager controls the deal and decides who gets the shares.

Although it is time-consuming, individual investors should pay attention to what's called the "league tables"—the lists of leading underwriters published at the end of every quarter in the *Wall Street Journal* and the *New York Times*. These tables will give you a good idea of how active a particular underwriter is and, more important, how well its deals have done. Beware of underwriters with bad track records. Bad track records mean the bankers have poor judgment in picking IPOs or fail to do their due diligence.

Also, a bad track record can mean the underwriter is too small to get a crack at the good deals. IPOs that are underwritten by small or regional brokerage firms should be looked at very cautiously. Although there are a handful of midsized brokerage firms like William Blair, which is known for its niche of underwriting mid-Western companies, there are many other inexperienced wanna-bes. Often, an IPO that is underwritten by a small brokerage firm was rejected by the more established players.

A small brokerage firm lacks the distribution of the major underwriters, and it also probably lacks a research department. So, even if the company has stellar results, there is no analyst to toot its horn, and the company falls by the wayside.

An IPO should have at least two underwriters. If a small brokerage firm sole manages the deal, the IPO is suspect for two reasons: First of

all, the offering may not be a genuine distribution to the public. There
are occasions when an IPO like this is simply traded among that
underwriter's brokers, who artificially boost the price with each trade.
This is called a "house stock." Second, with only one underwriter, no
other underwriter has any incentive to provide ongoing research.

VENTURE CAPITALISTS

Venture capitalists are playing an increasingly important role in determining which entrepreneurs receive private funding and, thus, which
companies are cultivated to the point of being ready to go public.
Venture capitalists raise funding from private investors, including pension plans and wealthy individuals. These monies are put in a partnership run by the venture capital firm and then invested in promising
start-ups. Venture capitalists diversify their investments so that if they
have a nasty surprise with one or two companies, it won't destroy the
investment returns.

Among the most active and successful venture firms are: Softbank
(invested in Buy.com, Critical Path, Net2Phone, GeoCities); Chase
Capital Partners (StarMediat, Kozmo.com, Lycos); Benchmark Capital
(eBay, Scient, eLoan); Oak Investment Partners (TheStreet.com, Exodus); Sequoia Capital (Shockwave); Austin Ventures (Southwest regional
technology companies); New Enterprise Associates (3Com, WebMD);
Norwest Venture Partners (Peoplesoft, Vantive); Polaris Venture Partners (Aspect Medical); and J. H. Whitney (Wellfleet Communications,
Compaq). Old-line firms include Kleiner Perkins, Mayfield Fund, and
Bessemer Venture Partners. Many of them are located on the now famous Sand Hill Road in Menlo Park, California.

To give you an idea of the magnitude of the influence of venture
capitalists, venture funds raised $4 billion in 1993. In 1999, that figure
had mushroomed to $47 billion. Venture capital fund-raising topped
$65 billion in 2000, with most of that going into Internet-related
companies.

Entrepreneurs seek out venture capitalists because they provide easy
access to significant amounts of money, more than the traditional "angel" investors of friends and family can provide. In turn, the venture

capitalists exact their pound of flesh by taking significant ownership in the company. To hedge against the risk that the start-up turns out to be a dud, the venture firms demand shares at dirt-cheap prices.

The venture capitalist's focus is always their "exit strategy." They want to be able to IPO the company or, failing that, to merge it with another company. Venture capitalists can't sell their stock for about six months after the IPO, so they are most anxious to get in at a low price, to have a good deal, to liquidate their holdings, and to move on to the next opportunity.

Young companies used to incubate for several years in venture firms. When the management and the company were ready for prime time, the venture firms would shop it around to Wall Street underwriters. With the Internet stampede, the process often takes months, not years, and the main function of the venture firms is to serve as a talent scout for start-ups. These days, some venture firms have an "entrepreneur in residence," someone who has previously run a company and who is waiting for the right start-up to come along.

The last time the venture capital business was white hot was in the early 1980s. Leading companies such as Cisco, Microsoft, and Sun Microsystems were funded. Fed by a boom in personal computers (PCs), peripherals, and software, inexperienced partners gave money to many dubious start-ups. Too much money chased too many look-alike technology companies. The inevitable shakeout happened, and the industry took 10 years to recover.

The venture capital world used to be a very clubby place. There was a handful of old line firms in California on Sand Hill Road, in Boston, and in New York. Today, the venture capital business has more money than it knows what to do with and legions of young turk new competitors. The old-line firms complain bitterly about the tactics of what they call "junior varsity" venture firms who steal deals at the last minute by taking the entrepreneur on a ski trip—that sort of thing. This is what happens when there is too much money sloshing around and too many eager venture capitalists. The investments don't get the attention they deserve. Instead of giving an entrepreneur a few years to develop the business, the venture firm's priority is getting the company processed to do its IPO. Too many me-too deals get done. Too many inexperienced venture capital guys are financing too many inexperienced entrepreneurs. You have to wonder why venture capital money guys with MBAs from Ivy League schools would throw money at companies like Ingredients.com, which competes with at least 50 other beauty-related sites, or VarsityBooks.com, one of legions of sites and stores selling textbooks to college kids.

Eventually, the IPO market turns against the venture capital companies and the entrepreneurs. The whimsically named WebSideStory, a Silicon Valley Web-site traffic analysis firm, couldn't get its deal done, despite the backing of well-known venture firms. Investors were turned off by its small size, shaky revenue model, and insider payouts. When deals go down in the dumps, as Internet retailers and the B2B companies did in the spring of 2000, investors are not going to want to throw more money at people who made bad decisions and at entrepreneurs with no track records. It may mean that entrepreneurs who actually have sound business plans for Internet retailing and B2B cannot get funding. What it means for investors is that they cannot trust the pedigrees of the venture capital firms as a proxy for good business and investment judgment, especially when coffers are overflowing with cash.

THE PROSPECTUS

So, having selected its underwriter, the IPO-to-be proceeds to work with its lawyers and bankers on the offering documents that it will file with the Securities and Exchange Commission (SEC). During this process, the underwriters and lawyers perform further due diligence. The product of all this work is an S-1 (or F-1 if the company is based outside of the United States). The S-1 has reams of information on the terms of the IPO, the number of shares to be offered, the company's business, and its financial statements. You can get a copy of this document at the SEC's Web site, edgar.gov, or at freeedgar.com. If you want to track filings, IPOhome.com has calendars of upcoming deals and of IPOs that have just filed with the SEC. For any upcoming or recent IPO you can easily link to the exact S-1 you want through IPOhome.com. Just search by ticker or company name, and you will get a brief company profile. On the bottom of every profile, there is a link taking you directly to the company's S-1 filing.

At this stage the SEC reviews the S-1. It is important to emphasize that the SEC does not *approve* the IPO; it reviews the prospectus to make sure the company has disclosed specific information about its financial position, business, risks, and management. Once this review is completed, the company will get a green light to publish and distribute what's called a preliminary prospectus—the "red herring," so-called because of the red band of legalese running vertically on the left hand side of the prospectus cover. A copy of the red herring can be obtained from the lead manager.

Just by being current on IPOs, you are way ahead of the rest of the pack. You have time to read the S-1. And you have plenty of time to make your interest known to your broker, if it is an underwriter.

PRICING THE IPO

Pricing IPOs is as much an art as it is an objective dollars-and-sense exercise. To figure out what the prospective IPO is worth, Wall Street bankers act just like real estate agents. If you are selling your house, realtors look at the selling prices of comparable houses in your neighborhood to establish an offering price. If your house is in a development built by the same builder, their job is easy. The differences between the houses may be slight. However, if the houses in your neighborhood were built at different times or are vastly different in size, the agents' job is harder.

IPOs are much the same. Instead of houses, the bankers look for companies similar to the prospective IPO. On Wall Street, these companies are called "comparables," or comps. Sometimes the job is easy. When Ralph Lauren went public, it was a snap to look to Tommy Hilfiger, St. John's Knits, and Warnaco as similar companies. The bankers then ask the research analyst to forecast revenues, earnings, and cash flows. They compare these statistics to the revenues, earnings, and cash flows being forecast by the research analyst in consultation with the IPO's management.

Using the forecasted growth rates of revenues, earnings, and cash flows, the bankers compare the IPO to the already public companies. They ask themselves if the IPO has a better or a worse brand, better or worse growth rates, and better or worse prospects. If the IPO is in a strong position, as was Ralph Lauren, with respect to its brand and the buzz surrounding the pending IPO, the deal may be priced at a higher price, usually based on price-to-earnings (P/E) ratios, relative to its peer group of the already public companies. If the IPO is a third- or fourth-tier player in the market, then the IPO will be priced at a discount to its peers.

It may seem obvious, but it is still worth stressing—the choice of comparables by the bankers can have a major impact on investors' acceptance of the proposed valuation of the IPO. For example, suppose the pending IPO is a biotech company doing research in genomics. The bankers would choose the hottest stocks in the sector, not the laggards, even if the laggards' businesses are closest to the IPO's business. That's Wall Street. Their job is to sell the deal, not to seek the truth.

Most of the time, investors docilely accept the proposed valuation, simply because most of them don't do independent research. If you are interested in an IPO, ask your broker what the comps are. If your broker doesn't know, have him or her call headquarters or talk to the research analyst. Most large brokers have highly organized procedures for doing IPOs, and the "selling memorandums" containing information about the deals, including comparables, are readily available. Be pushy. When you get the information, use your common sense to evaluate whether the banker has chosen the right comps.

The bankers set the price that's printed on the front page of the prospectus at the time they send the prospectus to the printer. Markets go up and markets go down, so the ultimate price of the IPO can be higher or lower. Also, if the drumbeat on the IPO heats up as a result of a great road show reception or rising stock prices of its peer group, the price can wind up being higher.

GETTING THE WORD OUT

The company's management is eager to go out and tell their story. Legally, they have to stick with the script in the prospectus. Few do. Management pitches the IPO at the road show breakfasts and lunches and at one-on-ones, meetings at which elite prospective investors get to grill management in private. They speak about their company's future and answer a few questions. More important, the Wall Street research analyst will opine about the company's revenue and earnings prospects.

One company, Webvan, an online grocer, let members of the press into its road show and then openly talked with reporters about information that wasn't in the prospectus. After the press published the interview, the SEC forced Webvan to delay the deal.

The road show process normally takes about two weeks. It starts with a "teach in" at the underwriter's headquarters, which is usually in New York. At these meetings, management makes their presentation, and the analyst runs through his or her financial model. The questions at these in-house meetings are often tougher than those at the actual meetings with prospective investors will be. Brokerage salespeople tend to be blunt and ask tough questions because they don't want to stick their important institutional customers with a bad IPO. Management makes any necessary nips and tucks in their presentation after the teach-ins and then may do a few key one-on-ones with elite investors to get the buzz going on the deal.

A large IPO that has U.S. and non-U.S. *tranches* (amounts of stock that are set aside for particular countries) can take longer. If the underwriters plan to sell the deal internationally, the next stops are London, Edinburgh, and Glasgow. And with the dramatic mergers of European stock markets, more IPO managements will be making the trip across the Atlantic and to the Frankfurt and the Paris bourses. Tokyo is an occasional stop, too.

On returning to the states, management may make a few more New York stops, due to the high concentration of large institutional investors. Then it's on to Los Angeles, San Francisco, Minneapolis, Chicago, Philadelphia, and Baltimore. Road shows almost always stop in Baltimore because it's the headquarters of mutual fund powerhouse T. Rowe Price. The next-to-last stop is Boston, home to giants Fidelity and Putnam. The last stop is New York for the big lunches and dinners in the five-star hotels.

Normally, only institutional investors are invited to the road shows, which take place in private hotel dining rooms. When the IPO market gets very active, bankers and investors joke that the only bottleneck to more IPOs is the availability of hotel dining rooms. These occasions can be elaborate. For example, celebrity designer Donna Karan appeared at the New York road show when her company went public and handed out goody bags of Donna Karan accessories for the invited. After cookie maker Keebler's packed New York luncheon, attendees were given duffle bags full of Keebler cookies and toys. We took extra boxes of Cheez-Its and Chips Deluxe back to the office at the request of our hungry staff.

The attraction of the adult goody bags handed out at the road shows means that analysts always have to be vigilant. At the Martha Stewart road show, large pastel canvas bags were handed out to attendees. The bags contained many Martha goodies, including magazines, cleaning instructions, a hat, and other items. In conversation with another attendee, our analyst spotted a man snatching up her goody bag off her chair and then furtively scurrying down the hall to the elevators. She took off in full pursuit and caught him at the elevator bank; but at five-feet-two-inches tall, she wasn't strong enough to wrest the bag away from the six-footer. So she took someone else's bag. Eat or be eaten.

The New York road show for the World Wrestling Federation was nearly a carnival. Voluptuous, scantily dressed women strutted around the hotel ballroom. Some of the male featured wrestlers were present. The normally staid Wall Street investment crowd was gaga. Many of them came prepared with cameras and asked for autographs. During the Q&A (question-and-answer period), one analyst asked Vince McMahon, the tough-talking CEO, how he was going to deal with the recent departures of featured wrestlers to rival World Championship Wrestling owned by Time Warner, which had recently acquired Ted Turner's Turner Broadcasting System. "I'd love to talk with that S-O-B about it," he responded, referring to Mr. Turner.

Instead of having to deal with these free-for-alls, elite investors get invited to one-on-ones. Other settings may be small private dinners, usually staged at private clubs. When Revlon went public, they had such a dinner, but the main attraction wasn't CEO Ron Perelman; it was several of the well-known fashion models who attended. Trying to unfairly influence the heavily male Wall Street crowd, perhaps?

As a sidelight, in the 1980s there was a big controversy about the locations at which these meetings where held. Many Wall Street houses favored having them at the private clubs to which the upper management of the brokerage firms belonged. Big problem. Many of these clubs didn't admit women. Sometimes the female bankers or investors had to enter the clubs through the back or kitchen entrance and scurry up the stairs to the meeting room.

With all of this road show activity, you might reasonably ask how institutional investors find the time to study each company. The answer is that they don't. Company managements complain that there are too many companies going public for investors to be knowledgeable. With hotel dining rooms crammed with competing IPOs, how does an investor decide which ones to go to? Basically, the institutional investors go to the presentations given by the companies with the most predeal buzz and maybe the best goody bags. Packaging the IPO is all important.

Regrettably, individual investors and members of the press are not invited to road shows. The process of attending road shows used to be very casual. Just about anyone in proper business attire could walk in. But fears of SEC scrutiny and increased demand to attend the limited-seating road shows forced underwriters to restrict attendance and to check guest lists carefully.

Feeling pressure from small institutions and high-net-worth individual investors, many underwriters have started Web road shows. These Web presentations almost always have the actual presentation given by the company's management. Some even have the live audio. However, access to this information is restricted by the SEC, so many underwriters won't give out the Web addresses and passwords to individual investors who don't have a certain threshold of assets at the brokerage.

Back to the road show. The IPO has just finished that last big New York road show. It's late afternoon, and the management team collects at their underwriter's headquarters to await the actual pricing of the deal. The stock markets close at 4 P.M. New York time. The price negotiations are about to begin. It took them six to eight weeks from filing with the SEC to get to this point. They're excited because many of them are about to become paper multimillionaires. They want the best deal they can get.

LEAVING MONEY ON THE TABLE

Management and their bankers are at IPO ground zero, the capital markets desk. By this time, the management is exhausted by the non-stop road show regimen but also more exhilarated than at any other time in their lives because they are on the brink of achieving wealth beyond their dreams.

At the capital markets desk, the managing directors of the under-writer review the key institutional indications of interest; this is called the "pot." They and the management go over the totals from the less well heeled institutional investors. If a portion of the deal will be sold to individual investors, then they review those orders from the retail sales force and from the co-managers. The head of capital markets discusses the orders with the heads of institutional and retail sales. Capital markets is effectively the middleman between the investors, who want the price to be as low as possible, and the company, which wants a higher price. All the head of capital markets wants is a successful deal.

As the former head of a major underwriter says, "IPOs go up, or they go down, they rarely stay stable. It's not in the nature of an IPO."

The capital markets desk and management work well into the evening. If the capital markets desk think that they can raise the price of the issue, they call around to key investors to see if they're still in the deal. Lesser investors are not called; they are informed the next morning if they got shares and what the price is.

The advent of the Internet changed the ways that IPOs are priced. The huge one-day pops on Internet stocks increased the stakes of getting IPO shares and made the process increasingly competitive. It also made it more difficult for the lead manager to gauge the real demand for an IPO. This is because investors, knowing that they will get a tiny amount of what they ask for, place orders many times greater than what they really want for hot deals.

One of the early Internet IPOs, theglobe.com, an Internet commu-nity that allows people to create their own Web sites and that was dreamed up by two Cornell University undergraduates, was originally set to price at $11 to $13 per share by its lead manager, Bear Stearns. However, because the market for both IPOs and small-capitalization stocks was rocky in late 1998, theglobe.com was priced at $9 in November 1998. Trading in the stock opened at 11 A.M. at a staggering $90 per share. What happened?

When Bear Stearns started marketing theglobe.com to investors, the stock market was still reeling from the near collapse of Long-Term Asset Management, a Greenwich, Connecticut-based hedge fund started by well-known Wall Street "rocket scientists." Shortening the tale a lot, the portfolio managers grossly misplayed computer-driven models for betting on interest rate movements and came close to causing a short circuit in the world capital markets. Only massive financial infusions from large Wall Street houses and the help of Federal Reserve Chairman Alan Greenspan staved off disaster.

So Bear Stearns knew that institutional investors were ultra cautious. And, they also knew that theglobe.com's founders, Todd Kriselman and Stephan Paternot, then 25 and 24 years old, respectively, were eager to price the deal and raise money. So did they get cheated by raising only $28 million when the public was willing to pay $90 per share for the 3 million shares offered, or $270 million? Was money left on the table?

These strange differences in pricing are part of the wonderful world of Internet stocks. Both Bear Stearns and theglobe.com had every reason to push the price up as much as they could. However, given the orders Bear Stearns had from institutional investors on the eve of pricing, the bankers decided it was better to have a successful deal than one that was aggressively priced. Indeed, under ideal circumstances, the offering price is set so that the IPO will trade above its offer price.

Sentiment on Wall Street can change in a flash. On the morning of the pricing, institutional investors decided that this deal was a winner and plunged in with aftermarket orders. And individual investors, excited by the deal, told their brokers to buy the stock. Many investors went through online brokers. Most of these buy orders from individual investors were "market" orders. All of these orders created a huge wellup of demand for the stock. The quoted stock prices were forced upward just as if a dam had broken. And, as is so common during episodes like this, the upward spiraling stock prices created even more demand. Many investors, able to get instant gratification by buying online, put in market orders; having to pick up the phone to call a broker often allows time for some reflection.

Again and again, this scenario was repeated in late 1998, all through

1999, and into 2000, as investors flocked into Internet IPOs. Was money left on the table? Theoretically, yes; but practically, no. Both the management and the underwriter want the IPO to succeed. So, they underprice a deal a little. That way the buyers of the IPO get compensated for the risk they are taking by owning an untested, new company. That's only fair. And the benefit to the company is that stockholders are happy. The positive returns from a successful IPO mean a lot to management in terms of branding and good publicity. Besides, they have only sold a small percentage of the company. If the IPO does well, they can come back for another round to raise more capital and sell insider shares in what's called an "add on financing."

As the industry veteran scoffs, "Money on the table? That's a convenient way for someone to second-guess you a couple of days later. It's advertising money."

One final observation about the process of going public. It is very time-consuming. The management of the company are focused on selling themselves, first to the bankers, then to the research analysts, and finally to the investors. They are not focused on their business. Smart managements set their business up to run on autopilot for six months.

THE POWER OF RESEARCH

Before an IPO is public, the management of the company and the underwriters are in what's called the *quiet period*. The SEC prevents the underwriter from issuing any research on the company and restricts management's comments to what is contained in the prospectus.

But 25 days after the IPO, the Wall Street underwriters can issue a research report on the IPO. And these research reports are always glowing paeans to the bright prospects of the company, the ability of management, and its focused business strategy. We have never seen a negative research report issued by a brokerage firm on a deal it has recently underwritten.

When companies go public, they typically have the next two quarters of revenues and earnings locked up by shifting the timing of booking revenues and expenses. And the company has sat down with the underwriter's research analyst to critique his or her model of the company's financial results for the next one to five years.

This information is made available to the institutional investors in the IPO prior to the actual offering. After all, if you didn't have a forecast of what the company's expected revenues and earnings are going to be, how can you value the IPO?

At the end of the quiet period, the analysts issue their reports. These reports typically don't have much long-term effect on the stocks. However, with some thinly traded OTC stocks, the market makers who buy and sell the stock try to goose the stock price about the time they expect the report to be issued. Institutional investors know that these initial research reports are always positive and contain little in the way of surprises, either positive or negative.

Even when the IPO in question has a problem early on, Wall Street research generally glosses the problem over and looks to the bright side. For example, Loislaw.com, an Internet-based provider of state and federal legal information, went public in late 1999. It competed directly against Westlaw and Lexis, both of which are large, well-established providers of case law and regulatory information to law firms. Enthusiastic investors pushed the stock up from its $14 offering price to a high of $47. Then, four months after going public, management announced that revenues would rise to $2.3 million for the final quarter of 1999, up 95 percent from $1.18 million the previous year.

Sounds good? Not really. That's because the key analyst was expecting more. And, the next day the analyst reduced the rating from a Strong Buy to a mere Buy, lowered the 2000 revenue estimate by 25 percent, and remarked that "revenue is taking longer to materialize than originally expected." Despite the dramatic reduction in the financial forecast, the analyst concluded that Loislaw's "land grab" (attempt to wrest market share away from competitors by giving product away for free) was the "right" strategy.

As in every case where an IPO disappoints Wall Street within months of its debut, the punishment was severe. Loislaw stock immediately dropped to the low twenties and then continued on its way south. Institutional investors apparently decided that Buy really meant, Sell, Sell, Sell.

If you are an investor at a full-service brokerage firm, you should insist on getting that firm's research on IPOs once they are out of the quiet period. Many discount brokers allow you access to Wall Street research for a fee. Other ways to obtain Wall Street research are highlighted in Secret 12, "Finding the Right Resources."

The entire IPO process, from finding an underwriter, drafting a prospectus, and meeting with investors to finally pricing the IPO, can take six months. Companies treat the process with much respect because it is time-consuming and may cost 5 percent to 7 percent of the funds raised plus up to $2 million in legal, printing, and accounting fees. That's $7 million to $9 million for a $100 million deal. They also know, or should have been told by their venture capitalists or underwriter, that the future of the company hinges on how well management presents itself during the IPO process and how well the company meets the expectations it laid out during the road show.

Now that you understand the IPO process and players, you will be able to position yourself to get IPO shares.

SECRET 2

The Way Wall Street Works

Why You Can't Get IPOs and
What You Can Do about It

I want my IPO! When telecommunications giant AT&T spun off its wireless division, AT&T Wireless, in April 2000, it rectified an omission it had made when it spun off equipment manufacturer Lucent in 1996 in a highly successful offering. This time, AT&T set aside a portion of the wireless offering for employees.

Dazzled by the returns of other initial public offerings (IPOs), AT&T employees drained individual retirement accounts (IRAs), pushed up their credit card limits, and borrowed money from family to get shares in what turned out to be the largest U.S. IPO ever—$10.6 billion. They were emulating what the employees/shareholders of shipping giant UPS did in 1999, taking advantage of the public offering. Regrettably for the AT&T employees, the wireless offering drifted below its IPO price for months after the offering. This was perhaps due to the telecommunications giant's much publicized problems in its long distance division, which were announced after the wireless offering.

Nevertheless, the AT&T employees acted like serious investors everywhere. They would have had to be blind and deaf not to know the power of IPOs. Awesome first-day debuts for Internet IPOs have aroused the global investing public. Their demand for IPO shares is unparalleled in intensity and longevity. The odds were highly favorable for AT&T's wireless division to be a success.

The IPO stars were what galvanized the AT&T employees: VA Linux up 698 percent on its first day of trading. theglobe.com up 606 percent. Foundry Networks up 525 percent. WebMethods up 508 percent. FreeMarket up 483 percent. Exhibit 2.1, "The 10 Biggest First-Day Pops," shows the 10 biggest first-day pops (sharp increases in price). With returns like these, competition for IPO shares is fierce. Wall Street has long referred to IPO allocations as "free money." IPOs are free money because getting shares of an IPO virtually insures a gain. It's free because you didn't work to get it. As legendary speculator Jacob Raskob said many years ago, "Everybody ought to be rich."

Despite the great returns and the hoopla, individual investors are left at the starting gate in the race to get IPO shares. And despite the fact that individual investors own about half of U.S. stocks, institutional investors and very high net worth investors, not individuals, get 70 percent to 80 percent or better of IPO allocations. This doesn't seem fair, but that's the way Wall Street works. Wall Street rewards its largest, most active clients with shares of IPOs. Individual investors are simply not able to deliver the millions of dollars of commissions that are the admissions price of getting IPO allocations. Individual investors are justifiably frustrated at not getting IPO shares and not understanding why they don't get shares.

Even among institutional investors there is a pecking order. At the very top of the roost is mutual funds giant Fidelity Investments. It's common knowledge on Wall Street that Fidelity demands at least twice as many shares as the next biggest allocation. Other IPO heavyweights are Janus Capital, Invesco, Putnam Investments, and Wellington Management.

An individual investor might reasonably conclude that to get IPO returns they should invest in the mutual funds of these giants. But these mutual funds are so large that the IPO effect is muted. And the giants manage many mutual funds, so they can't funnel IPO allocations into just a few funds. The other portfolio managers would howl. They want their IPOs, too!

Renaissance Capital's IPO+ Fund is solely focused on buying IPO shares on the offering and in the aftermarket. Because the IPO Fund is an institutional investor, it is able to get better allocations of IPO shares than would an individual investor acting alone. Other aggressive growth

Exhibit 2.1 The 10 Biggest First-Day Pops

Company	Description	Date	Increase
VA Linux	Linux-based software and services	12/9/99	698%
theglobe.com	Operates online communities	11/13/98	606
Foundry Networks	Networking products for enterprises and Internet service providers	9/28/99	525
webMethods	Licenses XML-based software that integrates enterprise applications	2/10/00	508
MarketWatch.com	CBS-backed financial Web site	1/15/99	505
FreeMarkets	Business-to-business online auctions of industrial materials	12/10/99	483
Cobalt Networks	Makes Linux-based Web servers	11/5/99	482
Akamai Technologies	Offers optimized Internet content delivery	10/29/99	458
Cacheflow	Makes Internet caching appliances for Internet service providers	11/19/99	427
Sycamore Networks	Makes optical networking equipment	10/22/99	386

Source: Renaissance Capital, Greenwich, CT (IPOhome.com).

mutual funds also invest heavily in IPOs. Morningstar, the mutual fund rating service, occasionally ranks mutual funds by their IPO holdings.

Yet the Wall Street system of handing out precious IPO allocations makes some sense. The Securities and Exchange Commission (SEC) wants to make sure that Wall Street is giving out IPO allocations fairly. Basing IPO allocations on the amount of commissions generated by investors is certainly an objective way of doling out IPO shares. However, it fails to take into consideration other factors that are important to the performance of the IPO and to the long-term success of the company.

Both the management of the IPO and the underwriters want to place the IPO shares in the hands of long-term holders, not institutional investors who will "flip" the stock within the first few hours of trading. Depending on the IPO, management and the underwriters may want to diversify the shareholders among large institutions, smaller institutions, and individuals. The management of the company certainly wants its shareholders to be knowledgeable about the company and committed to it as an investment. If the IPO is a retailer, selling products directly to individuals, management knows that the event of its IPO is a chance to build brand loyalty and to reward its customers.

When HomeShopping Network went public back in 1986, the bankers at Merrill Lynch told the chief executive officer (CEO) that demand was so strong he could boost up the price of the offering. However, he declined, saying that a pop in the stock was a way to reward loyal customers. A good return on an IPO is an advertising cost—investors with a nice gain in the stock were more likely to think favorably about buying his product.

Stock ownership is evenly split between institutional and individual investors. The managements of companies are aware of this. What they are not aware of is that individual investors are far more loyal to the stocks they own than institutions are. But somehow, at the time when the underwriter is allocating IPO shares, this very important attribute of the individual investor largely gets ignored.

This all being said, there are ways of bettering your chances of getting a piece of the 20 percent of IPO shares that, at best, is set aside for retail investors. Key to your strategy is where and how you do your brokerage business. The first requirement of IPO allocations is having a brokerage account. If you are just getting started or are moving an account, the purchase of an IPO cannot be the first transaction in a new account. We get hundreds of calls from investors wanting to get in on an IPO who don't have a brokerage account. Our first question to them is, "Who is your broker?"

STRATEGY 1: USE A FULL-SERVICE BROKER

You need to first decide who your broker is going to be. Which Wall Street investment house will best position you for IPO allocations? You need to have an account with the lead manger to have a good shot at getting IPO shares. If your brokerage firm is not an active underwriter, your chances of getting an IPO allocation are absolutely nil.

Institutional investors have accounts with many brokers. Very large institutional investors may trade on a daily basis with 30 different brokerage houses. The IPO+ Fund, too, has accounts all over Wall Street. But as an individual investor, you don't want accounts all over the Street. The paperwork would be impossible, and your assets would be spread too thinly. You need to concentrate your assets.

If you have significant assets, you might want to establish an account with one of the top underwriters' private investors group. Morgan Stanley Dean Witter, Goldman Sachs, Merrill Lynch, CS First Boston, and Salomon Smith Barney all have special portions of their brokerage sales force devoted to what they call high net worth individuals. These groups receive allocations of IPOs to hand out to their brokerage clients. The difficulty with this strategy is that the barrier to entry is high: most of these groups require a minimum of $5 million in liquid assets.

If you are fortunate enough to fall into this elevated category, press your broker on how many shares are actually allocated to his or her department. Question your broker on the timing of IPOs, and ask for projections of revenue and earnings. If your broker doesn't have the answers, that may mean that he or she is out of the loop on IPOs. If this is indeed the case, you must balance your loyalty—if any—to your personal broker against your desire to better your position to get IPO shares.

The single greatest edge that individual investors have in getting IPO shares is relating knowledge of the process to the practicalities of getting IPO allocations. Companies may indeed want their shares in the hands of individual investors, but it's the Wall Street bankers who are calling the shots. Knowing how the IPO process works is the starting point for strategies to increase your chances of getting IPO allocations. Even if you are not a high net worth customer, as a full-service account, you are still valued by the brokerage firm. You have chosen to stay with a full-service broker because you expect, well, full service.

Look at the amount of IPOs your brokerage firm is doing. If your goal is getting some shares on the offering, the only way you are going to accomplish this is by being with a firm that does a fair number of IPOs. With recent consolidations in the industry, there are now a handful of national brokerage firms. These firms do the bulk of the IPOs. Before you set up a new brokerage account, ask around. What are the broker's policies on allocating IPOs? If you have a relatively small account and the brokerage house's policy is to allocate strictly by commission volume, you probably aren't going to get allocations. Some brokerage houses use a strict commission rating system to decide what customers get IPO allocations.

However, if you are a long-standing customer of a large brokerage firm, you may find it helpful to have a candid discussion with your broker. Ask him or her why you aren't getting any IPO shares. You may discover that the problem lies not with you, but with where you are within the brokerage firm.

Allocations between institutional investors and retail investors vary from deal to deal, depending on what the company does and on the size of the offering. A rule of thumb is that 70 percent to 80 percent of the deal goes straight to institutional. On the hottest deals, the percentage is higher. The rest goes to high net worth individuals and to regular retail investors. Dividing up the retail side of the shares to be allocated is straightforward. Remember how the allocation process works: The powerful institutional investors' orders go into the shared "pot," and their allocations are made from the pot. Retail orders are made to each branch office by the capital markets desk. As the capital markets veteran explains, "First, the allocations go the highest producing offices. Second, they go to the best brokers. And third, they get divvied out to the best commission generating customers."

Most retail brokers are fairly low on the IPO food chain. If your broker is in the Altoona or Albany office, he or she is unlikely to have much access to IPOs. In fact, the entire office may fight over a measly allocation of 100 shares. The bigger the office, the more likely it is to get IPOs.

If your brokerage office is low on the IPO chain, there is another way you can get shares: Consider earmarking a certain percentage of your portfolio and moving those assets to an online broker. As we discuss in Strategy 5, the allocation process of online brokers may give you a better shot at IPOs.

If your broker is a big deal in a low-ranked office, there is still some hope—become important to your broker. You can accomplish this by having a high volume of transactions on which your broker earns commissions. Or, you can be a source of knowledge and information to your broker. If you regularly track the timing of IPOs by using the calendar at IPOhome.com and you study the prospectuses using our approach, you will be more knowledgeable about IPOs than your broker. Your early research on IPOs will permit you to place orders for IPO shares (called indications of interest) early in the process. Even if the office is getting the measly 100 shares, your chances of getting the shares are higher if you were first in line to place an order.

You can be on top of the IPO calendar by going to IPOhome.com and checking out our calendars. The IPO news will also keep you up to speed on new filings, price changes, and other items of interest.

STRATEGY 2: FIND OUT IF YOU ARE A FRIEND OR FAMILY

Another way to get IPO shares works for the lucky few. There is a category called "friends and family," which are quite literally the friends and family of company management. If you know someone who works at a pending IPO or if you are an important customer or supplier, you might possibly be able to get shares. Some underwriters will bow to management's desires to give out stock to friends and family. However, many large underwriters will disregard management's wishes unless the CEO or the president makes a strong case for a particular person.

STRATEGY 3: MAKE ASTUTE AFTERMARKET ORDERS

If you get IPO shares, buying more at the market price will get you brownie points with your broker. And make sure he or she is paying attention to your aftermarket purchases. However, as in any purchase or sale, make sure that the valuation is right and that you want to own the shares.

Regrettably, on some of the very hot IPOs, demand from institutional investors is so intense that the individual investors largely get "blanked," or shut out. There's not much you can do about that. However, you can be smart—and careful—about aftermarket purchases. For example, demand was high for the Ralph Lauren IPO, and underwriter Goldman Sachs priced it over the stated range on the prospectus. Aftermarket purchases drove it higher. At this point, knowing that Ralph Lauren was much more expensive than similar stocks, like Tommy Hilfiger, many institutional investors sold. But, the buzz on Ralph Lauren was so strong that it became a mark of status to be able to say that you owned Ralph Lauren; so some individual investors bought in on the highest prices of the day. They never saw those prices again because the stock drifted back to earth.

Wall Street brokers sometimes take advantage of individual investors on hot IPOs. Knowing that the deals are hot, they will call their clients telling them that the stock is moving up, which it is, preying on the individual's burning desire to be a part of the runup. If you get a call on a hot IPO to buy it in the aftermarket right after it prices, the chances are that you are buying the stock flipped by the brokerage firm's institutional investors. Think very carefully about giving in to the desire to own a hot stock.

The only time individual investors are courted by underwriters selling an IPO is when the deal is a dud. If you get a call from a broker singing the praises of a particular offering, the underwriters probably couldn't find enough institutional investors to swing the deal, and they are counting on the gullibility of individual investors. You should question the motives of the broker and scrutinize the IPO closely. If the broker really pressures you, the deal is probably a huge turkey. The only circumstances under which you would even consider taking the shares is if you get an ironclad guarantee from the branch manager that you can immediately sell the shares if the IPO is a turkey and that you will get shares of an upcoming hot IPO.

In tough IPO markets, underwriters have a hard time getting deals done. If you have analyzed the deal and come to a positive conclusion about its quality and valuation, you may be able to pick up IPO shares at big discounts. During periods like this, equity market psychology is bleak, making the purchase of any equity a scary decision. But the prices of the IPOs reflect that. For example, after the big Internet run-up in 1999, the valuations of Internet and other technology stocks collapsed in the spring of 2000. Nevertheless, there were a number of technology and biotechnology companies that were primed to go public. For example, Praecis Pharmaceuticals, which is developing treatments for hormone-related diseases, had its price dropped from a range of $15 to $17 to $10. To get the deals done, the underwriters had to chop the asking prices in half. At such times you can place orders for IPOs and often get them filled. Furthermore, if you are working with a full-service broker, you may develop a reputation as being a smart investor. And it is possible that your brokerage firm will reward you occasionally with small allocations of hot deals when the market starts improving.

STRATEGY 4: TRY A REGIONAL BROKER

Another way to get in on IPOs is to use a high-quality, regional brokerage firm like William Blair or Dain Rauscher Wessels. Firms like this are specifically added as co-managers in the underwriting because the IPO itself may be regional or because the regional firm's bankers have a relationship with the company. The regional firm may also have a top analyst who is expected to follow the IPO. The IPO's management wants the regional firms as co-managers, and thus it is likely that the regional firms will have stock specifically to allocate to individual investors.

STRATEGY 5: USE A DISCOUNT OR ONLINE BROKER

If you work with a discount or an online broker, bear in mind that the traditional, full-service brokers still get the bulk of IPO shares. However, Charles Schwab, DLJ Direct, E*Trade, and Fidelity Investments have well-publicized programs for IPOs.

Each of these large brokers has agreements with active underwriters to provide a certain amount of IPO shares to the discount brokers, who in turn allocate the shares to their customers. In these arrangements, the online broker is actually acting as an underwriter and is listed on the prospectus.

E-underwriting, as it's called, is in the early stages of development and accounts for no more than 5 percent, tops, of IPO allocations. The amount is small because the traditional firms have no difficulty distributing IPOs to hungry institutional investors and thus have little incentive. However, the parents of the online brokers have other relationships with the big Wall Street firms, and some of the big Wall Street firms are hedging their bets by investing in the online enterprises. These relationships have helped the e-underwriters to carve out arrangements for underwriting IPO shares. For investors willing to open an online account, the access to IPOs may indeed be greater, and the process is certainly more democratic.

Each of the online underwriters posts the upcoming offerings and disclosure materials on its Web site. Investors get to indicate their interest in IPOs electronically. Charles Schwab makes a point of making sure that its customers download the prospectus. (Charles Schwab and Fidelity also participate in traditional underwriting syndicates and make IPO shares available to their discount brokerage customers.)

The process of establishing IPO eligibility is similar for each broker. And although the individual firms won't go into detail about how the ultimate allocation decisions are made, the decisions are more objective because, by the nature of a discount broker, you don't have a relationship with a particular individual or office. So you are able to bypass the best-office, best-broker, best-customer approach that eliminates so many individuals.

To get IPOs through Charles Schwab, customers must have $1,000,000 in assets with Charles Schwab, or they must make 48 trades a year and have $50,000 in assets. Schwab's approach is egalitarian. A spokesperson from the company explained that because so many of their customers are in California, they are knowledgeable about technology companies and very tuned in to IPOs. "Our approach is to make sure as many customers as possible get 100 shares of an IPO. We do this instead of giving 1,000 shares to our very best customers." With Schwab, if you miss out on one IPO, their method of allocating shares takes that into consideration on the next offering, according to the spokesperson.

Schwab has had alliances with CS First Boston, J.P. Morgan, and Chase H&Q since 1997; but they are moving to generate their own supply of IPOs through a partnership with Epoch Capital Partners, which has backing from two other discount brokers, T. D. Waterhouse and Ameritrade. Epoch also has the backing of experienced venture capitalists Benchmark, Trident, and Kleiner Perkins. The idea is that Schwab's customers will have access to the IPOs that come out of Epoch.

Without overstating the amount of IPO shares that online investors are likely to get, this is an innovative approach for investors to get access to IPO shares without being dependent on the big underwriters, who have a vested interest in sticking with the old way of doing things.

E*Trade does not have any minimum account size necessary to participate in the program. All E*Trade asks is that the customer have sufficient cash to pay for 50 shares of the IPO. E*Trade has the most democratic process: it allocates the shares randomly. However, customers who have histories of short holding periods receive lesser allocations, and customers who own the shares longer get larger allocations. The IPOs come from relationships with Goldman Sachs and Robertson Stephens.

E*Trade has teamed with Wit/Soundview to offer access to IPOs through E*Offering, which was once a competitor that received financing from E*Trade. E*Offering also has backing from other brokers and well-regarded venture players General Atlantic Partners, SOFTBANK Venture Capital, and Battery Ventures.

Fidelity sets the gate a bit higher, requiring customers to have at least $500,000 in assets at Fidelity or to be an active trader. Fidelity has an alliance with Lehman Brothers to access IPOs.

Each of the online brokers has a policy against flipping (see the next section). Most require that customers hold the IPO shares at least 30 days or face punishment. Flippers in E*Trade's program are denied IPO access for 60 days. Other online brokers are harsher and forever kick a flipper out of their IPO program.

W. R. Hambrecht, which is associated with E*Offering, has truly tried to democratize the IPO process by using a Dutch auction to price IPOs. Under this method, investors make bids on IPOs, and the IPO is priced at the highest price that will sell all of the shares. W. R. Hambrecht underwrote Ravenswood (a vintner), Salon.com (a network of content sites), and Andover.Net (a provider of Linux products). Of the three, only Andover.Net produced strong returns early on. Apparently, both companies doing IPOs and investors prefer the traditional method, which often produces the large, first-day jumps in price.

For individual investors, using a Dutch auction would be a much fairer way to allocate shares. Indeed, if investors placed orders at what they thought the company was worth, the IPO could pull in more proceeds. However, powerful Wall Street participants have little interest in democratizing the IPO process because so much money is at stake.

It's hard to firmly land on how many IPO shares are going to online brokers. Certainly, demand outstrips supply for nearly every IPO. The online brokers won't divulge what percentage of their customers get IPO shares. However, the relatively egalitarian means of allocating IPO shares to customers is a big step forward from the best-office, best-broker, best-customer approach of the traditional brokers.

STRATEGY 6: KNOW THE RULES

Both traditional brokers and discount brokers discourage the practice of *flipping*, or selling IPO shares immediately after the offering and reaping a quick profit. Some people try to outsmart the brokers by setting up new accounts when an existing one is tagged for flipping. But this is a lot of work.

Traditional brokers who do a lot of IPO business will subtly let you know what their firm's sensitivities are. They may care somewhat less than online brokers about flipping, particularly if the stock has risen a lot. But even with a traditional broker, if you flip every IPO you get, it doesn't look good and you will get cut off the "A" list.

Another thing you should know about is *penalty bids*, which underwriters use as a way to discourage its brokers from allowing customers to sell IPOs prematurely. If you get shares in an IPO that has a penalty bid and you sell those shares, your broker doesn't get a commission. In some of the worst cases, brokers have been known to refuse to sell customers' IPO shares or to not answer the telephone. Several state securities watchdogs are looking into the practice.

In contrast, institutional investors flip with relative impunity. Institutional investors centralize their purchases and sales of securities through the Depositary Trust Company or through a prime broker. Every night these organizations take all of the purchases and sales made by institutional investors through every Wall Street firm and make sure the transactions are posted to the right accounts and credited to the correct brokers. So, if an institutional investor does get an IPO allocation and wants to flip it, the investor would not sell the shares through the underwriter. Rather, it would sell through the "side door" (one of the many firms that specialize in dumping IPOs). Although the underwriters electronically track IPO sales, the tracking isn't perfect, and it is done for only a limited time. With a really hot IPO, the underwriter may be very happy to buy back the shares, usually selling them to a retail investor.

STRATEGY 7: BUY INTO INCUBATORS

Another way to receive IPO allocations is to buy the stocks of incubators. These are companies that act partly as venture capitalists, by purchasing private start-ups and assisting them with their business until they are ready to do an IPO. The incubators also own the shares of companies that have already done their IPOs and are publicly traded. The interesting thing about the Internet incubators is that when one of the privately held companies is IPO'd you get an allocation of the IPO.

When U.S. Interactive and Opus 360 did their IPOs, parent Safeguard Scientific allocated shares of the IPOs to shareholders of Safeguard Scientific. Other incubators are CMGI and Internet Capital Group. Owning these stocks, which hold diverse portfolios of many Internet companies, is one way of indirectly having a portfolio of Internet and technology IPOs.

However, the downside of owning Internet incubators is obvious.

Their valuations are totally dependent on the valuations of the companies in their portfolios. In ebullient times, the prices of the incubators were sky high. However, as investors became skeptical about owning Internet stocks, the incubators became "incinerators," in Wall Street parlance, falling dramatically in price. The top of the market for Internet incubators was when the curiously named divine interVentures did its IPO in July 2000. With most of its investments in development stage, a change of underwriter, and a downsized valuation, investors were not anxious to pony up money in a weakening dot.com market. The deal had difficulty pricing and even more difficulty in the aftermarket. Of course, if you believe in the long-term survival of the underlying companies, the strategy of buying incubators while they are down might pay off in the long run, as long as the companies in incubation go public. Expect incubators to make a comeback in the next up cycle.

STRATEGY 8: WATCH OUT FOR UNSCRUPULOUS BROKERS

Many unscrupulous brokerage houses use IPOs as bait to lure naïve investors into their lairs. There are many sad stories about individual investors buying shares of little no-name IPOs and losing all of their money. Some of these unscrupulous brokers are "bucket shops"—the brokers might as well be sitting on buckets in a basement, making telephone calls to prospects. The ones you really have to watch out for have a veneer of respectability. The brokers will call you and cultivate you—maybe take you out to lunch, invite you to see their offices. They show you how well their IPOs have done. Don't be fooled. The IPOs these companies do are not real IPOs. They are stock promotions and not true underwritings.

The brokers for these organizations simply trade the stock amongst themselves. One classic technique is the "pump and dump": Small stocks are hyped and then sold to naïve investors. Then the brokers, who own shares, sell the stock and the price comes down. Left with worthless stock are the unsuspecting customers.

The Web has increased the number of scams. Cruising the Internet looking for IPO-related sites, we have uncovered many start-up brokerages that try to attract investors with the possibility of getting IPOs. There are a growing number of other online e-brokers, some of which have elaborate ways of allocating IPO shares. Several brokers use a "point" system, much like accumulating frequent flyer miles, in which customers have to reach a certain "point" level before they can get access to the firm's IPOs. However, before signing up with one of the new brokers, check out the list of IPOs that they've underwriten. Chances are you won't recognize a single name. These are little companies that no one has ever heard of, and they are much worse than the bad IPOs we write about in Secret 6, "How to Avoid Bad IPOs." They are the IPOs that couldn't get in the doors of the first-tier underwriters, were rejected by the second- and third-tier brokers, and finally found a home at the dubious start-up online brokers.

The Web sites of these e-brokers often have "IPO" in their name and promise that they are "revolutionizing the initial public offering distribution process." This is an altruistic goal. But don't be fooled. This is a classic bait-and-switch marketing ploy. Their object is to gain more customers for their regular brokerage services and to expand the number of naïve investors on which they can dump IPOs that no one else will touch.

As an aside, it is not that difficult to become a broker. There are people who sell shells of broker-dealers, that is, a broker-dealer license with no operations. A couple of years ago, you could buy one for $50,000.

Although the FBI and the SEC target fraud in the stock markets and have been successful in uncovering unscrupulous brokers and even organized crime connections, their motivation is to stop the bad guys, not to protect the victims. So even if the scam is stopped, customers often discover that the brokerage has gone out of business and has declared bankruptcy. There is virtually no chance for victims to recover their money.

If the brokerage house is not a well-known firm, check the company's track record—much can be found out via the Web. You can also call the National Association of Securities Dealers (NASD), the industry watchdog, to check on the company or go to www.NASD.com. One way of stopping a fraud in its tracks is to ask for the broker's central registration depository (CRD) number. This is the unique identification number that the NASD uses to identify all brokers. With the CRD number, you can get a record of any complaints and rulings against the broker, if there are any. An unscrupulous broker will always hang up the phone as soon as you ask for the CRD. It's a trick we use to stave off the unsolicted calls we get at home from brokers asking us if we want to make "big money."

The moral of the story is to stick with the large brokers, whether full-service, discount, or online. If you have a dispute with them on your portfolio, at least they are staying in business.

STRATEGY 9: OTHER SUGGESTIONS

Consider spin-offs and large IPOs. Because of the significant number of shares to be distributed, the first day pop is less. However, these companies tend to be leaders in their industries. Consequently they are guaranteed Wall Street research coverage and broad institutional ownership. Often, after six months of the IPO they are added to the critical Standard & Poor's (S&P) 500 index because they are industry leaders. That action adds an additional constituency for the stock because investors whose portfolios mirror the S&P 500 must now buy shares in the company. The management of these spun off companies, freed of being buried within a large parent, is now independent and can focus on growing the new company.

Examples of spin-offs are Lucent, the telecommunications equipment manufacturer that was spun off from AT&T, and Genentech, the leading biopharmaceutical firm, spun off from Roche.

Look for *privatizations of foreign companies*, which have been some of the largest IPOs. The European privatizations of Portugal Telecom and Swiss Telecom have proved to be good investments. This is because these companies were once government owned, bloated with costs and employees. When the government decides to sell shares to the public, it allows professional management to come in and cut costs. It's not as exciting as owning a high flying Internet business-to-business provider, but many of these large companies have been very rewarding investments.

Whether you are trying to snag IPO shares at the offering price or are buying in the aftermarket, the real edge any investor has is knowledge—special knowledge of IPOs. Because IPOs have defining characteristics that are different from regular stocks, knowledge of the process, company fundamentals, management, and valuation are worth more to individual investors when deciding whether to buy or to sell these unseasoned companies than when buying any other type of equity.

In good IPO markets, individual investors don't stand much of a chance of getting in on hot IPOs, unless they are related to the company's CEO, are the CEO's best friend, or are lucky with an online broker's lottery. But in bad IPO markets, the institutional investors usually slink off to the sidelines, leaving more opportunities for smart investors willing to take the risk of buying equities when market momentum is poor or the economic outlook is dicey. The most money is made when the IPO market is facing tough sledding. Prices are cut and knowledgeable investors face far less competition to get IPO shares. In tough IPO markets, the knowledge edge is worth more. Having decided on your best strategy, use the steps in Exhibit 2.2, "Five Steps to Improve Your IPO Allocations."

You now understand the initial public offering process. You know who the players are and what they do. Now we will dig into the process of understanding the individual companies and learning how to distinguish between the good deals and the bad ones.

Exhibit 2.2 Five Steps to Improve Your IPO Allocations

Step	Timing	What to Do
1. Set up one or two brokerage accounts.	Now	• Check out Appendix B of this book for a list of active IPO underwriters. • Contact the underwriter that is best for you, and set up an account. • Also consider opening an online account.
2. Search for pending IPOs managed by your broker.	Weekly	• Check the *IPOhome.com* filings and calendars section. –Coming Attractions (for IPOs further out).
3. Develop an IPO short list.	One month before IPO	• Review all IPO profiles of your broker's pending IPOs. • Weed out the bad deals from the good deals by using techniques from this book. –Secret 3: How to Have IPO Intelligence. • Prepare an IPO short list to track potential investments. –Limit the number of IPOs that you analyze and ask for. • Call your broker with early indications on deals you like.

| 4. | Complete your research and call your broker to request an allocation. | Two weeks before IPO | • Do more intensive IPO research.
  –Secret 4: Mining the IPO Prospectus.
  –Secret 5: What Makes a Good IPO
  –Secret 6: How to Avoid Bad IPOs
• Starting at the company's profile on *IPOhome.com*, you can:
  –Link to and analyze the prospectus (on EDGAR).
  –Consider buying a Renaissance IPO Research report.
  –Link and review the IPO's Web site.
  –Keep checking *IPOhome.com* calendars for IPO timing.
• Check the *IPOhome.com* calendars for deal timing.
  –This week's IPOs.
  –Next week's IPOs.
• Reconfirm with your broker that you want an allocation.
  –On hot deals, you will only get if you ask.
  –Remind the broker of your prior interest. |
| 5. | Call your broker. | Morning the IPO starts trading | • Keep checking *IPOhome.com* news and calendars to see if your deal priced.
• Call your broker the first thing in the morning to see if you got shares and to confirm your interest in the deal.
• Read Secret 10: How to Trade IPOs. |

Source: Renaissance Capital, Greenwich, CT (IPOhome.com).

SECRET 3

How to Have
IPO Intelligence

Investors have long sought a secret formula for making money in the stock market. While we're not alchemists able to turn lead into gold, Renaissance Capital has a tried-and-true way of looking at the world of initial public offerings (IPOs) and making sense of them. In this chapter, we will discuss our IPO investment philosophy and the four-step process that we use to rank IPOs.

Over the years, we have analyzed thousands of IPOs. We've analyzed everything from Chinese bicycle manufacturers to riverboat gambling companies and business-to-consumer (B2C) Internet providers. During an average year the analysts and portfolio managers at Renaissance Capital study about 500 individual deals. After analyzing that volume of IPOs we have developed special insights into what makes individual IPOs work and how the IPO market as a whole functions.

Prominent mutual funds, investment advisers, and hedge funds pay us substantial retainer fees to get our Renaissance IPO research reports on individual companies and our commentary on the IPO market. They value our research because they know our process is remarkably reliable in distinguishing the good deals from the bad ones.

When we developed our Renaissance IPO research approach to analyzing IPOs, we culled best practices from investment banking and traditional stock analysis. For example, investment bankers look at IPOs as if they are buying the whole company. Bankers are concerned about the enterprise value of a company— what it is worth to an independent buyer? Traditional stock analysis relies more on forecasting earnings growth rates, looking at return on equity, and comparing price-to-earnings (P/E) ratios. Traditional analysis focuses more on what a single share is worth.

THE FOUR STEPS

The heart and soul of our approach are the four key criteria we consider when evaluating IPOs.

1. *Fundamentals.* What does the company do? How good is their business plan? What are its prospects for the future?
2. *Management and Control.* Does management own stock? Are they experienced? Are they totally focused on making the IPO a success?
3. *Valuation.* How is the IPO priced relative to other publicly traded companies? Does it merit a discount or a premium?
4. *Group Momentum.* How well are similar companies performing in the stock market? Is the group momentum strong or weak?

Fundamentals and management/control issues are long-term factors. Your assessments on each will remain valid unless there are dramatic changes in an IPO's strategy, industry conditions, or management team. Valuation and group momentum are short-term factors and can change in a single trading day. The attractiveness of a company's valuation will depend on where the underwriters price the IPO. If the price goes up a lot, the valuation may be too expensive. The same goes for group momentum. A particular sector can fall in or out of favor faster than a video game with teenagers. Remember what happened to the e-tailers?

For each of these criteria, we ask ourselves whether an IPO is above average, average, or below average. If an IPO has an above average overall rating, it's a potential buy. If it's below average overall, it's a potential sell.

Our whole philosophy is to apply rigorous investment standards to established companies as well as to unproven start-ups. Even though it sounds like an oxymoron, we are conservative IPO investors.

By going through this thorough four-step process of evaluating an IPO, you will be able to separate the good deals from the bad deals. You may not *always* be right. But if you use Renaissance Capital's system of rating IPOs, you will be correct in the majority of cases. An added benefit of using the four steps is that we can guarantee that you will be more knowledgeable than 99 percent of all IPO investors, including many supposedly smart institutional investors. Lack of understanding of an IPO's business plan and strategy by institutional investors is a major frustration of IPO managements.

The systematic four-step process of evaluating IPOs is all the more important because the forces driving IPO investing aren't always rational or based on facts. More so than with investors in seasoned stocks, investors in IPOs let their emotions guide their decision making. They decide that they must own a particular IPO because they are devoted fans of the product or service. The huge success of donut maker Krispy Kreme, whose stock shot up in the stratosphere, is a good example of how investors can ignore comparable valuations of other food retailers. They desperately want to own an IPO because its stock performance is strong. Online investors, enamoured of the potential of the Web, propelled Internet stocks to previously unseen valuations. Although familiarity with an IPO's product or service can point you to good stocks, it can also blind you to glaring corporate weaknesses and overly pricey valuations. Because IPOs are extremely volatile, much money can be lost very, very quickly. More so with IPOs, it pays to be disciplined.

Well-researched conclusions about IPOs are far more valuable than investment research on broadly held stocks. Why? Stocks in the Standard & Poor's (S&P) 500 are widely followed by Wall Street analysts. Trying to get a leg up on IBM or General Electric is nearly impossible. Hundreds of analysts follow these companies. When Coca-Cola or Gillette makes a major announcement about the state of its business, everyone gets the information at the same time. Information on stocks in the S&P 500 is immediately absorbed and usually correctly interpreted by investors. New information is immediately reflected in the stock prices.

But not with IPOs. Prior to an IPO's debut and for nearly a month after the offering, Wall Street cannot issue research. The public may not have heard of the company's products and services. This means that few investors are knowledgeable about the company. With so many uninformed investors, new information is not instantly absorbed and correctly interpreted. That's why you see wide swings in IPO prices. Knowledge is power. Specialized knowledge about an IPO through research gives you an edge.

The independent research you do on IPOs is worth even more after the company goes public. How come? The reason is that Wall Street analysts never, never, never issue a negative research report on an IPO that their firm has underwritten. These research reports are invariably positive, even for the biggest clunkers. Cynics call Wall Street analysts "cheerleaders" for their industries. Even when an IPO stumbles early on in its public life, the Wall Street analyst is an apologist for management and its strategy.

The reason for this "see no evil" approach is simple—*survival*. Sell-side analysts are under special constraints. How independent do you think an analyst can be in his or her investment conclusions if the company under scrutiny is a banking client? Wall Street analysts are under great pressure to be positive. They are pressured by the investment bankers, who are looking for follow-on business from management. They are pressured by the stockbrokers, who get angry when investment recommendations are reduced and stocks fall. Few Wall Street analysts have the internal corporate clout to completely resist these pressures. The majority of Wall Street analysts care about the integrity of their work and the correctness of their investment calls. So they avoid the problem of being negative on IPOs that are supported by the investment bankers by doing exactly what their mothers advised: "If you don't have something nice to say, don't say anything."

Company managements are known for using strong-arm tactics on errant analysts. Analysts who issue negative investment opinions or who write something critical about a company's accounting procedures are stricken from conference calls and sometimes physically prevented from attending meetings.

We were on a conference call once for a London-based online airline ticketer, eBookers.com, that was holding its first post-IPO earnings announcement. Just from the questions asked, you could tell who the players were. The analyst for the underwriter served up big, slow puff balls. "Great quarter. Congratulations," he gushed. Those who were short the stock asked a few "when was the last time you beat your wife" type of questions. Management responded in an interesting way. The chief executive officer (CEO), who was not a native English speaker, but spoke perfect Oxbridge English, didn't answer challenging queries. Instead, he directed the chief financial officer (CFO), whose English was difficult to understand at best, to respond to the negative questions. Finally, the CEO said there were no more questions and terminated the call. Actually, there were more questions pending, but they weren't acknowledged. The conference call system either wasn't working or had been cut off.

Even knowing that Wall Street coverage of its own IPOs is invariably positive, it helps to decode the recommendations that the analysts place on their reports. In Wall Street lingo, only a "Strong Buy" is really a buy recommendation. A mere "Buy" recommendation could mean one of several things: "The stock is overvalued, but I like the company." Or, "The stock is overvalued and management is so-so, but the company just did their IPO and I have to issue this research report or else." Or, "Darn. I had it as a strong buy right after the IPO and the management has already screwed up. I'm toast if I reduce the rating to a hold, so I'll make it a buy." A hold is Wall Streetese for a "sell."

These are the reasons why you can't use most Wall Street research to help you in your quest for good IPOs to buy in the aftermarket. The analysts are motivated to be cheerleaders for their IPOs. In the IPO market, more so than anywhere else, you are really on your own. You have no Wall Street research to guide you in deciding which IPOs to go after. And you can't trust the Wall Street research that is published after the IPO's debut. You must rely on your own judgment. In the remainder of this chapter, we will show you how to do just that.

STEP 1: ASSESS FUNDAMENTALS

Our philosophy is that fundamentals always win out in the end. Because the IPO market is the place where new ideas get their chance to prove their commercial viability, there are many contenders vying for financing and investor support. Good business plans that are well executed will be quickly rewarded. IPOs that prove to have faulty business models or those that encounter early problems will be swiftly punished. In an area where innovation is rewarded, small companies have the opportunity to challenge the bigger players. While future events outside of management's control, like a competitor that stumbles or a recession, can determine whether the IPO is ultimately a success, it pays to evaluate the IPO's fundamentals as best you can. How good is its business and how well equipped is it to face the challenges of success?

Fundamentals is a broad concept. It encompasses many issues: business model, defensible niche, market size, competition, pricing, stage of development, burn rate, expansion, customer concentration, geographic diversity, crazes, and accounting and other issues.

The starting point for analyzing IPO fundamentals is *figuring out what the company does*. On the surface, this may seem to be obvious. But in fact, with so many companies involved with new technologies, figuring out their business models can be difficult. The test of whether you understand what the company does is being able to describe it in your own words in one or two sentences.

If you cannot understand what the IPO does, take a pass. Not being able to describe the business could mean you lack the technical background needed to understand the company and its prospects. Prospectuses generally include enough industry background and descriptions of the product or services to give you a basic understanding of the business and its environment. However, if you don't understand the business, it may not be your fault. Some prospectuses are poorly written on purpose. Stay away from these companies.

Business Model

Once you have figured out what the company does, the next thing to assess is the company's *business model*, in other words, where its revenue comes from and the costs and mechanisms of delivering its products and services. Companies can sell to individual consumers, to other businesses, or to both.

Under our investment discipline, companies with the strongest fundamentals face a large, definable, and growing opportunity. They have a strategy for attacking the opportunity, and they have management who are up to the task. They are typically first movers and are actively erecting barriers to entry. For example, Amazon.com was the first large retailer of books on the Internet. When we analyzed Amazon.com at the time of its IPO, there was much to like: the fact that it was the first in the space, the fact that the book market is large, and the strong trend for consumers to purchase books on the Web. We cautiously ignored the lack of profits in the near term with the expectation that volume would eventually translate into earnings over time.

In investing in Internet and technology IPOs, it is absolutely critical that the company be the first one to develop a new business opportunity. When money is abundant, you have to assume that other entrepreneurs are also trying to develop the same concept. The powerful combination of ready financing and the speed at which technology is developing today has cut the time that managers have to develop business concepts down from years to months. Being first to raise money through an IPO gives a company a priceless lead time and an advantage over competitors. In the case of eBay, there were certainly other auction sites. However, with its branding and its robust technology, eBay had established itself at the top of the pile. Competing with eBay would require much capital for promotion and a Web site infrastructure that was at least equal to eBay's standard.

When Yahoo! went public in 1996, it faced tremendous competition from Alta Vista, then a subsidiary of DEC, which was poised to go public. But Alta Vista bagged its IPO and was sold to CMGI by Compaq Computer in 1999, which itself had acquired DEC. When Alta Vista tried another IPO in early 2000, it had completely lost focus and momentum and was unable to complete the offering.

In boom times, there is so much venture capital and other private investment capital sloshing around that many wacky business concepts can get financing. When the IPO market is very strong, venture capital firms and Wall Street bankers get overextended. Junior bankers with little experience throw money at start-ups that would have been sent packing in calmer times. The axiom is that when there is lots of capital, there is less due diligence.

That is why you as an investor have to exercise due diligence and common sense. Few Internet companies are profitable. However, it is possible to make reasoned judgments about an IPO's business model. Particularly with Internet and technology companies it is critical to try to separate the ones that have staying power from the ones that will crash after they've burned through your money.

For example, many e-tailers went public in 1999. All lacked profits. Some, though, lacked positive gross margin. In other words, they were giving their products away below cost. If you throw shipping costs, selling and promotional costs, and general overhead on top of that, you have to ask the question of whether such a company will ever be profitable. Indeed, many investors reached the same conclusion that we did about Web retailing. Until the Internet retailers can figure out a way to teletransport merchandise—Beam me up, Scotty!—shipping costs will consume profits.

Here's how we evaluated eBay, the online auctioneer. eBay was a hot IPO, no question. It had the huge advantage of being the first company to use the online auction method to allow people to engage in a cyber flea market. Unlike other online merchants, who had the problem of shipping big bulky things that mostly benefited the bottom line of United Parcel Service (UPS), eBay had sidestepped the whole issue of shipping costs by requiring the two parties—the seller and the buyer—to take care of that detail. While we were concerned about high payments to America Online (AOL) and legal liability on sales of items that were misrepresented by the seller, eBay's use of the Internet for commerce was unique and, unlike other e-tailers, profitable.

The focus of a business model is also a concern. If the company has a well-laid-out strategy, it is far more likely to be successful than a company that is trying to be something for everyone. Priceline.com, the online purveyor of "name your price" airline seats and hotel rooms, was successful as long as it had its eye on the ball. As long as they tried to scale their proprietary technology into markets that embraced the "name your price" concept, Priceline was likely to succeed. The other ingredient for success was willing partners with airlines and hotels to offload perishable merchandise. Priceline stumbled badly when it plunged into the grocery and gasoline businesses. The technology to support the online retailing was different, and the food products and oil companies never bought into the enterprise. Not only did that venture fail, but it badly tarnished the whole Priceline concept in the process.

Market Size

When you assess a company, give high marks to a company that addresses a *large opportunity*. The e-commerce market that eBay addresses, online auctions of personal items, is a very large opportunity. The communications market addressed by optical network provider Sycamore Networks is also large. Large market opportunities allow companies to have breathing room for trial and error and to have high market valuations. Companies that address more limited markets must be even more focused and have significant advantages over competitors and the ability to produce high margins. The prospectus will almost always give you information pertaining to the dollar value of the market today and in the future.

Defensible Niche

We also look at where the company has staked its claim. Ideally, the company should be number one or two in its category, and there should be *high barriers* to entry into the category.

An example of high barriers to entry would be Amazon.com, the online bookstore and general merchant. By building a proprietary Web infrastructure and establishing agreements with powerful suppliers early on, Amazon.com made it difficult for others to follow. That's because the capital investment required was high and the Amazon.com brand had been established.

An example of low barriers to entry would be Web communities and content sites. As drkoop.com, the online health Web site established by former U.S. Surgeon General C. Everett Koop, and quepasa.com, a Spanish online community, quickly found out, all it takes is a high school student with a knowledge of HTML (hypertext markup language, the web programming language) to set up a Web site. The business model based on selling advertising to support a Web site simply doesn't work.

We recently analyzed a small company that had developed a chip to deliver digital amplification for consumer electronics, like digital video disks (DVDs). The amplifiers would replace the 60-year-old analog technology and would allow smaller and more cost effective devices. In theory, that sounds great. One big problem was that the tiny company faced larger potential competition from the Japanese electronics manufacturers. So, despite the fact that this little company had developed a credible technology, we concluded that its strategy of selling the chips below cost to the large Japanese electronics makers was a fatal sign of weakness. The Japanese companies, we believed, would do what they've done for years—reverse engineer, and mass produce a cheaper product. End of story.

Competition

A related concern is *competition*. Unless an IPO is the number-one or -two company in its space, it had better have a significantly better mousetrap than the established companies. Another concern is the size of the company. A small company competing against large, powerful, existing companies is often in an untenable position to compete on pricing and on the amount of resources it has. While we generally agree that smaller companies are fleeter of foot and more likely to innovate, the competitive environment in which they operate is important.

Pricing

Pricing trends are particularly important when the company's product is a commodity. Although people tend to think of mundane products like metals, cattle, and cement as commodities, many new industries can face commodity pricing. This occurs when new entrants converge on a new market at the same time. For example, the provision of Internet access is also a commodity, with internet service providers (ISPs) competing largely on price.

Declining average selling prices can also be a concern, unless the IPO in question is demonstrating that it is rapidly innovating its products. A very good example of a company being able to flourish in a declining pricing environment is chip maker Intel, whose development of new chips was so far ahead of competitors that it was already selling the next generation of chips when the average selling prices for the old chips was starting to decline.

Stage of Development

These days companies are going public at ever earlier *stages of development*. We refer to this as "public venture capital"—IPO investors take all of the risks of an early company but have none of the advantages of the venture capitalists, who bought in at cheap prices.

We firmly believe that investors should be compensated for the risks they are taking for purchasing the shares of small, risky, developmental-stage companies. With very few exceptions, the fundamentals of these companies are below average. The company has an unproven and probably changing business plan. If it is a biotechnology company, it faces the risk that the Food and Drug Administration (FDA) may refuse to approve its drug or medical device or may delay in doing so. A recent start-up means that management is not only new but also inexperienced in working together. Over the years, we have seen many biotechs go public three, four, and even five years before they expect their drugs to hit the market. When you are asked to be a venture capitalist, think like one. Don't buy unless you get in at a dirt cheap price.

Competitive reasons are supposedly forcing today's rapidly developing Internet commerce and technology companies to seek financing at ever earlier stages of development. We suspect that the main force here is greed, too much money sloshing around in venture capitalists' hands and the desire by entrepreneurs to hit it rich quick. That's fine. Just don't let them do it with your money.

Burn Rate

How fast the IPO is going through your money is called the *burn rate*. You can get an idea of the magnitude of how quickly the company will spend your money by looking at its accumulated losses compared to revenue. If the losses are very large and the revenues are very small, you can be certain that management is spending money like a contestant in a grocery shopping contest.

Managements of Internet start-ups argue that they have to spend money on establishing their brands. Far too many of them threw investors' money away on glitzy but untargeted television and radio advertising campaigns. One company, pets.com, bought time on the Super Bowl and the World Series. Whoops! They succeeded in making the cute black-and-white doggie puppet a media star. But even sales of the $20 sock puppet couldn't save this ill-conceived dud. It went to doggie heaven in late 2000.

Tales also abound about young Internet executives spending investors' money on expensive office furnishings, free Palm pilots for all, and travel. These immature executives can burn through the $40 million raised in a typical Internet IPO in under a year.

iVillage Chairman and CEO Candice Carpenter did not like our conclusions about iVillage and insisted on coming in for a personal visit to try to change our minds. She did, and we became more convinced of our initial concerns about iVillage's sizable losses, fast rate of cash burn, and low management ownership.

Companies that burn through investors' cash quickly are betting that when they've spent the money, they'll be able to go back to the trough for more. Trouble is, unless the IPO has achieved significant success in a short time frame, the stock price will be below $10 a share, and the company will be unable to raise more money. When the money shortfall is announced to the investment community, the stock usually dips under $5 a share. At that point, the only hope the long-suffering remaining shareholders have is a merger with a stronger player.

Expansion

Obviously, investors want to see their company grow. However, very rapid *expansion* puts pressure on company resources. The company's operating and financial systems should be up to the task. One retailing IPO, Eagle Hardware, which had an aggressive plan for expanding its hardware superstores in the Pacific Northwest, blew up after announcing a series of accounting irregularities. Apparently, it expanded so fast it was having trouble tracking how many items it had in its stores.

Rapid expansion also puts pressure on a company's ability to hire and manage staff. Many recent Internet companies have added staff, going from having a handful of employees to hundreds of employees. It is reasonable to question how well a staff of people who barely know each other will be able to execute the business plan.

In addition, rapid expansion strains the supply chain. This is especially true with restaurant chains. A regional restaurant chain decides to roll out nationally. But the single regional distribution network cannot handle the far flung operations, so other distribution networks are established. These must be skillfully managed, which is a problem for small companies, which may lack the resources to find and train local managers.

Customer Concentration

The main concern is whether revenues are *highly concentrated* in a handful of key customers. If one of the customers cancels or reduces its orders, sales are surely at risk. They can demand discounts and special deals. There are some industries in which customer concentration is a given. For example, suppliers to the large auto-mobile companies have among the highest customer concentration.

Customer concentration isn't always bad. When Sycamore Networks, the provider of light-wave telecommunications technology, went public in 1999, it had a single customer, Williams Communications, a leading telecommunications services provider. However, Sycamore was a technology leader in this category and would shortly be adding additional customers to diversify its customer base. Both customers and revenues ramped quickly after the offering.

Geographic Diversity

Geographically concentrated operations are also a source of concern for investors. At the height of the frenzy over casino gambling, companies that operated a single floating riverboat for gaming were able to successfully complete IPOs. The risks of having a single location seem obvious. What if the local economy tanks? What if state or local officials give the company a hard time? It has nowhere else to turn for revenues.

Restaurant IPOs often have limited operations, sometimes in a single state. A single restaurant entrepreneur, having created a successful concept at one location, will try to replicate it elsewhere. A tiny Florida chain, Pollo Tropical, decided to raise money through an IPO to expand its operations northward. However, the concept didn't click well outside southern Florida and the company was deleted from Nasdaq trading in 1998.

In 1996 and 1997, the medical profession began a massive and frenetic consolidation. So enamored of these stocks were investors that toward the end of the cycle, even small partnerships of dentists and orthodontists were able to pull off IPOs. Buyers of these IPOs were purchasing the equivalent of two or three single dental practices. It might be a good private investment, perhaps, if the dentist is your brother-in-law. But the IPO glow quickly wears off companies like these.

Crazes

Throughout the history of IPOs, there have been *crazes* in which a company pioneers a new technology or opportunity and is soon followed by copycats and then a host of dubious wanna-bes. In the 1920s, it was airlines. In the 1990s, it was biotechs in 1991, casino gaming in 1993, virtual reality in 1994, roll-ups in 1997, and the Internet beginning in 1998. In nearly every instance, the initial companies performed the best, and the last IPOs to the trough performed the worst.

Roll-ups are a good example. The concept is simple: a number of companies in a fragmented industry seeking economies of scale join together under a centralized management. In 1997, investors had 21 new IPO roll-ups to choose from. Among the first were roll-ups of large physician practices, staffing services, and industrial equipment renters. These did reasonably well at first because they were consolidations of fragmented industries and could claim economies of scale. But as time went on, financiers began to scrape the bottom of the barrel for roll-up concepts and produced roll-up IPOs of regional bagel companies, pallet providers (a pallet is the wooden platform on which goods are shipped), courier dispatch management companies, and auto-towing companies.

The most active financier in this area was Jay Ledecky, a high-energy ex-Wall Streeter and founder of U.S. Office Products. He swiftly produced IPO roll-ups in the flower-distribution industry, USA Floral and the then new ISP area, One Main. He topped off his accomplishments with a roll-up of roll-ups, Consolidated Capital, which was designed to use the proceeds of its IPO to invest in roll-ups. The returns from these were undistinguished, at best.

One of the many problems inherent in roll-ups is that the financials are what's called "pro forma." Management presents the consolidated companies as they *might* have operated together. Trouble is, management has much discretion over making assumptions and multiple adjustments on revenues, expenses, and assets. Very few roll-ups work as long-term companies because of the problems of integrating formerly independent operations and egos. Another problem is that in some cases, one or more of the companies is unprofitable.

Accounting Issues

Look for conservative revenue and expense recognition. One obvious area to look at is the amount of *goodwill* a company has on its balance sheet. When a company makes an acquisition, it can put on its balance sheet the actual value of tangible assets—things like warehouses, computers, and inventory. The difference between the acquisition price and the value of these tangible assets is called goodwill.

Watch out for companies that have more goodwill on their books than equity or negative tangible equity. Acquisitive IPOs with lots of cash from their recent deal are notorious for overpaying for acquisitions and then writing off the assets. When a company writes off assets, it reduces its equity. Shareholders do not like this practice, and these companies pay a stiff penalty in a plummeting stock price. Acquisitive companies that take write-offs of the assets of their acquisitions are also a turnoff. Some companies overpay for acquisitions, fail to achieve the hoped-for returns, and then purge the assets from their balance sheets to make results look better.

Other Issues

There are also industry-specific factors that will affect reaching a judgment on the quality of a company's fundamentals. In the media and Internet content provider arenas, significant "bartering" is a negative. When a company barters, it offers its advertising space for goods and services instead of cash. However, the company will recognize the bartering as revenue. With established radio and television companies, it may not be a big issue; but with a small, cash-starved Internet company, bartering effectively overstates revenue.

Finally, when assessing overall fundamentals, ask yourself these questions: Is the market opportunity large enough to support a significant company? If the size of the market is $100 million, you won't get an IPO with a $1 billion valuation. Are there barriers to entry? Is the company a first mover? Can it be number one in its market? Does the business model as you understand it make sense? Do you think that the company has the potential to deliver future cash flows significant enough to produce a stock price substantially above what it is now? Can it overcome the company-specific and industrywide obstacles in its path? Are there legal liability issues?

If you conclude that the company has the potential to do all of these things, then rate it above average. If you're not sure, rate it average. If you think it's a risky piker, rate it below average.

STEP 2: MANAGEMENT AND CONTROL

Management is just as important as fundamentals. If the management of an IPO lacks the background and the capability to execute on its strategy, the company will ultimately fail. We also examine the incentives that management has to do well because that will play a part in determining success. Our goal as an investor is an IPO that produces a strong return. We want to invest in companies whose managements share that goal and have the resources to accomplish it. In that sense, management's interests are closely allied with ours.

The principal areas to review are management's experience, its incentives, its stock ownership, and the manner in which it conducts business. With more established companies it is relatively easy to judge whether someone is capable of doing the job. If the CEO has years of relevant background in positions of increasing responsibility, then management likely fits the bill. Top executives with experiences of successfully starting up previous companies are also highly likely to produce the results you want.

However, beware the marquee name unless he or she is surrounded by strong supporting players. CEO Jim Clark, who had founded Netscape, was the main reason why Healtheon, the medical information company that was the first to use the Internet to exchange data and to execute transactions, took off like a rocket. But other name IPOs have been less successful. Donna Karan, Ralph Lauren, and Martha Stewart are all examples. In each case, the CEO was the creative spirit behind the company, not someone known for managerial expertise.

Also suspect are companies in which too much control rests with one person. If one person is chairman, CEO, and president, the company probably has problems delegating power, a weakness that will become more of a problem as the company grows.

Internet and technology company managements play by much the same rules. Relevant background and past success are key. However, the management of some Internet start-ups are untested. You used to be able to judge management's capability by the company they keep, that is, the venture capital firms backing the company. If industry biggies like Kleiner Perkins or Benchmark were investors, that said a lot about the quality of those controlling the company. However, the surge of billions of dollars into venture funds has made the venture investors less picky, so their presence is a less reliable indicator of quality.

Management incentives are another important barometer of whether management is properly motivated and whether his or her interests are allied with yours. The top management should be appropriately compensated. In established companies look for the CEO or the president to be pulling down somewhere between $250,000 to $500,000 in base compensation, with a possible cash bonus. However, some of management's compensation should be tied to the IPO's stock price, so he or she should own a significant amount of shares. Companies that pay their top executives $1 million or more in cash should be suspect. It's okay if the executives are billionaires. But their wealth should be in stock holdings—the same stock you own. You want the top brass's feet held more to the fire.

Young technology and Internet companies usually pay their top executives in the $125,000 to $150,000 range, with most of their compensation coming from stock options. Look closely at those options. If many of the options are dirt cheap, management is motivated to cash them out at the end of the lock-up period for a quick profit.

Unless management owns a big piece of the company, they are not properly motivated to work for you, the public shareholder. The worst thing you could see is a CEO who cashed out of most of his or her shares on or before the IPO, being paid generous cash compensation, and now owning little stock. Holdings of less than three percent are suspect.

It is also our philosophy that a public company should be run with the public shareholder's interests at heart. Management should devote 100 percent of its attention to the company and not have outside interests. Red lights should go on if the CEO of an IPO is also the CEO of another company. As a potential shareholder of the IPO, you want the CEO totally focused on making your stock a success. The CEO can't do that if he or she is spending time running another company. That person has too many balls in the air. Management and directors should have few, if any, inside deals amongst themselves.

If you can answer an emphatic "Yes!" to the questions "Is management qualified to do the job?" and "Are their interests riveted on a higher stock price?" then rate the management above average. If your answers are less enthusiastic, rate them average. And, if you see a pattern of abuse in compensation, perks, and insider dealings, the management is below average.

STEP 3: ASSESS VALUATION

When you buy an IPO on the offering or in the aftermarket, you do so with the expectation that the price will go up and that you will make money. The way we gauge the attractiveness of the *valuation* of an IPO is to compare it to the most similar comparable companies we can find. For example, when we evaluated Ralph Lauren, we compared it to already public Tommy Hilfiger and Nautica, both designers of upscale sportswear, mostly for men and boys. Because Ralph Lauren not only designed clothing but also licensed its brands and had a number of Polo stores, comparables Tommy Hilfiger and Nautica were close because they, too, had stores and licensing agreements in addition to their traditional clothing.

A deafening drumroll preceeded the Polo Ralph Lauren offering in the spring of 1997. Underwriter Goldman Sachs, whose founders ironically had financed the Sears, Roebuck chain where no Ralph Lauren item is likely to be found, gave the upscale designer an upscale valuation. Goldman Sachs proposed to price the stock between $22 and $25 per share, giving it a $2.3 billion valuation, compared to a $1.6 billion valuation for Tommy and a $1 billion valuation for Nautica.

We compared the three companies side by side. Both Tommy Hilfiger and Nautica had growth rates that were twice Ralph Lauren's and margins that were superior.

Here's what we told our clients: "With a focus on adding licensing revenues, the company should grow at 20 percent to 25 percent for the next two years. Although its margins are now much lower than competitors Hilfiger, Gucci, and Nautica, the company is being priced at a premium to them, largely due to the proven equity value of the Polo Ralph Lauren name. Like Estee Lauder, Polo Ralph Lauren may be a must-own for growth investors."

Balancing the positive (the brand) and the negative (lower margins and growth rate), we gave it an average on valuation.

At the pricing, Goldman pushed harder on the valuation, and the deal was priced at $26. Polo Ralph Lauren quickly charged into the low thirties, where droves of institutional investors bailed out. The stock later settled back into the mid-twenties, in line with its peers.

Picking the right comparables is all important. If we had picked lesser lights in the rag trade, Ralph Lauren would have looked even more expensive. Over time, the stock has traded right in line with Tommy Hilfiger and the other upscale apparel designers and suffered through the same industry downturns.

When an IPO is the first to go public in a new industry, it is obviously impossible to find close comparisons. When Priceline.com went public in 1999, we scratched our heads to find other analogous companies. Obviously, the right comparable had to be an Internet player, but there were no candidates that filled the bill precisely.

We finally settled on eBay and Amazon.com because each was a first mover and an industry leader in its own right, addressing separate online retailing opportunities. Further, we believed each had scalable business models, which means that they can be easily leveraged and applied to other applications.

Because only eBay was profitable, we resorted to comparing the three on the basis of projected sales. Priceline.com was projecting sales to grow to $500 million in 2002, which was less than Amazon but better than eBay. And yet, we noted that Priceline sported a mere $1.4 billion valuation, a tenth of Amazon's and eBay's. Relatively speaking, Priceline was a bargain.

The advent of the Internet supposedly brought with it a new paradigm of investing, where profits mean nothing and opportunity means everything. There have been innumerable times throughout history when investors completely abandoned traditional ways of placing a value on a company. In *every* instance, the market crashed back to reality. Investors are interested in opportunity; but they are really valuing a company off the future cash flows that a company will ultimately produce.

Some traditional investors scoff at the idea of valuing a company based on revenues or profits many years in the future. They want to stick with the tried-and-true methods of book value and dividend yield. However, the companies that are going public today are very different from yesterday's rubber and automobile manufacturers. Companies that are involved in heavy-duty manufacturing have most of their assets tied down in plant facilities, high-ticket inventory, and other fixed assets. In contrast, the new technology company's value is intellectual capital, not plant and equipment. Patents, new ideas, and innovative employees drive the valuations.

The biggest weakness in valuing companies based on comparables is that the valuation is relative. Traditional investors call it the greater-fool theory. In times of rampant speculation, the comparable companies could be inflated, as many of the Internet companies were in 1999. This means that a high valuation for the IPO is reasonable only in the context of other high-priced companies. The Internet craze of 1999 is an object lesson in the perils of using this approach, but the method has its roots in many industries, including real estate. Value is set by the price that buyers and sellers are willing to pay at that point in time. So long as you accept this risk, using comparable companies to value an IPO is an objective method. Our philosophy is, understand the fundamentals first, then look at valuation. A superior company should be priced at a premium to its peers; a below average IPO should be priced at a discount.

Each industry also has its quirks of valuation; for example, retailers and restaurants look at same-store sales, and ISPs and cable television companies are valued by populations served and by miles of cable backbone. With a new or unfamiliar industry, figure out what is the most important measurement of the company's progress. For example, when the Internet portals and communities burst on the scene, investors were perplexed about how to value them. Along came new media companies to measure page views, eyeballs, and registered users. It soon became apparent how unsatisfactory these metrics were, largely because they were not tied to any measure of profitability and because they were reported inconsistently by the Internet companies. The investment community finally settled on revenues as the primary point of comparison among young, fast-growing, but profitless companies.

Although none of these methods of valuing IPOs are completely satisfactory, they do provide a basis for an objective comparison of an IPO with its publicly traded peers.

STEP 4: DETERMINE GROUP MOMENTUM

We define *group momentum* as the performance, relative to the broad market indexes, of companies similar to the IPO. We define the group as the companies that are closest to the IPO in their business plan and product or services.. The theory behind using group momentum as a criteria to a successful IPO is simple. If other similar companies are performing well, investors generally feel good about the sector, and this IPO should do well, too. If the comparables are trading poorly, the IPO may have tough sledding.

Group momentum isn't the single most important criteria, but it is a way to predict the IPO's near-term performance. If the IPO has strong fundamentals and management but weak group momentum, it may turn out to be a great long-term investment. Because the stocks in its sector are trading poorly, it may take time for other investors to notice it. Conversely, if the group is white hot, the IPO should be strong right out of the gate. However, because the valuations of the sector are high relative to other areas, an investor should be cautious near-term.

In any case, group momentum is but a short-term predictor of an IPO's performance. Group momentum can change on a dime. However, it is invaluable to look at the charts of the IPO comparables to know whether the stocks are in or out of favor. We also look at other technical indicators to judge the strength of the group.

Our Renaissance IPO research process works because it is systematic and provides a relatively objective way of assessing, comparing, and contrasting IPOs. It provides you with a game plan when you read the prospectus.

SECRET 4

Mining the IPO Prospectus

There is an anecdote about legendary investor Benjamin Graham when he was in college. In researching how statistics could be used to analyze stocks, he came upon a young company that was developing a machine that put financial information on punch cards. The company was called Calculating, Tabulating, and Recording, and Benjamin Graham was impressed with how it made bookkeeping more efficient. When he went to Wall Street after graduation, he told his boss about this terrific technology company. His boss told him, "Forget about it. We have looked at that company, and its balance sheet is water—the assets are phony, there are financial accounting improprieties, and we do not want to go anywhere near that company." Graham dutifully followed his boss's advice and avoided the company that later became IBM.

With initial public offering (IPO) investing, there is often a tug-of-war between the company's potential and its current state. A young technology company with good products and a sound business model may have financial issues that a more developed company may not have. A seemingly high growth restaurant chain looking to expand may have fatal problems that are just below the surface.

This chapter is designed to help you use the information provided by the company at the time of its IPO to understand the fundamentals of the company, its financial underpinnings, and the ability of its management to pull it off.

Before you read further, you should know that this is the most difficult chapter in *IPOs for Everyone*. It will teach you step-by-step, detail-by-detail, how to mine the IPO prospectus and decide whether the company is the mother lode, a short vein of ore, or fool's gold. This chapter will get into specific accounting and financial analyses that are necessary to understand the workings of companies. We will dissect a typical prospectus. We will get technical. So, if you are looking for only a top-down perspective on IPOs, skip this chapter.

THE PRELIMINARY PROSPECTUS

One of the beauties of investing in IPOs is that you have at hand the single best, most informative material on a company that you will ever get—the *preliminary prospectus*. When a company does an IPO, the Securities and Exchange Commission (SEC) forces the company to offer more disclosure of operations, strategy, finances, management compensation, and insider transactions than it will ever have to provide in the future. The version filed with the SEC is called the S-1. The version distributed to prospective investors is called the preliminary prospectus. This document combines disclosure material required by the SEC and the company's marketing pitch. Ignore it at your peril.

In O. Casey Corr's book *Money from Thin Air* (Times Books, 2000), there is a story about Craig McCaw, whose McCaw Cellular Communications is a legendary example of entrepreneurship. In 1987, when McCaw Cellular went public, McCaw described it as the "worst day in the history of our company." What? The man had just raised $2.39 billion. Was he crazy? Craig McCaw was angry that the price he paid to raise those billions was the disclosure of McCaw Cellular's company secrets— how it had been so successful.

It's pretty amazing to know that companies have been providing investors with this information only since the 1930s. Before that, most companies kept their investors in the dark. As you read an IPO prospectus, keep in mind that there are real philosophical differences among companies about providing company information to the investing public. Some companies believe that full disclosure is good public relations. Other companies think that the bare minimum is all the public deserves.

By the way, all of this information is available for free from the underwriter and on the Internet from EDGAR (Electronic Data Gathering and Retrieval), which is the SEC's electronic file room. Go online to our site, IPOhome.com, where we have a link to the prospectus on each IPO profile.

In recent years, the SEC has made considerable strides to making the preliminary prospectus more readable and accessible to the general public. The so-called "plain English" prospectus forces companies to explain their business and their strategy as clearly as possible. Although the prospectuses are indeed easier to read, they are still pretty daunting documents. It takes years of reading IPO prospectuses to sort out what's important and what's boilerplate (required but routine material).

Before taking you step-by-step through the prospectus, we want to emphasize our belief that one of the surest ways to make investing mistakes is to ignore information. Investors who buy an IPO without reading the preliminary prospectus are setting themselves up to lose money. Since 99 percent of investors fall into this category, the minority who study the prospectus have a significant edge.

Even many institutional investors have their first encounter with a prospectus when they attend the road show luncheon and find one at the place setting. They, like most individual investors, rely on tips and opinions of stockbrokers and friends.

So, even though the prospectus looks like a boring legal document— which by the way, it can be—each prospectus contains secrets about the company, many of which are being reluctantly revealed.

FRONT COVER

Just like the front cover of a book, which shows the title and author, the front cover of a prospectus gives key, basic information: the IPO's name, the anticipated ticker symbol, the number of shares to be offered, and the proposed price range. It may also try to lure you with snappy graphics. And, in the fine, usually italicized print, the company must disclose any insider buying and selling. If there is a significant amount of insider selling, consider rejecting the deal.

Listed at the bottom of the cover page are the lead manager and any co-managers, arrayed from left to right in order of importance. Do you recognize any of the names? If only one underwriter is named and it doesn't ring a bell, find out more before proceeding. The dangers of buying a sole-managed IPO are great, particularly if the underwriter is small, has managed only a few offerings, or has a checkered past.

In some cases, you will see the name of a well-known, large underwriter like Goldman Sachs, CS First Boston, Merrill Lynch, or Salomon Smith Barney paired with a less well known underwriter. This is important because it indicates that the smaller firm is the one with the tightest relationship with the company (maybe the chief executive officer went to school with one of the underwriter's bankers). And because of that relationship, the smaller underwriter is likely to get a decent chunk of stock to distribute. If you have an account with that brokerage firm, you stand a chance of getting stock.

Even in a strong equity market, being with a reputable broker is key to your financial well-being. There are countless examples of investors who rue the day they ever got involved with a third-tier brokerage firm. These small firms often lure investors with promises of IPOs and enormous profits on little-known small-cap stocks. But when faced with the inevitable regulatory problems and investor complaints, these brokers just close up shop. That leaves customers with few ways to recover their money. Many individuals have no access to their accounts while the regulators work the company carcass over. These days, most brokerage firms have Web sites and advertise the number of deals that they have done.

PROSPECTUS SUMMARY

Turn the cover page, and you will find the Prospectus Summary. This is where you will find a basic description of the company's operations, its hopes and dreams, how it fits into the industry, its achievements, and its strategy for growth. The IPO will also list who their top customers are and will cite recent accomplishments.

The description of Amazon.com was simple: "Amazon.com is the leading online retailer of books." It tells you how many SKUs (stock-keeping units) it sells: "The Company offers more than 2.5 million titles, including most of the estimated 1.5 million English-language books believed to be in print." And the prospectus gives key reasons why an online book retailer is better than the old-fashioned kind: "Amazon.com's high inventory turnover, lack of investment in expensive retail real estate, and reduced personnel requirements give it meaningful structural economic advantages relative to traditional booksellers." It is very clear what Amazon.com is all about.

Of course, Amazon went on to apply its business model to many other types of online retailing—compact disks, housewares, and gardening. But the example is a good one; successful, fast-growing companies change over time. The prospectus gives you an opportunity to study what is often the IPO's initial business and may offer clues to the future strategy.

However, one trick that prospectus writers use is going to great lengths to explain the business the company *wants* to be in and then glossing over what the company actually does. For example, a company may describe itself as an e-tailer or business-to-business (B2B) provider of software solutions, while it actually derives 99 percent of its revenue from traditional businesses. IPOs that pull these stunts are usually companies whose old line of business is under some kind of pressure. They want to use the occasion of an IPO to raise capital to change their colors, usually by shifting to new products and services. Product transitions like these are generally risky.

To figure out what the company actually does, you will refer to the "Management's Discussion and Analysis of Financial Condition and Results of Operations"—the MD&A section, as we call it—which occurs later in the prospectus. There you will find a discussion and a breakdown of sources of revenues.

THE OFFERING

In this section, which immediately follows the Prospectus Summary, you'll find a synopsis of how many shares the IPO is offering in the

United States and overseas and how many shares the company will have outstanding after the IPO. Getting a grip on the number of outstanding shares is critical. Most emerging growth companies pay management principally in stock options. While the chief executive officer (CEO) and other key top executives may have monetary compensation of $125,000, they also get thousands of options, usually at very low prices. An option gives the holder the right to purchase a share of stock at a set price that is generally lower than the offering price in the prospectus, so options are issued to executives partly as compensation and partly to encourage them to perform well.

Look for the option prices and the number of options. Very low priced options are free money to insiders. Very low priced options used to be the exception. Now they are standard issue.

IPOs usually exclude the option shares from their calculation of the common stock to be outstanding after the offering. This is wrong. The existence of lots of low-priced options inflates the valuation of the company, diluting public ownership. The impact can be huge. Mortgage.com, an online provider of residential mortgages, listed 41 million shares of stock to be outstanding after its August 1999 offering. However, in the footnote below the summary table, it disclosed that there were another 19.4 million shares exercisable at a low $0.98 per share. The option shares increased the market valuation of the company by nearly 50 percent.

To calculate the effect of option shares on the market capitalization of the IPO, you need to add the option shares to the number provided by the company. The right way to do this calculation is to find the percentage difference between the midpoint of the IPO price range and the low option price and then multiply that "free compensation" times the number of option shares. Add the resulting shares to the shares outstanding. If you had trouble following this, you are not alone. Most financial analysts ignore dilution.

You can approximate the number by rule of thumb. If the option price is very low, add all of the shares back. If it is about 50 percent of the offering price, add half of them back. And if it's close to the offering price, you can ignore the options. The theory behind this is that if management has options at, say, $0.50 a share and the IPO goes public at $10, management is highly likely to exercise those cheap options at the first opportunity. If the options are issued at $9 (which is close to the offering price), management will wait until the stock price is higher.

Remember, we warned you this would get technical.

SUMMARY FINANCIAL DATA

Immediately following the description of the offering is a short presentation of the company's income statement, showing whether the company is earning money. Here, the company reveals what its revenues have been for the past three to five years. This is usually not a very detailed presentation. However, you will be able to tell whether the company is profitable, what its revenue trends are, and if the company has taken any charges against income.

The IPO may also present other key ratios and data. For example, a retailer should show you same-store sales, which tells you how sales are trending in stores open more than one year. Companies that have high debt or capital expenditures will almost always show earnings before interest, depreciation, and amortization (EBITDA). They prefer that you look at EBITDA rather than at earnings because their earnings are unimpressive or nonexistent.

Finally, the IPO will present its balance sheet, showing cash, working capital, total assets, debt, and shareholders' equity. The company will give you a before- and an after-the-IPO look. The balance sheet items before the IPO are listed under the header "Actual"; the post-IPO balance sheet items are listed under "As Adjusted." Not all IPOs show the cash available, pre- and post-IPO. Make sure you know the cash available and how long it will last if there are annual losses.

Sometimes, the IPO's financial statements are straightforward. But many times they are perplexing, even for experienced analysts. Usually, confusing financial statements are the result of acquisitions, restatements of earnings, or recapitalizations.

In any case, this presentation is just the tip of the iceberg. IPOs present themselves as they would like to be seen. You can still glean some things from this summary. Are revenues growing? Is the company profitable? If it is a retailer, are same-store sales trends positive? On the negative side, you may find items that you will want to study further in other parts of the prospectus. For example, if the company took a restructuring charge, you will want to find out why. Negative same-store sales trends may be a turnoff.

A confusing pro forma financial presentation may also signal a company with things to hide. Pro forma income statements are used when a company has made an acquisition and wants to show what the revenues and income might have been had it owned the new company a year ago. The trouble with pro forma statements is that there is too much wiggle room for management. They can make too many assumptions about what might have been.

With Internet and other emerging growth companies, expect to see losses. There are three areas on which you should focus in the income statement. First, are there any revenues? IPOs that totally lack revenues are probably too early stage and too risky for investment. Look at the revenue growth. It should have a strong ramp. With biotechnology companies, sometimes their revenues represent collaborative fees from large pharmaceutical houses, not product sales. You will have to look in the MD&A to get to the bottom of the source of revenues. Second, is the gross margin positive or negative? Gross margin is the difference between what the good or service sells for and what it costs the company to produce. Even in Internet investing, it pays to have standards. If the company's gross margin is negative, it is giving its goods or services away for free, which is never a good sign. Third, how much money is the company losing? This will give you an idea of how fast the company is likely to spend the IPO proceeds. The financial presentation should also divulge "accumulated deficit." This is simply the total amount of money the company has lost since its inception. Compare revenues to the accumulated deficit. It's the Internet version of the traditional price-to-earnings (P/E) ratio. If the accumulated losses are much larger than the revenue the IPO has managed to produce, it doesn't augur well for the future.

The bottom line—you should make note of any things that are positive or potentially negative for later analysis.

RISK FACTORS

This is the scariest part of the prospectus. The lawyers want to enumerate every potential problem—real and imagined—that could arise with the company, the industry, and the offering itself. They want to do that as insurance against getting sued by irate shareholders in the future. "It was in the prospectus," is the ultimate defense.

Naturally, the Risk Factors section presents the company in the worst possible light. Because of that, IPO managements fight not to disclose unpleasant facts and negative "what if" scenarios. A common strategy is to disclose the negative information, but to sneak it in after a particularly boring section of boilerplate.

When you start reading prospectuses, it is often difficult to separate the real risks from the boilerplate risks. We will outline several real and several routine risk items as a guide for you. After reading a few prospectuses, you will be able to boil down "prospectusese" into plain English. See Exhibit 4.1, "Translating the Prospectus into English," for some examples.

First of all, *what are the real risks?*

IPOs generally put the most important risks first.

- *Accumulated deficit.* Before the Internet age, there were few profitless companies, maybe just the occasional biotech with a drug nearing approval by the Food and Drug Administration (FDA). But today, the first thing we look for is how much money the company has lost since it started business. This is called the accumulated deficit. In all likelihood, an IPO with an accumulated deficit will also confess that it will lose money for the foreseeable future. This is one of the most important risk elements you need to consider before investing in a profitless company. IPOs with huge accumulated deficits have gotten used to spending money without focusing on profits, and they are likely to burn through the proceeds of their IPO quickly.
- *Limited operating history.* A recent start-up, a roll-up, or a company that has just made a big acquisition has little track record to show investors. The products or the services are new and have unproven acceptance. Management has not worked together before. With the onslaught

Exhibit 4.1   Translating the Prospectus into English

What They Said	What They Meant
Planet Hollywood: "During the initial period following its opening, a new unit (Planet Hollywood restaurant) typically realizes higher revenue than in subsequent periods of operation, depending in part on the season in which it is opened."	People eat here once and don't come back because the food is mediocre and expensive.
Planet Hollywood: "On a same-unit basis, Direct Revenues for the first quarter of fiscal 1996 are expected to be approximately 4% below those for the first quarter of 1995."	See above.
eToys: "The online commerce market is new, rapidly evolving, and intensely competitive. Increased competition is likely to result in price reductions, reduced gross margins, and loss of market share, any of which could seriously harm our net sales and results of operations. We expect competition to intensify in the future because barriers to entry are minimal."	With so many other competitors, it's unlikely that we're going to make it.
Value America: "Our product gross margins are small or sometimes negative, and we will not become profitable unless we significantly increase purchases from our online store at acceptable gross margins."	We're giving the merchandise away to make our sales increases look good.
New Power: "We have incurred net losses since inception, and based on our current business plan we expect to continue to incur substantial losses for a significant period of time. To date, we have	Don't expect profits anytime real soon. We're too busy figuring out what we're doing. But we've got big plans on how to spend money.

Exhibit 4.1 *(continued)*

What They Said	What They Meant
recognized minimal revenue and our ability to generate revenue is subject to uncertainty. In addition, we intend to increase our operating expenses significantly to develop our business, including brand development, marketing, and other promotional activities and the continued development of our billing, customer care, and Internet Web site infrastructure."	
New Power: "We have broad discretion in how we use the proceeds of this offering, and we may not use the proceeds effectively."	We can do whatever we want with the money. Please call my chauffeur and make sure he has the Taittinger's chilled for the ride home to Greenwich.
@Road: "We anticipate that our available cash resources combined with the net proceeds from this offering will be sufficient to fund our operating needs for the next 12 months. . . . Thereafter, we expect to require additional financing in an amount that we cannot determine at this time. If our plans or assumptions change or are inaccurate, we may be required to seek capital sooner than anticipated. We may need to raise funds through public or private debt or equity financings. If we need to raise additional funds, we may not be able to do so on commercially reasonable terms, or at all, and may not be able to continue to fund our operations."	We're going to burn through the money really, really fast. This time next year we may be out of business. Take your chances.

Source: Renaissance Capital, Greenwich, CT (IPOhome.com).

of the Internet deals, this section has become almost boilerplate, but it isn't to be ignored.

• *Ongoing losses.* "We have a history of losses, we expect to incur losses in the future, and we may not achieve or maintain profitability." Although this is the mantra set forth by every Internet company and many technology and biotechnology start-ups, as investors in failed Internet IPOs will attest, it is a key, real risk. If an IPO is unable to put its IPO proceeds to effective use in a relatively short period of time, ongoing losses may prevent the company from raising additional capital and, thus, seal its fate. While Internet and technology investors are willing to put up with ongoing losses while the fledgling company builds its brand and ramps up sales, smart investors set mental milestones. Web site IPOs like drkoop.com and quepasa.com, which failed to deliver on revenue expectations, saw their stock prices swoon. In contrast, Amazon.com and Yahoo! remained unprofitable for years but saw their prices rise. The Risk Factors section, regrettably, usually doesn't provide any insights into what it will take to become profitable and serves only as a warning.

• *Customer concentration.* A most important risk is having just a handful of large, but key, customers. What if one or more of them stopped ordering the product or service? How would the IPO replace those sales? The IPO may tell you who their largest customers are and what percent of sales each comprises. Customer concentration may not be a deal killer for young start-ups that are likely to add customers quickly, but it is worth reading this closely. For example, Sycamore Networks only had one customer, Williams Communications, when it launched its IPO. But it was actually selling commercial-grade optical products to Williams. On the other hand, if the IPO is selling products to customers who are merely testing them, this puts those future revenues at greater risk. The customers haven't decided whether they want to use the product on an ongoing basis.

• *Lengthy sales cycle.* Needing a lot of time to sell a product means that the product is expensive and its purchase is a major decision on the part of the customer. For a small company, this can mean "lumpy" quarterly revenues—a lot of revenue can fall in the June quarter due to timing, and the September quarter could be lower. In growth companies, investors want to see consistent, sequential revenue growth. Revenue disappointments can wreck havoc on a stock price.

• *Product acceptance.* If a product or service is new, the company cannot be sure if customers will buy it. This seems simple, but it's important. A small technology company competing to gain market share away from established companies must have a much better, much cheaper mousetrap. However, a small technology company that is the first mover, or first to offer a particular product that addresses a large opportunity, is far more likely to be successful. Medical device companies are prone to this issue. A medical device company must earn not only acceptance from physicians, who are cautious in adopting new technology, but also reimbursement approval from insurers. We once analyzed a company that was developing a helmet that would allow surgeons to perform surgery by looking at a magnified image projected inside the helmet. The underwriter said it was a hot deal. But when we called a potential customer listed in the prospectus, an assistant told us that the device was so unwieldy that they had put it in storage, where it was gathering dust.

• *Operational or financial control issues.* If an IPO discloses that it is having internal control problems, that its computers crash a lot, or that its management information system needs to be upgraded, there are serious problems. A company with problems might entitle such disclosure as, "In order to manage our growth and expansion, we will need to improve and implement new systems, procedures, and controls."

• *Rapid growth.* Small companies have finite resources. And even if being small makes them nimble, growing from 10 employees to 200 employees in a year can be a challenge for a young, untested entrepreneur. Another issue is the availability of qualified workers. Yellow flags for investors might go up if a small, regional restaurant chain that is about to embark on a national rollout has no executives with relevant experience. Another yellow-flag raiser is fast-growing Internet companies with dubious business plans and inexperienced managers.

• *Customization.* Software and systems companies have high margins because their products are "shrink-wrapped," or right off the shelf. If an IPO has to employ costly consultants to install, customize, and test the product, margins fall. If an IPO has this issue, it may refer to "sophisticated" products that are "deployed in complex environments" and have "errors or defects that we find only after full deployment." If a software company has to send in legions of consultants to correct glitches, not only does it incur the expense of these consultants, but it may not be able to book the product sale until the installation is complete.

• *Sole-source contract manufacturers.* If an IPO outsources its products, as many apparel manufacturers and technology companies do, the principal risk is if the company relies on a single manufacturer. What if the manufacturer has a strike? What if it experiences an earthquake? What if there's a war, or unrest, or a hurricane?

• *Geographic concentration.* If an IPO has all of its operations in a narrow geographic area, it is prone to economic downturns and—not joking—adverse weather. For example, the casino industry in Las Vegas, even though it draws customers nationally, occasionally experiences severe weather in the mountains, preventing gamblers from entering from California. Another industry generally prone to this risk is homebuilders.

• *Insider transactions.* If a company discloses any leases or sales of property relating to insiders, these transactions are generally egregious and should be studied further in the prospectus. Any other insider transactions that are disclosed in this section are usually there because the SEC wants to emphasize the potential conflict of interest. For example, if the chairman or other insiders benefit substantially from the deal by cashing out, that will be disclosed here. Additionally, if members of management have substantial outside interests, like running another company, for example, that will be cited here. Even if no insider transactions are highlighted here, make sure you refer to the "certain transactions" section, located after the description of "management."

• *Litigation.* Any lawsuits mentioned in this section must be examined thoroughly. To warrant mention in this section, the potential implications must be serious. Litigation at best is a distraction and at worst is a company killer.

• *Other industry-specific disclosure.* Retailers will provide information about same stores. If same-store sales have been particularly strong, the prospectus will warn of their unsustainability. But, in the prospectus for

Planet Hollywood, the company warned that same-store sales for celebrity-based restaurant chains were turning negative. The IPO was a complete flop. Smart investors figured out why people visited Planet Hollywood once, never to return. The food is mediocre and expensive; the chain is dependent on tourists, not locals.

Next, what are the routine risks?

Every prospectus is full of boilerplate, put there by lawyers for the IPO, the underwriter, and the SEC. You should still read these sections, however, because the management of the company may sneak in relevant information in the middle of a particularly dreary section. The boilerplate doesn't shed any particular light on the IPO that you are investigating. As you read prospectuses, you will see these sections appearing over and over. In fact, when the lawyers are preparing the company's first draft of the prospectus, they cut and paste good material from other companies' prospectuses. In school, plagiarism is bad; in prospectus writing, it is good because it means that the SEC has vetted the language.

Here are some typical boilerplate sections:

• *Fluctuating results.* "Our quarterly results may fluctuate and are difficult to predict, and if our future results are below the expectations of public market analysts, the price of our stock may decline." This is not intended for your enlightenment. It's intended to stave off potential class action suits by listing everything that could possibly go wrong. The prospectus will then list a bunch of things that could go wrong, from new-product introduction timings to political instability or natural disasters.

• *Product acceptance.* "We may not achieve anticipated revenues if the introduction and customer acceptance of our new product is unsuccessful." True enough. If a company can't sell product, it will have no revenue. Again, the company will list a number of factors.

• *Key executives.* "The success of our business depends on our key personnel whose knowledge of our business and technical/creative expertise would be difficult to replace." This is in every prospectus. In the case of a company that does really rely on one person, such as Donna Karan, Martha Stewart, or Ralph Lauren, it is a real risk.

• *Litigation and patents.* Companies try to cover themselves by cautioning that they could be subject to litigation and challenges of their patents. But unless there are actual law suits mentioned, it's boilerplate.

• *Failure to hire and retain personnel.* It goes without saying that if a company can't hire and retain personnel, it will have trouble growing. Good technology employees are hard to find. If a company mentions this and has specifics to support it, only then is it a real risk. Most prospectuses have this risk, but you should read it thoroughly to determine if it is company specific or put in there by the lawyers.

• *Additional capital.* Clearly, if the company needs to raise money shortly after the IPO, that is not a good sign. If this section is vague, it's probably boilerplate. You'll have to wait to get to the "Liquidity" section further along to find out.

READ THE BOILERPLATE

An IPO is also required to list the major risks in the industry in which it operates. It is usually stuck toward the end of the section, just when a reader's attention may be waning. Even if you are familiar with an industry, read the section because sometimes an IPO sticks a nasty little item in the midst of a tedious description of industry risks and regulations. For example, a large alternative power company, NRG, disclosed that it was losing close to $100 million in revenue due to a change in regulations in New York State. Not only did they stick the disclosure in the third paragraph of a mind-numbing disquisition on the Federal Energy Regulatory Commission, they disclosed the $100 million impact as $8 million in February, $8.2 million in March, and so on. While not incorrect, this type of disclosure lulls an inattentive reader into concluding "only $8 million," and the investor might not take the next step of assessing the entire impact of $100 million over a year.

SEC REQUIRED RISKS

Finally, the SEC requires companies to detail the risks relating to the offering. Experienced investors know these risks. But investors new to buying IPOs and equities should review them.

- *Volatility.* "Our stock price may be volatile." True, all stocks go up and down. This is a risk you take in owning equities, particularly small-capitalization stocks.
- *Liquidity.* "An active trading market may not develop." Absolutely a real risk. If a small company fails to develop a following among Wall Street analysts, the brokerage firms will not make a market in the shares. It will "trade by appointment only" in the pink sheets, which list illiquid securities.
- *Use of proceeds.* "Our management may apply the proceeds of this offering to uses that do not produce profitability or increase market value." While management is required to state what they intend to use the IPO proceeds for, in reality they have tremendous discretion on where the IPO money is spent.
- *Control.* "Insiders will continue to have substantial control." Absolutely. We'll look at how much in a later section.
- *Antitakeover provisions.* "Antitakeover provisions could prevent a change of control." Most U.S. IPOs incorporate in Delaware, which is known for its sophisticated and management-friendly legal system.
- *Substantial sales of future stock.* With nearly every IPO, management and other insiders who own substantial blocks of stock are prevented from selling stock for a period after the offering. This is called the "lockup period." It is not an SEC restriction but an agreement between the management and the underwriter. A typical lockup period is 180 days. However, the underwriter can release management earlier. The number of shares subject to this provision used to be listed here. The SEC has moved it to another part of the prospectus. Look it up in the prospectus's table of contents.

USE OF PROCEEDS

This section immediately follows the Risk Factors. Here, the IPO spells out how it plans to spend your money. Ideally, you want the IPO to invest it in growing the company. Because technology and Internet companies generally don't have any debt, they will use the IPO proceeds for research and development (R&D) and brand development.

However, some high-growth companies are saddled with accumulated losses and, perhaps, debt from making acquisitions. In those cases, the management will elect to pay down the debt. The question then arises, "Whose debt?" If the company is paying off the debt of insiders, like management or other investors, this is a negative. The company must tell you if the money is going to insiders. Sometimes the prospectus will say that the proceeds are paying down the "11 percent subordinated note." If that is the case, turn to "Certain Transactions," which will indicate who owns the 11 percent subordinated note. You have just become an "IPO Detective." Companies that go to that amount of trouble to hide where the money goes usually have other warts. Be wary of companies that have done recent leveraged recapitalizations or leveraged buyouts (LBOs) in which a lot of money was borrowed. It is likely that the money borrowed was used to pay off insiders before the IPO. The proceeds of the IPO are going to go to pay off this debt. It is exactly the same thing as having the IPO proceeds go directly to pay off insiders.

Very squishy explanations of the use of proceeds are also suspect. Not being able to precisely identify uses of proceeds is generally okay in a fast-growing company because you are hoping they will put it to work profitably. Perhaps for competitive reasons, they don't want to publish their intentions. But a slow-growing company whose use of proceeds is "general corporate purposes" and "liquidity" usually plans to feather its own nest. Those reasons for going public bring into question whether the offering is just to create a public market for the stock for future insider bailouts.

Other turnoffs include paying large dividends to insiders and, in the case of a spin-off, turning the money back to the parent.

MANAGEMENT'S DISCUSSION AND ANALYSIS OF FINANCIAL CONDITIONS AND RESULTS OF OPERATIONS

This is the heart of the prospectus. This is where management must tell you where its revenues come from and where they go. You should read it alongside the detailed financial table that immediately precedes it. This section is usually two pages and is immediately followed by explanations of the financial results of the past two or three years. Here is where the IPO describes exactly what it does, where the sales come from, how it recognizes revenue, and what its expenses are. This section will provide you with the reality check on how the IPO presented itself initially.

Chief financial officers (CFOs) can and do use accounting to make their companies look good. And what more important time to look good than the occasion of a company's public debut—its IPO? The MD&A section will describe the company's significant accounting policies. The first thing that experienced analysts look for is revenue recognition—what does the company record as sales and when does the company record these sales?

Many Internet companies recognize the full value of items they sell, even though they never actually hold the goods in inventory. This has the effect of inflating revenues many, many times over what they actually are. Examples of companies that booked the gross ticketed prices of nonpublished airline tickets as revenue are eBookers (a London-based provider of cheap seats) and Cheap Tickets (a Honolulu-based seller of excess airline capacity). Because the commission on the tickets is relatively small, putting the gross bookings in revenue arguably inflates revenues many times over what they should be. Internet companies are understandably sensitive about their sometimes-small revenues, and the practice is currently permitted. It is a practice used by some business-to-consumer (B2C) commerce companies, as well. However, it is misleading to investors. This manner in which revenues are booked will be disclosed in the MD&A.

The Financial Accounting Standards Board and the SEC are looking into this practice. It is likely that many Internet companies will be figments of their former selves.

Pushing the envelope on accounting standards is one of the dangers of investing in IPOs. New industries are notoriously liberal with their accounting. There are no standards. It may take many years for the accounting industry to catch up with them.

Another issue is when an IPO recognizes revenue. A conservative company will recognize the revenue from software sales, for example, over the life of the contract. An aggressive CFO might book all of the revenue right away to make the company appear profitable. It will eventually catch up with the company, but that may take years.

A well-publicized recent example of that practice is MicroStrategy, which sells "data mining" software, or programs that help businesses collect and analyze the buying habits of customers. The company booked revenue from large contracts immediately, rather than over the life of the contract. MicroStrategy had to go back and redo all of its past financial statements, reducing its revenue significantly. Its stock price plummeted from a high of $333 to the single digits.

And don't count on accountants to enforce conservative revenue recognition. MicroStrategy's books were audited by Pricewaterhouse-Coopers, an industry leader. MicroStrategy, in fact, was "outed" by reports issued by the Center for Financial Research and Analysis in Rockville, Maryland, and then by *Forbes* magazine.

The prospectus may also describe any recent trends or changes in policies. Study any changes closely. They may have been made for the sole reason of making the company look good right now. For example, sometimes acquisitions are timed to manipulate earnings or revenue increases. Be wary of companies that are in the habit of making acquisitions and then writing them off a year or two later. That should tell you that the IPO's management not only has bad judgment about the companies it acquires but also overpays for them.

Next, the prospectus will describe for each of the past two or three years its results of operations. If the IPO is occuring in the middle of a year, this section will begin by presenting what's called the "stub" period (the year to date, compared with the previous year's comparable period).

The prospectus will first describe why its revenues went up or down. Next it will describe gross profits trends, and finally, operating income trends. When reading the revenue section, focus on the source of revenue growth. Is it from new products and services? Increases in same-store sales? The result of adding salespersons? When buying a growth company, it is important to zero in on why the company is growing.

This is where you look at what the company says it is doing and compare that with actual results. For example, if an IPO touts its new enterprise software at the beginning of the prospectus, you'd better see it racking up sales here. If an IPO is making a product transition, the

"Results of Operations" section will give you some clues as to whether the transition is occurring. Time and time again, we have seen companies whose software or systems have become obsolete try to raise money through an IPO to finance their entry into a new business. This is risky for the company and financially dangerous for the investor.

Some companies grow mostly through acquisitions. Oftentimes, the prospectus will gloss over this fact. Try to figure out if there is any internal growth by subtracting the revenue from the acquisition. If there isn't, you may want to take a pass.

Once you've analyzed the company's sources of revenue, move on to the discussion of what it costs the company to produce its products or services. First, the IPO will describe the basic direct costs—the cost of goods. For example, if the company is a software vendor, gross margin will be high because the per unit cost of software is a CD-ROM and shrink-wrap. In contrast, the gross margin for an Internet retailer will be very low because the costs of acquiring the goods it sells are relatively high. Beware of negative gross margins. If a company has negative gross margins, it is giving its goods or services away. During the height of the Internet craze, we actually came across some e-tailers that successfully went public with negative gross margins. Stamps.com, the venture-backed provider of Internet postage, took first prize with *infinitely* negative gross margins. They had no revenue at the time of the IPO, so dividing expenses of $8 million by zero produced that result. Following in second place was e-commerce PartsBase.com, which offered one-stop shopping for aircraft parts, with gross margins of –787 percent. And coming in third was Neoforma.com, a B2B marketplace for medical products, with gross margins of –453 percent, which blamed its results on its very early stage of development. More recently, Web-accessible global-positioning-system provider @Road went public with gross margins of –84 percent and net margins of –868 percent, because they were selling hardware below cost. But with $39 million in losses at the time of the IPO and additional financing required, it seemed @Road had a very big pothole to dig itself out of.

Operating margins show how profitable the company is after it includes sales and marketing, overhead, and depreciation. It goes without saying that these trends should be positive. To make the comparison, ignore one-time charges. Be on the lookout for any telltale signs of expense manipulation, for example, reductions in depreciation and changes in inventory valuation. Remember that expenses can be pushed off into the future but not buried forever.

The prospectus will then proceed to discuss net income, which is the amount left over after taxes. However, as an investor you are primarily interested in the operating results.

After you've satisfied yourself that you understand recent operating results, turn to the financial statements at the end of the prospectus. The numbers at the bottom of the pages begin with "F-1." First read the report of the independent auditor. It is always found on the second page of the "Financials" section. It should be issued by a major firm and should be *unqualified,* which means that the audit was prepared in accordance with generally accepted auditing standards and free from material misstatement. If the report contains words like *going concern* or *except for,* run for the hills. *Going concern* means that unless the company raises cash fast, it's out of business. And *except for* means that there was some aspect of the company or its financial controls that concerned the auditor.

Next, go to the balance sheet. The balance sheet is a snapshot of the IPO at a point in time. It lists assets and liabilities.

Look at inventory levels, which are found in "Assets." Are they rising at the same rate as sales? If they are rising much faster than sales, the IPO's revenues are questionable. This is a common problem for fashion-oriented and technology companies because the risk of obsolescence is high.

However, an IPO may have perfectly logical reasons for the high inventory levels. The company may be expanding rapidly. If the IPO does have a *good* reason, you can be sure it will be highlighted in the MD&A section.

The next balance sheet item to look at is "Accounts Receivable." This shows the amount that the company is owed by customers for the sales of its products. If it has risen much more than sales, beware. The IPO may be recognizing shipments of goods or services as revenue well ahead of when customers are likely to pay. Some technology and fashion apparel IPOs have been known to "stuff" the distribution channel, which means that they shipped higher levels of goods to stores or distributors to boost near-term revenues. The retailers and the distributors will then need more time to work through the higher levels of product, so revenues in subsequent periods will be hurt because the retailers and distributors won't continue to accept the shipments.

Returning to the MD&A section, look for quarterly results. IPOs should disclose quarterly results—but they don't always do so. If no information is available, this is a yellow flag. If a company has made a recent acquisition, they will probably not report comparable quarterly results. In a growth company, you want to see not only year-over-year growth, but also sequential quarterly growth. If a quarter declines sequentially, the company may be highly seasonal or may sell high-ticket products, which produce "lumpy" revenues.

Look also at the revenue mix from quarter to quarter. Software companies that have rising professional-services revenue as a percent of total revenue almost always have declining gross margins because professional services are so labor intensive.

LIQUIDITY AND CAPITAL RESOURCES

This section describes the IPO's cash flows over the past two years. Cash flows are important because they are the true cash generated by the business. The cash flows for nearly all Internet companies are, of course, negative. That means they are consuming rather than generating money. If the IPO is still a money-losing enterprise, this section will explain how it's managing to stay afloat.

The IPO will also detail just how it has spent its money over the past two years. It may also indicate what it expects to spend over the next year. With this information, plus the size of the accumulated deficit and annual losses, you can figure out how fast the company will go through the IPO proceeds plus its existing cash. It is unusual for a company to admit it may have to raise more money within 12 months. Companies like this are highly risky because the cash burn rate is high and management is under tremendous pressure to perform and keep the stock price up. High burn rates were the cause for the demise of many once-high-flying Internet companies. The IPO graveyard is full of big-spending dot.coms.

BUSINESS

The "Business" section of the prospectus goes into much detail about the IPO's operations and the industry background. In many cases, the discussion of the industry itself will help you understand the market opportunity and how the IPO is positioning itself. Some IPOs have really useful industry presentations that include statistics on the size of the market and on projected growth.

The company then generally elaborates on its strategy. These sections are true marketing pitches. The text points out a problem in its industry, and then it proceeds to describe its innovative solution to this market opportunity. With most IPOs, even technology companies, a thoughtful reader can piece together the so-called market opportunity and reach an educated judgment on whether this particular company is the horse to ride. Granted, some prospectuses are so badly written or the area is so highly technical that the uninitiated really can't understand them.

The rest of the Business section goes into detail on subjects that were touched on in the Summary.

The IPO will take you through:

- Products and services
- Customers
- Product technology and architecture
- Sales and marketing
- Manufacturing (if relevant)
- Product development (R&D)
- Customer support and services
- Competition
- Strategic relationships
- Patents and intellectual property
- Employees
- Legal proceedings

MANAGEMENT AND CONTROL

Who is running the company is as important as the financial results and business. As you read the biographies of the management and directors of the company, ask yourself whether these individuals have the backgrounds necessary to run the company. Have they worked for similar companies in the past in increasing positions of responsibility? Have they ever been involved in a start-up? You want to see a history of success.

If members of top management have checkered pasts, watch out. Past bankruptcies, felony convictions, and violations of U.S. securities laws should be taken very seriously. These crimes speak volumes about how they will operate in the future.

Other obvious turnoffs are a job-hopping CEO, lack of relevant experience, and lack of significant stock ownership. Also check for familial relationships. Who wants to be a public shareholder of a company that has fathers, mothers, in-laws, cousins, and children on the payroll? Another concern is the age of the CEO. If the CEO owns a lot of stock and is close to retirement, make sure that a line of succession is clear and that the CEO isn't planning to liquidate.

A board typically consists of officers of the company, the representatives of large shareholders, and people who are neither employees of the company nor shareholders. The officers of the company and the large shareholders are insiders and can be expected to make decisions in their own best interests, which may not be the same as the interests of the public shareholders. That's why most companies ask people who don't work for the company, don't have a financial interest in it, and aren't related to company officers to sit on the board and represent the interests of the public shareholders.

The trouble with a good many IPOs is that they have been run by the insiders —the venture capitalists and the founders—since day one. The only reason these IPOs put independent directors on the board is pressure from underwriters and potential investors. It simply looks bad if an IPO lacks one or two outside directors. With no independent people sitting on the board, investors conclude that management will simply feather their own nests.

In truth these outside directors usually do have some ties or interests in the IPO. They almost always have some relationship with the IPO's management or large shareholders. They are asked to be on the board because they will bring business connections, will offer sound advice, or have highly regarded technical expertise. The board of directors of a biotech IPO, for example, should have several medical heavyweights from well-known universities and medical centers.

Exceptions to the outside director rule are companies that have strong venture capital backers. Although there may be no outside directors, the strategy of the venture capital firm is to ensure that the IPO is successful as a public company. Only if the IPO is successful in its debut and first year as a public company will the venture firm be able to liquidate its holdings, which is their endgame. Venture capital firms have people sitting on the board of directors to hold management's feet to the fire. Venture firms are unforgiving. They will replace top management if they aren't performing.

Most IPOs offer their nonexecutive directors, as the independent directors are called, fairly minimal compensation for their efforts. It's not uncommon to see directors paid in stock, and not cash. However, when director compensation hits the $20,000 level, warning bells should go off. Cushy compensation for attending four meetings a year may make the "independent" directors more interested in siding with management than in representing the public shareholders.

Management compensation, as well, should be realistic. Salary levels of $100,000 to $150,000 for start-up IPO executives are appropriate. If the executives are successful, their payoff will be in the stock options they hold. In a more established company that is going public for the first time, the top executives should have a balance between cash and stock compensation. A top executive making anything close to $1 million a year in cash compensation is far more likely to be interested in his golf handicap than in launching a new product. Public shareholders want management to be hungry for success.

CERTAIN TRANSACTIONS

The last place you check for unseemly relationships among insiders is "Certain Transactions." In this section you will find all of the stuff the company would rather not disclose about relationships with insiders, cushy agreements, cozy employment contracts, loans to officers, cheap option grants, company-paid-for vehicles, extra fees paid to insiders, and leases of office space from insiders. While almost every company has some deals that look bad in the light of day, the judgment call is the number and the monetary significance of the deals.

For example, one acquisitive IPO had agreed to pay its chairman a percentage of every future acquisition. Because the chairman would get a percentage of each acquisition price, it was in his financial interest to have the acquisition prices be high. Not only would he get paid more by overpaying for acquisitions, but the more overpriced acquisitions he brokered the better . . . for him. That IPO was scuttled because investors objected to these fees. The IPO came around for a second attempt—without the incentive fees.

In the cases where the IPO is a family-owned or closely held company, you will come across leases, dividends to insiders, and other non-arm's length transactions. However, if these transactions stop once the company does its IPO, the company is making an appropriate transition from what's acceptable for a private company to the standards of a public company.

This section will help you put to rest any possible confusion about the use of proceeds if the proceeds are being used to pay off debt. The "Use of Proceeds" section should indicate whose debt is being repaid. Sometimes, the prospectus writers refer to the debt as the "11% Notes" or the "12% Subordinated Debt." If you can find debt that was given by insiders to the IPO that matches precisely the debt being paid down in the Use of Proceeds section, then go to the footnotes of the audited Financials to confirm where the money is going.

PRINCIPAL STOCKHOLDERS OR PRINCIPAL AND SELLING STOCKHOLDERS

The acid test for investors is the amount of stock owned by management. The executives of the company must have a significant financial stake in the company. This keeps their feet to the fire and keeps them working for you. In a venture-backed IPO, the venture firms may own the bulk of the shares. That's okay as long as management's stake is financially significant to them. However, be concerned if only one person owns stock. This is sometimes true with family-owned businesses. How enthusiastic and hardworking are the top executives going to be if they own no shares? How is the stockholder going to dispose of his or her shares?

With old economy companies and closely held businesses, it is likely that some of the shareholders will be selling their shares in the IPO. This is not necessarily a bad thing. The significance of shareholder selling depends on who the seller is and how many shares of stock are sold. Clearly, the executive officers shouldn't be selling. But if they are, is it a lot? If they still own a significant amount of stock, they may be selling for perfectly understandable and human reasons—liquidity, college bills, or need for cash. There is a difference between cashing out and selling a few thousand shares. If the top executives are cashing out, they do not think much of the company and its prospects. You should follow their lead.

Venture capitalists usually do not sell on the IPO. Selling by the venture firms on the IPO is a deal killer, and it indicates that the venture firm is frustrated with its investment and wants out fast. They may have concluded that the company is a dud. If so, they are likely to bail out completely at the end of the lockup period, which will put selling pressure on the stock. Because the venture capital firm has had plenty of opportunity to work with management and to understand the company's business, it knows more than you do about the IPO's prospects. Venture firms can make mistakes on their initial assessments of companies. And, with record pools of cash, they are highly pressured to make investments and some of them are made in haste.

Sometimes, there will be long lists of selling shareholders. Start-ups are often financed by friends and family. These investors have had an illiquid security for some time and are eagerly taking advantage of their first opportunity to cash out. This is not a negative by itself.

FINANCIALS

If you have read through this much of the prospectus and if you are still seriously interested in the IPO, look at the company's financials. As mentioned earlier, you should see if the inventories and the accounts receivables are growing at about the same rate as revenues. You should also read through the notes to the financial statements. These notes may clarify any remaining questions about the company's business model and financial practices.

CONCLUSION

Everything in a prospectus is there for a reason. The company clearly wants to put its best foot forward and convince potential investors of its great opportunity, bright prospects, and capable management. Management also wants to downplay anything that is potentially negative. The underwriters, who have dollar signs on their eyeballs because of the fees they'll reap with a successful offering, are intensely aware of the threat of lawsuits and punishment for violations of SEC requirements. So, they do their due diligence and insist on certain disclosures and changes in company practices. And the SEC reviews the document to make sure that it conforms to its standards for operational and financial disclosure.

The prospectus contains the most disclosure a company will be forced to make in its public career. Just by reading it carefully, taking notes, and thinking about what was presented, you will know more about the company than 99 percent of the investing public. Use this process to reach conclusions about whether the company is a fundamentally sound one or a dud. You will also be able to assess management's ability to carry forward. Taken together, you will be able to reach a reasonable judgment about whether the IPO has a big enough market opportunity, has a competitive product, and has the managerial resources to win.

If you read the prospectus and reach conclusions about the valuation of the IPO and decide to buy stock, you will be able to respond knowledgeably to future news and events. You will have an edge because most of the other investors out there make ill-informed and emotional decisions. Information is your best weapon against costly investment decisions.

SECRET 5

What Makes a Good IPO

After studying Amazon.com's prospectus in 1997, we concluded, "This is a winner." Against prevailing wisdom that much bigger Barnes & Noble would eat Amazon.com for lunch, we told our clients to jump in.

Barron's headlined, "Web's Biggest Bookstore? Don't Make Book on It." The article went on to note that Barnes & Noble wasn't rolling over dead and unplugging its espresso machines. It quoted an investment expert who contended that Amazon.com was a bookseller, not an Internet retailer.

We bravely stuck to our guns. We were quoted in *Barron's* as a fan of Amazon.com, saying, "Amazon is one of the killer applications on the Web."

Our thinking was that the bricks-and-mortar booksellers, Borders and Barnes & Noble, would enter the market reluctantly because they were afraid of cannibalizing their existing business. Why would they abandon their land-based franchises and jump into the unknown?

Our initial public offering (IPO) research opined, "We think there is an opportunity for a very focused firm to pull a market share coup over established booksellers who are naturally dragging their feet."

In his year-end wrap-up, the *Barron's* reporter admitted that we "got it exactly right."

The most emotionally satisfying and financially rewarding IPO picks are those that go against the prevailing wisdom. And even in frothy markets, those companies exist. Because the thundering herd of institutional investors hasn't stampeded demand for the IPO, when a company like this is priced, the price is right—right for the buyers, that is. In down markets good IPOs are easier to pick, because underwriters are forced to raise their standards.

Good IPOs are like happy families—they share a number of characteristics. We've identified 10 success factors. Every IPO won't have all 10, but will likely possess a majority of them.

SUCCESS FACTOR 1

Winning IPOs address a significant market opportunity. With Americans buying $30 billion worth of books a year and the rest of the world buying another $60 billion, online book sales are clearly a big potential market. The idea of transforming a bricks-and-mortar bookstore into an online store with unlimited shelf space gave Amazon the opportunity to address the global book buyer, not just the potential customers who live within 10 miles of a physical store. Amazon's store was open 24 hours a day: it was as close as a book lover's computer, and it offered 2.5 million titles, including most of the 1.5 million English language books in print. This was a significant market opportunity.

E*Trade, the online discount broker, is another example of an innovative company addressing a large opportunity. In 1997 at the time of the E*Trade IPO, Forrester Research, which is a technology consulting firm, forecast that online accounts would hit 10 million by 2001. E*Trade and its competitors were already well past that milestone by 1999. Cheaper, more efficient online trading was such a hit with leading-edge investors that by early 2000, online customers numbered 15 million. Moreover, it was clear from the E*Trade prospectus that it had a well-defined plan for expansion, proprietary technology, and a strong brand identity.

IPO investors need to be more focused on the significance of innovation than do investors in large-capitalization, established companies. By its nature, the IPO market is populated by companies that are trying new things. But what is new is not necessarily innovative. And what is innovative is not necessarily financially significant or commercially viable. For an innovation to make money for its investors, the new idea must address a commercially significant unfilled need and improve productivity.

Truly great innovations are few. Exhibit 5.1 lists the engineering achievements that have the greatest influences on life and commerce. The National Academy of Engineering ranked the 20 greatest engineering achievements of the twentieth century. Topping the list was electrification, which occurred around the turn of the century; it was quickly adopted by industry but took nearly 20 years to make its way into homes. Next on the list was the automobile, which dramatically extended and speeded up the distances that could be traveled. Close on its heels were the airplane, safe water supply and distribution, and electronics (mean-

Exhibit 5.1 The Greatest Engineering Achievements of the 20th Century

1.	Electrification
2.	Automobile
3.	Airplane
4.	Water supply and distribution
5.	Electronics
6.	Radio and television
7.	Agricultural mechanization
8.	Computers
9.	Telephone
10.	Air conditioning and refrigeration
11.	Highways
12.	Spacecraft
13.	Internet
14.	Imaging
15.	Household appliances
16.	Health technologies
17.	Petroleum and petroleum technologies
18.	Laser and fiber optics
19.	Nuclear technologies
20.	High-performance materials

Source: Copyright 2000 National Academy of Engineering. All rights reserved.

ing the microprocessor). It is interesting that the engineers ranked the Internet a lowly 13th on the list, just after highways and space-craft. Perhaps as the Internet matures and the commercial significance of it becomes better understood and realized, the Internet will move up the list.

Each of these breakthroughs was so powerful that it created other products and technologies that were extensions of it. This created even more value. Many of the companies that launched these breakthrough technologies are still around today. Consolidated Edison (electrification), Kodak (imaging), and AT&T (telephone) launched IPOs around the turn of the century. The 1920s saw the debuts of innovators IBM (computers), Chrysler (automobiles), Phillips Petroleum (petroleum), and Warner Brothers (radio and television).

Time after time, major innovations like these are pounced on by small, new companies that try to leverage (advance) the technology. The introduction of the computer chip by Intel in 1971 spawned opportunities for computer makers and software writers. Fledgling Microsoft was one of the early purchasers of Intel's second-generation chip, the "8008." Likewise, the advent of the Internet has produced a long line of new companies trying to cobble together products and services that play off it.

One of the characteristics of a truly innovative technology is that it is like a large and growing family that flourishes generation after generation. The original computers were huge expensive devices that were suitable only for large applications within very large organizations. The invention of the microprocessor was the step that permitted the first personal computers to be introduced in the 1970s. And further advances in microtechnology have produced new generations of handheld devices that have more computing power than did the early models in the 1970s. The development of the Internet will likely follow a similar pattern, with clunky first attempts at businesses finally giving way to successful and profitable products and services.

The genomics area is developing along the same lines. Most of us don't have a Ph.D. in biochemistry and can't recite from memory the proteins that comprise DNA. However, we all know that the charting of the human genome is a major breakthrough, offering tantalizing possibilities of cures or vaccines for cancer or diabetes. The problem is how to distinguish the good biotechnology companies from the bad ones. For the lay person, there is really no good way. One reason why most of the biotechnology IPOs performed very well was that investors were buying portfolios of these companies. Unable to tell the companies apart, investors bet on the opportunity itself, not the individual companies. One way to increase your chances of selecting winners in this category is to bet only on the companies that have commercialized their product. That reduces risk considerably.

Like a blast from the past, the need for inexpensive, alternative sources of electricity is a major investment opportunity for the twenty-first century. In the 1980s, opponents of nuclear power, incompetent state and federal regulators, and high interest rates stopped the nation's electric utilities from building additional electricity generating facilities. Today, some electric utilities are faced with inadequate generating capacity and aging plants. Coming to the rescue are developers of fuel cells and smaller, more efficient generators. Reserve margins (the amount of unused generating capacity) have plummeted from 33 percent during the 1960s and 1970s to under 15 percent today.

Fuel cell technology has been around for 50 years, but researchers have not been able to build commercially viable fuel cells that are efficient and reliable. A fuel cell combines hydrogen from natural gas or methane with oxygen from the air to produce power without combustion. They generate power through a chemical process that produces water, useable heat, and negligible pollutants. They are an environmentalist's dream. Individual homes and apartments could have their own fuel cells, thus reducing demand from the power grid. Automobiles could be powered by fuel cells, which would mean a reduction in carbon dioxide pollution. There have been a number of fuel cell IPOs, all several years from launching a commercial product. Investors have been snapping up Plug Power and Ballard Power in the hope that these will be the first to break through with a viable device.

Other electric-power market opportunities are companies that make efficient power generators that use a variety of nonpremium fuels such as kerosene, sour gas, and diesel fuel. Capstone Turbine, founded in 1988 by Asea Brown Boveri alumnae, makes environmentally friendly

Exhibit 5.2   IPOs Addressing Significant Market Opportunities

Telecommunications	Opportunity	Solution
Sycamore Networks, Corvis	Faster backbone networks	Optical fiber switch
Global Crossing 360 Networks	More bandwidth	Global fiber-optic networks
Sonus Networks	Convergence of voice and data networks	Packetized voice over Internet
Juniper Networks, Avici Systems, Brocade	Faster data networks	High speed switches, routers
Palm, Aether Systems	Mobile internet	Handheld internet devices

Biotechnology/ Healthcare	Opportunity	Solution
Affymetrix, Invitrogen, Bruker Daltonics	Genetic analytic tools	Chips, systems, and reagents
deCode Genetics, Diversa	Gene/protein target discovery	Proprietary research and databases
Intermune, Tanox, Praceis	Drug development	R&D
Healtheon	Medical paperwork inefficiencies	Internet-based solutions

Internet Commerce	Opportunity	Solution
eBay, Yahoo!, Amazon	Consumer-to-consumer	Internet interaction and shopping
Ariba, FreeMarkets	Business transactions	Online buyer/ supplier services
E.piphany, Kana, Broadvision	One-to-one marketing	Personalized software and security
Tibco, Verisign	Internet-based corporate networks	Internet software and security
Transmeta	Handheld intelligence	Specialized chips

Exhibit 5.2 IPOs Addressing Significant Market Opportunities *(continued)*

Energy	Opportunity	Solution
NRG	Need for power	Private power generators
Capstone Turbine, Plug Power	Environmentally friendly power	Alternative solutions

Technologies	Opportunity	Solution
Globespan, Broadcom	High speed local service	Cable and DSL chips
Avanex, Finisar, New Focus	High-speed networks, components	Fiber-optics components

Source: Renaissance Capital, Greenwich, CT (IPOhome.com).

microturbine generators that can be used by utilities, by small businesses, and by vehicles. Capstone went public in 2000 at $16 and soared upward as investors realized its potential. These and other significant market opportunities are shown in Exhibit 5.2.

On the other hand, great IPOs can also be found in niche markets. The size of the market niche is important. The size of the company is limited by the size of the potential market. For example, a biopharmaceutical company may have developed a drug to treat an "orphan disease," that is, a rare one with few sufferers. Though the biotech may have a truly effective drug to treat a horrible affliction, as a public company, it will not likely amount to much because its niche is too, well, nichey.

A defensible niche in electronics is handheld organizers. Palm and Handspring both make personal digital assistants (PDAs). Their operating systems and marketing were so good that they established themselves as market leaders, shutting the door on Microsoft and others. The keys to isolating a successful player in a niche market are a superior product and limited competition.

Another example of a successful niche is specialized consulting. Corporate Executive Board, which is the leading provider of "best practices" research on corporate strategy and general management, provides this research to 1,300 of the world's largest corporations. Although their market is limited to large corporations that can afford the $30,000 annual subscription fee, it is a profitable area of consulting with few competitors.

SUCCESS FACTOR 2

The IPO should be a first mover or category killer. The virtues of being first in an industry are obvious. An IPO can establish its brand and gain loyal customers ahead of competitors. Palm established itself as the leader with a suite of spiffy handheld devices and great marketing, grabbing 80 percent of market share. Then Handspring, founded by Palm alums, created a device with a twist—add-on modules that allow Handspring users to download and play music or to access the Internet. Handspring priced its PDAs aggressively and captured most of the remaining share. With those two aggressive players dominating PDA sales, it is very difficult for a new entrant to compete. Even Microsoft, with its billions of dollars of marketing clout, retreated from the field.

Another example of an early mover is Affymetrix, a maker of microchips that identify and analyze gene sequences. When it went public in 1996, it was one of the first companies to figure out how to apply computer technology to the daunting task of identifying the human genetic code. Not only did Affymetrix's devices work well, they also speeded up the time it took to analyze genes—from months to hours. Numerous other companies have tried to enter this area, but Affymetrix's early product lead, capital raised during its IPO and subsequent financings, and recognition as the gold standard proved impossible for competitors to break.

Even in other areas not as technologically advanced as genomics, the first to debut as an IPO has an advantage. In 1995, Petsmart, the pet superstore, launched its IPO. Its New York road show, held at the Palace Hotel on Fifth Avenue across from St. Patrick's Cathedral, attracted hundreds of portfolio managers and analysts. Seeing the success of Petsmart, other pet superstores followed suit. But none have done as well as Petsmart did in terms of stock price or picking up market share.

Petsmart was also a leader in entering the online arena. Its name recognition and powerful distribution system proved an impossible mission for pets.com, the online retailer that IPO'd in 1999. Today, pets.com is best remembered for blowing its IPO proceeds on an ill-considered television advertising campaign and the cute sock puppet that made the rounds of the late night talk shows.

The same thinking holds true for other sectors. Capstone Turbine was the first to introduce the small, efficient microturbine for commercial use. While competitors are gearing up their own versions of these generators, Capstone is several years ahead of the crowd and will be rewarded with market share.

SUCCESS FACTOR 3

The product or service must be superior.　Today's blinding rate of new-product development leaves no room for mediocrity. Buyers want it here, they want it now, and they want it right. The companies going public know that they must be among the first to offer new technology or services or some other new company will beat them out permanently. Failure to produce a superior product is now a death knell because there is so much competition and so many bright entrepreneurs looking for opportunities, if a company can't do what it promised when it went public, investors and bankers move on to a company that can deliver the goods.

The companies and their employees are keenly aware of the heightened pressures to perform. The *Wall Street Journal* recently described the extreme effort that Sycamore Network went through to deliver a state-of-the-art fiber-optic switch for AT&T. The stakes were high. Start-up Sycamore was up against giants Lucent and Cisco. At great personal sacrifices, Sycamore's engineers delivered a switch that simultaneously processes 2 million phone calls, twice the capabilities of existing devices.

One Sycamore supervisor internalized the competition so much that he kept waking his wife up all night long to talk about the project. He criticized his wife for not having the swimming pool sticks aligned properly, smallest to largest. After his team successfully delivered the switch to AT&T, Sycamore chief executive officer (CEO) Dan Smith assembled his troops and assigned the supervisor to lead yet another tough project.

Technology companies are not the only ones for which excellence is a basic requirement. A retailer needs to have great product selection, pricing, and customer service. Me-too companies need not apply. That's why Amazon is around today and buy.com and pets.com are battlefield debris. The only way online broker E*Trade was able to take on industry leader Charles Schwab was by offering cheaper trades through a reliable, online site. E*Trade innovated by putting more and more full-service-type features on its Web site, including research, quotes, and news.

Companies with superior products almost always keep improving and refining their products and services. By doing this, they keep ahead of competitors and maintain the loyalty of their customers.

SUCCESS FACTOR 4

The IPO needs to have a reasonable size, given its market and competitors.   David and Goliath notwithstanding, a company needs to be big enough to take on the competition. As the dot.com debacle of 1999 proved, having revenues and a route to profitability matter.

When Amazon.com went public, it had $32 million in revenue. By producing that level of revenue, Amazon had demonstrated that indeed its concept of an online bookstore was credible. In contrast, a record number of dot.coms were able to go public with little or no revenue.

Pets.com, with only a couple of million in revenue, was in a weak position to take on industry giant Petsmart. Likewise, a small chip manufacturer is unlikely to be successful in competing in the market for commodity-type chips because the market is highly price competitive. Stamps.com was in a similarly weak position with *no* revenue and a powerful competitor in Pitney Bowes.

Growth investors know that small companies are the first to embrace and exploit new technologies, but even small companies need to have the resources to stay in the game. The high anxiety among Internet companies and venture capitalists to grab the lead forced many IPOs to debut before they were ready for prime time. Although these companies were able to do their IPOs and to gather capital, many spent the money unwisely and were left without revenue or market share.

Size also plays a part in how much attention Wall Street will give the IPO. We recently looked at a little oil services company that was preparing a public offering. It wasn't a bad company, and the management seemed smart. The underwriters were knowledgeable oil patch players. But the company had only $58 million in revenue and because it was highly labor intensive only warranted a $98 million valuation. Lacking liquidity, institutional investors stayed away.

SUCCESS FACTOR 5

The management of the company should have relevant backgrounds and be up to the task.   At the height of the Internet frenzy, little attention was given to the credentials of management. Far more important were fuzzy concepts like vision and webcentricity. But, as investors in Internet stocks quickly found out, the companies that had the best chance of success have capable, experienced management. For example, Handspring founders Donna Dubinsky and Jeffrey Hawkins, had left Palm, where they had headed the company. Even with "old" economy companies, management background matters. This is a very important topic, and we will focus on specifics in Secret 9, "How Management Helps or Hurts an IPO."

SUCCESS FACTOR 6

Barriers to entry should be high.   Palm, eBay, and Amazon each succeeded in establishing itself in its respective market because it created high barriers to entry. They did this by developing proprietary technology for customer interaction that was superior to that of rivals. eBay developed a unique auction model and supporting infrastructure to allow millions of auctions. Palm pioneered PDAs and became the industry standard. Amazon spent millions to insure that its Web site was vastly better than others. The personal welcome when a customer revisits the site, the customized suggestions for future purchases, and the frequent e-mail product offerings drew customers to Amazon. So, even though PDAs, bookselling, and online auctions are competitive arenas, each company developed technologies that made it the gold standard within its industry.

SUCCESS FACTOR 7

A focused company is more likely to be a successful company. A company that has figured out what it does best is a far better bet than a company that has several initiatives going at once. This is particularly true of small companies, which have limited human and financial resources.

E*Trade, the pioneering online brokerage firm, has a singular mission: to be the largest online brokerage firm. E*Trade intended to accomplish this through service innovations, advertising, and knowledge of its customers. Its service innovations were dramatic for low-cost brokerages—price charts, research, news. In a particularly astute move E*Trade also added IPO information from Renaissance Capital! And these services were free. It advertised like crazy on national television.

It paid off. E*Trade knew that its customers tend to trade more heavily than other online brokers and certainly traditional brokers. E*Trade's customers are more active because E*Trade invested money in services and ease of use. And finally, E*Trade knew that the time to establish itself as the premier online broker was when online trading first started. It knew that Merrill Lynch and others were reluctant to enter the market because of internal opposition from the full-service brokers. But E*Trade also realized that the big brokers would eventually move in. And when they did, E*Trade wanted to be a contender. That's a *focused* company.

Another highly focused company is Radio One, the first operator of radio stations targeting African Americans. The company's strategy is to acquire underperforming urban radio stations that reach a black audience and then improve their ratings through better programming and financial management. The mother and son who run the company have demonstrated their ability to make and then integrate acquisitions into the radio network. If they deviated from plan and began snapping up Hispanic radio stations, investors would react negatively because management does not know the Hispanic market.

SUCCESS FACTOR 8

To reach a high valuation, a growth company must have sustainable growth. In valuing growth stocks, investors look to future cash flows, sometimes many years in the future. If the expected upward trajectory is relatively smooth, expect the company to be rewarded with a premium valuation.

Sustainable growth can come from a number of sources. The IPO may have demonstrated an ability to continue to improve its product, thereby building customer loyalty. Or the IPO may have a shaver-blade business model; that is, the company sells a relatively high priced system but has ongoing revenues from providing its installed base of customers with consumables.

IPOs don't even have to have off-the-charts growth. Look at IPO United Parcel Service (UPS). It focuses on next-day delivery of parcels. UPS's growth comes from economic expansion, entering new geographic markets, and being one of the two principal deliverers of online purchases.

SUCCESS FACTOR 9

Strong brand identity is a necessity in both consumer and business markets. Remember Christmas of 1999? Tiny Internet retailers spent millions on advertising. Most of that money went down the drain because there were just too many of them and consumers tuned out.

A strong brand is as important for UPS and Kodak as it is for smaller IPOs. Palm, Amazon, eBay, and Yahoo! established their brands before their IPO debuts. That not only made it easier to raise money, it also made it easier to raise more money than a no-name competitor. Investors are more comfortable with a new company that has already put its stake in the ground with its name.

Brands and names are also important to technology companies who are selling largely to other businesses. When we do our research, we call the IPO's competitors and try to get a bead on who's who in the sector. If we hear positive things, even if they are grudging, we are more confident about the IPO. We also try to touch base with customers. When we researched Copper Mountain Networks, which makes high-speed, digital-subscriber-line (DSL), web-access concentrators, we realized that they were a clear leader in this area. For Web sites that are clogged with traffic, Copper Mountain's solutions were becoming the standard for optimizing Web traffic.

SUCCESS FACTOR 10

Having a low cost structure allows an IPO to survive the expected pricing and competitive pressures as its market develops. For a more developed company, having a low cost structure cements its position as industry leader and permits it to weather the inevitable economic downturns.

A low cost structure is less important to a young company that is throwing off losses as it begins its initial growth trajectory. However, there should be clues in its business model and results to date of how it intends to position itself against competitors. An IPO that has a low-cost model has thought through its operational costs and will be quicker to adroitly pursue opportunities and correct mistakes.

Being able to produce products and services more efficiently than others do gives a company more flexibility in pricing. It also serves as a barrier to entry to potential competitors.

The Internet, by its nature, can support efficient communication, but not necessarily low-cost-structure delivery of products and services. For example, fashionmall.com faces the same UPS delivery charges that a land-based apparel shop or catalog company must pay. But software and information can be efficiently delivered to customers. The *Wall Street Journal* online has features not available in the newsprint version— archived articles, data, and stock quotes. The trick will be to figure out what business models are successful on the Web.

We like a company that has wrestled with its cost structure and pricing strategy. It means it understands the dynamics of its industry, the mechanics of getting its product or service out the door, and the wants of its customers.

IPOs come in all shapes and sizes, flavors and colors. But common to all good IPOs are the traits we have described in this chapter. The U.S. and world economies are moving too fast and are so performance-based that companies new to the public markets have little room for error. Of the IPOs that we review every year, perhaps 15 percent make our cut. The stock market is an unforgiving place, so you should be just as tough on passing judgment on IPOs that want your money.

SECRET 6

How to Avoid Bad IPOs

Lousy initial public offerings (IPOs) are examples of "I told you so!" Their failings are brilliantly clear in the rearview mirror. The objective of this chapter is to show you how to get these IPOs in your headlights.

Every truly bad IPO we have ever looked at disclosed its future Achilles' heel in its prospectus. That's why our mantra is, "It's in the prospectus, stupid."

Unlike good IPOs, which share many positive attributes, bad IPOs are lousy in their own special, individual ways. Although there are a handful of general, common sense rules, the warning signals of bad IPOs are company specific. The media seems to think that the invasion of the dot.coms in 1999 provided the market with the epitome of bad IPOs. In reality, crash-and-burn bad IPOs are not a new phenomenon related to the Internet. They have been around all the time. Fatally flawed companies go public all of the time due to bad judgment, greed, and hubris. More bad deals get done in euphoric markets than in bear markets. When stock market momentum is strong on the upside, underwriters are eager to take as many companies public as possible. As the pace gets hectic, the warts on companies are overlooked.

Company managements feel the pull of a strong IPO market. "If that company can go public, why not us?" they ask. They know that the IPO window for their industry sector will not stay open for long. And so, they try to tap the public markets. There is no understating the tremendous sense of urgency that surrounds going public. Personal fortunes can be made overnight. Much is at stake.

Entrepreneurialism is a global phenomenom. The Bombay, India, chief executive officer (CEO) of an information technology (IT) consultancy shares the same "grab the moment philosophy" as his or her American or British counterpart. Every company deserves a shot at going public. At the present time, the desire by companies to tap the public markets coincides with the investing public's willingness to be tapped. Thus, many companies are drawn to the IPO market. And when so many companies have a shot at the brass ring, not all of them are going to survive and thrive. So a good many of the IPO crop in any one year are duds and worse.

Some people erroneously think that the Securities and Exchange Commission (SEC) approves IPOs. Although the SEC is an effective watchdog on disclosure and polices against stock market baddies, its staff does not review deals for the sanity of the business plan or the competence of management. That's your job. The SEC's job is to make sure that everything relevant about the company is contained in the prospectus. So, the only thing standing between making a good investment and throwing your money on a really ridiculous IPO is you (see Exhibit 6.1, "The 10 Worst First-Day Returns").

There are many ways in which a company can be fundamentally flawed. It can have a questionable business model, face daunting competition, or be a little fish in a big pond. The reasons why an IPO is particularly bad fall into one of two categories: (1) fundamentals and (2) management issues. Here are some "flop" predictors.

FLOP PREDICTOR 1: NO BARRIERS TO ENTRY

Let's look at a once high-flying IPO, Discovery Zone, which has since filed for bankruptcy. Discovery Zone, which went public in 1993, was priced at $22, and soared to $35½ at the close of its first day of trading, then an incredible return. Discovery Zone operated indoor recreation centers for young children, offering play areas with plastic balls and space to crawl and greasy pizza. You may remember visiting one. They were usually located in suburban malls. They catered to the baby boom

Exhibit 6.1 The 10 Worst First-Day Returns

Company	Description	Date	Decrease
eChapman.com	Investment and banking services geared to minority groups	6/14/00	−43.3%
VIALOG	Operator-attended audio/video teleconferencing services	2/4/99	−32.8
Trader.com	Classified advertising via 230 publications, 41 Web sites	3/30/00	−32.2
Golden Telecom	Facilities-based Russian telco services to businesses	9/29/99	−28.6
Allos Therapeutics	Biotech firm with cancer drug starting Phase III in 2000	3/27/00	−27.8
iAsiaWorks	Internet access, hosting, co-location in Asian-Pacific	8/2/00	−26.9
Interland	Web application hosting to small and midsized businesses	7/24/00	−25.5
Cobalt Group	Internet marketing and data aggregation for auto dealers	8/4/99	−24.4
Streamline.com	Online provider of groceries and errand-related services	6/17/99	−23.8
US SEARCH	Public record info search services via the Web and phone	6/24/99	−22.9

Source: Renaissance Capital, Greenwich, CT (IPOhome.com).

parents who wanted high-quality playtime for their tots. Discovery Zone even hired teachers to work on the weekends. The typical scene in a Discovery Zone was one of kids running around the bright plastic balls and the parents wearily trying to find a place to sit in the overcrowded eating area. And for this you paid $5 to $8 a child.

The drum roll preceding the deal was deafening. The ex-chief financial officer (CFO) of Waste Management, a once high-flying stock, was the chairman and CEO. Blockbuster Video had a 19 percent stake in the company. The concept was that management would roll out cookie-cutter Discovery Zones across the country, just as they did with the Blockbuster Video chain.

Sounds great? Not really. First, the company was losing lots of money, and this was before the Internet deluge made it acceptable for an IPO to lose money. Second, management was brand new—they had no record of being a successful team.

But these things weren't what ultimately killed Discovery Zone. The single biggest problem Discovery Zone faced was the lack of any barriers to entry. They disclosed in the prospectus that a competitor, Leaps and Bounds, which is owned by fast-food powerhouse McDonald's, was rolling out a similar type of indoor gym. Discovery Zone said that while indoor recreational facilities were a new business, it was already highly competitive. Indeed. Shortly after reviewing Discovery Zone, we stopped by a Burger King in Danbury, Connecticut. The restaurant had devoted about a quarter of its floor space to an enclosed Discovery Zone–like indoor recreational area. It had things to crawl through and plenty of bright, plastic balls. Just like Discovery Zone. Only it was free.

You could have used your common sense to figure out that if Burger King and McDonald's are opening *free* indoor playrooms, why would young families *pay* to go to Discovery Zone? Advancing that train of thought a bit more, you might wonder about competition from community and school playgrounds, which at the time were sprouting up everywhere, due to the baby boom of the mid-1980s.

Further, an investor could ponder what it would take to create his or her own Discovery Zone knockoff. Let's see: order a bunch of colorful plastic balls from a catalog, rent some space at the strip mall, hire a couple of carpenters to make a few crawl spaces, and hire a couple of college kids. It shouldn't take more than a couple of months from inception to finish.

FLOP PREDICTOR 2: FINANCIAL CHICANERY

But low barriers to entry weren't the problem for poultry restaurant chain Boston Chicken, another class of 1993 IPO brought to you by the Blockbuster bunch. Boston Chicken promised consumers rotisserie-basted chicken with home-style fixings like mashed potatoes and gravy, all at a reasonable price. Boston Chicken was a promising concept. The demise of the company was entirely due to management, which dug its own grave by committing a series of financial operations sins to gloss over the fact that its units weren't making money.

The chicken chain was one of the hottest IPOs of 1993. The company made much of the fact that CEO Scott Beck hailed from Blockbuster and that other members of management had impressive fast-food pedigrees. When we issued our IPO Intelligence report on the company, which was largely favorable, Beck called to get it within hours of its release. A CEO on top of things, or so it seemed. But, we, like others, had the yolk pulled over our eyes.

For nearly three years, the poultry purveyor grew dramatically, from 175 stores at the time of its IPO to more than 1,000 in 1996. Investors included many big-name mutual funds. Not us. Boston Chicken borrowed lots of money. Then a few analysts began to squawk over accounting irregularities. It turned out that the poultry restaurant chain was feathering over operating losses by making huge loans to its large franchisees, some of whom were insiders, and booking the interest on those loans as revenue. Also they were moving annual operating expenses into overhead to make it look like the individual stores were profitable. They ultimately had to fess up in quarterly filings made to the SEC; but until they filed for reorganization, executives were calling the allegations, "Baloney." But as it became abundantly clear to investors, Boston Chicken had an insatiable appetite for new financing because it was raising capital to fund losses. In 2000, the scrawny remains were picked up by McDonald's.

Looking back at the original prospectus, we did find a few clues to the company's ultimate demise. Boston Chicken did reveal that they had begun to generate interest income from loans to certain developers. Had we been as cynical then as we are now, that reference, coupled with the fact that the CEO's father and other company officers controlled three large franchisees, should have at least sparked some tough questions.

FLOP PREDICTOR 3: HISTORY REPEATS ITSELF

Incredibly, even as the criticism mounted on Boston Chicken's accounting practices, Boston Chicken's management was laying another egg. Directly across the Golden, Colorado, parking lot from Boston Chicken, world headquarters for bagel restaurant chain Einstein Noah was being built. Backed by Boston Chicken, which owned 62 percent, Einstein Noah hoped to become the Boston Chicken of bagels. In fact, the game plan was to use the Boston Chicken model of rapid expansion to roll out Einstein and Noah bagelries across the United States. Many of the executives had moved over from Boston Chicken, and Scott Beck was chairman.

And guess what? Einstein was using the exact same financing technique that Boston Chicken used. Most of the stores were franchises, financed by Einstein Noah. At the time of the IPO in 1996, Einstein Noah had agreements to open an astonishing 924 new stores over three years. So Einstein was using the $81 million it raised in its 1996 IPO, the $85 million it raised in an add-on, and millions more in debt to loan money to franchisees. If you didn't look at the numbers too closely, the revenue growth looked great because it was getting one-time franchise fees for each new store opened and interest on the money loaned to the franchisees, who by the way were largely insiders. The biggest franchisee was owned by Bagel Funding, an entity directly controlled by Beck and other insiders. Beck's dad owned another franchisee. Effectively, this financial structure allowed Einstein Noah to push off the losses to the franchisees.

Although all of this was disclosed in the prospectus and the chickens were starting to come home to roost for parent Boston Chicken,

Einstein Noah's stock soared from its IPO price of $17 to $36. Although the short sellers were stalking Einstein Noah by early 1997, it wasn't until late 1999 that the bagel caper blew up. By that time, the company had a new CEO, who was trying to resurrect the struggling chain. With too much debt and faltering stores, it filed for bankruptcy protection in 2000.

In figuring out the fatal flaws in Einstein Noah, it also helped to be New Yorkers. Bagels outside New York? Blueberry bagels? Fahgettaboutit.

FLOP PREDICTOR 4: OVERLY HIGH EXPECTATIONS

Accounting irregularities aside, some truly bad companies are greeted like the next new, new thing. Planet Hollywood was the buzz of suburban cocktail parties and Hollywood. Demi Moore, Arnold Schwartzenegger, Sylvester Stallone, Bruce Willis, and Whoopi Goldberg were stockholders. If you read the celebrity gossip columns of the big city newspapers or *People* magazine, you couldn't help but notice that these stars were making appearances at Planet Hollywood publicity parties.

To put Planet Hollywood in context, theme restaurants, especially those with a celebrity association, were hot. The House of Blues and Hard Rock Café, both private, were drawing crowds. Rainforest Café had many fans. Planet Hollywood was the first major one to IPO. The Planet Hollywood restaurants featured memorabilia from movies, pictures of movie stars and models, and casual food. In the early days, the shareholder stars did indeed show up occasionally. The restaurants were opened in large U.S. and European cities that draw many tourists.

The hype spread beyond the normal group of IPO stock market investors. "That Planet Hollywood IPO," blurted the father of a Cub Scout at the annual "Blue and Gold Banquet" for the pack, "I've got to get some of that deal. It's going to be hot."

When Planet Hollywood finally launched its deal in 1996, the prospectus prominently featured Sly, Bruce, Demi, and Arnold in front of a Planet Hollywood, with arms linked. Inside, there was a shot of Whoopi on a sedan chair being carried by some hunks wearing Egyptian outfits. All of this celebrity backing served to increase the din.

The company was also launching a sports-oriented chain, the Official All Star Café. Its "active" shareholders were Andre Aggassi and Monica Seles. Again, Planet Hollywood held out the possibility of an appearance by a star. As was the case with other highly touted brand-name stocks, like Ralph Lauren and Boston Chicken, results could not possibly live up to the hype. However, the hype allowed underwriters in each of these cases to put premium prices on the IPO, puffing up the valuation so much that any flaw would be fatal to the stock price. Investors in IPOs like this are like people who go out carousing on Saturday night and have to deal with the unpleasant consequences on Sunday morning.

But hype aside, there were other serious problems in the Planet Hollywood story, if only you looked.

FLOP PREDICTOR 5: WHEN THE INSIDERS ARE BAILING OUT, YOU WATCH OUT!

From an investor's perspective, the Planet Hollywood deal was loaded with negatives. First, $71 million of proceeds was going to insiders. The money had been loaned to Planet Hollywood by a key director and personally guaranteed by the chairman, Keith Barish, and the president, Robert Earl. Essentially, the director got repaid, and the two executives were released from a large obligation. Not good. It shows lack of confidence in the future.

FLOP PREDICTOR 6: CUSTOMERS ARE UNDERWHELMED

What was most worrisome about the Planet Hollywood deal was described in the management discussion. The new restaurants have their highest period of revenue in the initial period following their openings. This meant that the company created a lot of first time hype and then had no follow through. A curious investor might wonder about same-store sales—a critical statistic for a restaurant chain.

But whoa! The increases or decreases in revenues year over year for individual restaurants opened more than a year were not disclosed. This is *highly* unusual. Nearly every other retailer and restaurant chain proudly displays its growing sales, as proof that the concept draws in more and more new customers. So this was something Planet Hollywood would rather not advertise. Hidden away in a section most investors gloss over was the disclosure that on a same-unit basis, Planet Hollywood expected revenue to be down 4 percent. Moreover, they said that first-quarter 1996 net income would be 12 percent lower due to higher interest expenses.

So, here we had a restaurant chain that had been profitable only in its most recent year admitting that results going forward were deteriorating! Why? No explanation was offered. But a diligent investor doing a little bit of field research might conclude that overpriced, mediocre food served in noisy tourist traps is not the ticket for repeat, satisfied customers.

Outcome? Planet Hollywood got priced at $18 and by the end of 1996 had only risen to $19.75. While it had several rallies in 1997, word was getting out about the company's sluggish sales. By first quarter 1997, Planet Hollywood was $13.63. And by year end 1998 it had sunk to $2.38. Apparently Whoopi, Sly, or Arnold could do nothing to whip up sales. Planet Hollywood then reevaluated its strategy, laying off employees and shuttering units. But by late 1999, at which time its stock was $0.05 per share, management threw in the towel. Planet Hollywood filed for Chapter 11 bankruptcy protection. *Hasta la vista, baby.*

Moral to the story: When a company does its IPO, it has prettied itself up as much as possible. Management and its bankers choose the most auspicious timing. So when a company admits in its prospectus that results are deteriorating, this is a very, very bad thing. Investors in Planet Hollywood were so awed by the concept and the celebrities that they neglected to look objectively at the company's sales trends and product.

FLOP PREDICTOR 7: ABANDONING THE FRANCHISE THAT ONCE MADE A COMPANY GREAT

Another example of an IPO that went public when its trends were deteriorating was Loehmann's, the famous seller of off-price designer clothing. Started in Brooklyn in 1921 as the "Original Designer Outlet" by Frieda Loehmann, Loehmann's drew crowds of shopping cognoscenti to the mother store, which featured racks and racks of heavily discounted merchandise from New York City's Seventh Avenue. And the "Back Room" even attracted wealthy but penny-pinching suburbanites, who reveled in being able to pick up trendy designer items at rock bottom prices. The rich and not so rich tried on clothes in the open because Loehmann's was so no-frills that it lacked dressing rooms.

The heavily discounted merchandise was such a success that Loehmann's expanded nationally and went public in 1964. Then, in the 1980s the company went through a series of ownership changes. By the 1996 IPO, it was a shadow of its former self.

Loehmann's new management decided to follow an aggressive new-store-opening strategy. The problem was that they were opening stores in existing markets, causing what the rag trade calls "cannibalization," which means that the new stores were stealing customers from the old stores. Not only did the company fail to disclose same-store sales, which was a telling omission, but they said that same-store sales "experienced significant fluctuations." No further details were provided. Translated, this means that sales trends were rotten.

In fact, what management was doing was veering away completely from the tried-and-true Loehmann strategy—great bargains, low-cost strategy. Management was picking prime center-city locales for its new stores, which meant high rent and high store expenses. Investors who visited a "new" Loehmann's store would find racks of well-organized blouses, pants, and dresses by no-name designers. Where was Donna? Where were Steven Tyler and Fendi???? The Loehmann's of old had been stacked with racks upon racks of somewhat disorganized apparel. But discriminating shoppers knew that somewhere in the piles of clothing were fashion gems at bargain prices.

At first, Loehmann's IPO performed well, rising from its $17 IPO price to $30.25 a few months later, mostly on the strength of the store rollout and few analyst questions about its same-store sales trends. But by the beginning of 1997, it was apparent that things weren't going well, and management was forced to admit to declining sales and profits. The stock quickly fell to the bargain basement price of $6.

This story is more than a sad reminder about the fickle world of off-price fashion. It is a story about a company that completely threw away its valuable franchise. For investors, it should have been apparent from the downtrending results at the time of its IPO that Loehmann's was a loser. By 1999 Loehmann's had filed for Chapter 11, was delisted from the Nasdaq, and was trading at under $1.

You may ask why Loehmann's is such a good example of a lousy IPO if it nearly doubled in the first few months of trading. It's a good example because the fundamentals of a company always win out in the end. Crafty managements and clever CFOs can do the blue-smoke-and-mirrors act for only so long, usually a couple of quarters. After that, any reserves that were carefully stashed away are depleted, and the company's true colors come out.

But what is the value of painstakingly ferreting out bad IPOs when you don't buy them? First, the opportunity cost of owning a bad IPO is huge because they are new companies and the shareholder base is not yet knowledgeable or committed to the company. They will sell at the first whiff of trouble. Bad IPOs don't just take a little dive. End-game can be less than $1 a share, as Loehmann's and Discovery Zone proved.

Second, what many people fail to realize is that there is much money to be made in bad IPOs. Another benefit of landing on truly terrible companies is that a knowledgeable investor can short the stock. When you short stock, you borrow shares from a broker, anticipating that you will be able to cover (or buy back) the shares at a lower price. Shorting can be riskier than buying shares. When you buy shares in a stock, your downside is the amount of money you paid for the stock. But when you short stock, your risk is unlimited. Theoretically, at least, a stock could keep soaring forever.

The IPO+ Fund shorts stock to hedge (or to offset) our long positions in IPOs. When our analysts come across a really bad IPO, it becomes a candidate for the portfolio. The trouble is that shares of recent IPOs are difficult to borrow. It generally takes a few days for the shares to show up at brokerage houses to be borrowed. Shorting stock has definitely added return and reduced risk for the IPO+ Fund's portfolio.

Individual investors are just starting to realize the potential in shorting stock. Most of Wall Street is geared to the long side, largely because people are generally optimistic and betting that something is going to go wrong is against most people's nature. Because of the risk, when shorting stock, it is imperative to do your homework.

A financial Web site featuring many well-known columnists held a seminar for individual investors and small hedge funds on shorting. During the question-and-answer period, one individual asked, "How do I get information on a company if it's down a lot and there's no news?" The hedge fund guys chuckled. The fact is that individual investors don't have access to the whisper circuit of upcoming news on companies, as some institutional investors do. That's why it's imperative for individual investors to investigate an IPO thoroughly before wading in. When a stock goes up or down a lot, you'll be confident enough about your conclusions in the company to hang on in the face of volatility.

FLOP PREDICTOR 8: THE EMPEROR HAS NO CLOTHES

But Loehmann's, Discovery Zone, and Planet Hollywood were all land-based companies, with real revenues and profits. How can you figure out if a company is fatally flawed if it's a developmental stage company and lacks revenues?

One of our favorite clunkers was Earthshell Container, a developmental-stage company that licenses technology to make organic food-packaging products. Earthshell planned to make disposable food-service items, such as cups, plates, and hinged-lid containers, from a mixture of limestone, natural potato, and starch. The politically correct and maybe environmentally better packages were meant to appease environmentalists.

At the time of its 1998 IPO, the company had not generated one dime of revenue, lacked manufacturing facilities, and had a going concern opinion from its auditor due to its $74 million of losses and a stockholder's deficit of $45 million.

But even with all of these negatives, incredibly, it was a hot deal. Earthshell had an agreement with McDonald's to supply the fast-food chain with Big Mac sandwich containers. However, if you read the fine print, which most analysts didn't, McDonald's had the right to discontinue development at any time. It was a supply agreement, but not really.

It did not have a contract committing McDonald's to buying a specific amount of product from Earthshell.

There were also management issues. Earthshell did not own the technology. It was licensed from a separate company controlled by Earthshell's founder and chairman, Essam Khashoggi. Part of the proceeds from the IPO were intended to repay $37 million of debt owed to Khashoggi's company. And finally, there were a lot of insiders bailing out by selling stock on the offering.

None of this troubled some of the many investors who piled into the ballroom on the top floor of the St. Regis Hotel in midtown Manhattan for the road show lunch. The tables were packed. The Renaissance Capital analyst attending the lunch sat down near one of the Wall Street analysts who would be covering Earthshell after its IPO. The table was littered with Earthshell's prototype biodegradable plates and cups. The Wall Street analyst proposed a toast, holding up an Earthshell cup filled with hot coffee. The cup, aloft in the air, began leaking coffee onto the table below. The embarrassed analyst quickly put the cup back on the table, where it continued to ooze coffee onto the white tablecloth, a reminder throughout the lunch of the gaffe.

In the meantime, a buy-side analyst rose in the back of the room to ask a question of Khashoggi. Known for his sarcasm and questions that cut to the quick, the analyst posed: "Please tell us how you arrived at a $2 billion valuation for Earthshell. You have no revenues, no customers, no manufacturing. Why $2 billion? Why not $5 billion? Or $10 billion?" Management responded that they thought $2 billion was a fair price, but they didn't elucidate. When we interviewed the CFO of a comparable packaging company, he volunteered that when his CEO saw the Earthshell valuation, he raced into the CFO's office, slammed the door, and demanded, "Get me this valuation!" They both had a good laugh.

Our analyst brought several Earthshell cups and Big Mac containers back to the office after the road show. The cups were brittle and broke easily. Then we dunked the containers into a pitcher of water. After a few hours, bits of the containers had precipitated into a slimy, greyish blob on the bottom of the pitcher. We decided that seeing regular McDonald's paper or styrofoam-box discards was a lot less disgusting than the greyish slime into which Earthshell containers partly disentegrated. Besides, can you imagine the combination of limestone, potato, and starch becoming a gelatinous part of your coffee or Coke?

How many other analysts took the time to test the product and ask themselves, "Does this story hold water?"

The bulls had their day, briefly. Priced at the top of its range at $21, Earthshell went up, briefly. By the end of the year it had dropped to $12 and recently traded around $3.

As of this writing, McDonald's was still testing Earthshell products in a hundred restaurants. It's questionable whether Earthshell will ever be rolled out. The moral: Concept stocks with no revenues, customers, or relevant experience are to be avoided.

FLOP PREDICTOR 9: THE PROSPECTUS MAKES YOU LAUGH

The Internet craze in 1999 and 2000 produced many wonderfully bad concept stocks. We all take our analysis of IPOs very seriously. So when the analyst who was reading a prospectus began laughing uncontrollably, we knew something was up. Prospectuses aren't supposed to be funny. The analyst was reading the prospectus of PNV, which provides cable television and Internet access services to truck drivers at truck stops. In the convenience of their cabs, the drivers could log on to PNV's portal Web site, which had trucking-related content.

What was ridiculous about this IPO was not what the company was intending to do—offering cable television and Internet access on the road is a legitimate enough niche service. Trucking companies are using the Internet to streamline logistics. But the turnoffs were legion. First, here's a company that is providing a very simple service, entertainment for tired truckers. But did trucking fleets want their truckers entertained? "I don't want a guy looking at a computer screen while he's driving," grumbled an industry executive. Also, PNV had racked up $62 million in losses and had negative cash flow. And it was loaded with debt. What was going on?

There were many other questions. How big was the market for their services? Only 24 percent of truck drivers have personal computers

(PCs). Would the cable channel "Drivers' Entertainment Network" attract viewers? Nearly 18 percent of subscribers dropped the service after a month or two. Do truckers really want to read PNV's lifestyle magazine, *Connect*? Advertisers were not flocking to the Web site. Is selling subscriptions through payroll deductions and through truck-stop vending machines effective?

Poor PNV also had operational problems. Drivers experienced problems in connecting to the network due to accumulations of moisture in the parking lot access points. Hey, it rains! PNV was also being sued by a long list of people for "slip and fall" incidents, in which the victims alleged that they tripped over an access point to the PNV network in a truck-stop parking lot.

The sad saga didn't stop there. PNV faced tremendous competition from AT&T, MCI WorldCom, and others. Qualcomm and Highway-Master offer wireless access, thus neatly eliminating the pesky access-point tripping problem.

Only an euphoric IPO market can carry a company like PNV. It was priced in late 1999 at $17, the top of its proposed range. We promptly called Bear Stearns, one of the brokers we use to borrow stock, and asked them to find some PNV for us to borrow. We covered the short at around $6.

PNV is an example of a company that was not ready for prime time. While it is addressing what seems to be a niche market, it was not the right part of the niche. When investors realized that the main area of opportunity in the industry was providing wireless logistics services, PNV's many problems and disappointing results after going public caused the stock to plummet. When an IPO trades much below $10 a share, it is pretty much precluded from dipping into the equity market again. Its strategy must be to either find a partner or merge with another company before its money runs out.

Finding and shorting bad business concepts works best in ebullient markets. When stocks are flying, even iffy companies can get lifted by the rising tide. What's frustrating is finding IPOs that you know are destined for failure, like the revenueless Internet e-tailers, only to have them drop to single-digit prices before we can borrow them. In some cases they are out of business before you can remember what they did.

FLOP PREDICTOR 10: A SMALL COMPANY WITH HUGE CAPITAL SPENDING REQUIREMENTS

The 1998 IPO of USN Communications made a quick trip from raising lots of money in its IPO to bankruptcy and class action suits. USN was a reseller of local telecommunications services to midsized businesses in Illinois and four other states. It got its start in 1996 when Congress passed a new telecommunications act, permitting competition in local telephone service. Though unprofitable, USN had $67 million in revenue at the time of the offering. Its revenues were ramping rapidly, due to the pent-up demand by businesses to have a low-priced alternative to the former telephone monopoly.

Alas, USN suffered from the classic problem of the start-up entering a capital-intensive business already dominated by established players. USN already had lost $132 million and had lots of debt. From the service problems and the need to upgrade its technology, it was apparent that USN was behind the curve.

On the other hand, USN had some nameplate investors. Merrill Lynch (also the underwriter), HarbourVest, Chase, CIBC Venture, BT Ventures, and Fidelity each owned at least 5 percent of the company. It was similar to Motorola's Iridium, which planned to create a global wireless network, in that it had goldplated backers.

Things quickly spun out of control. In an effort to boost revenue, USN added salespeople and customer support personnel and invested in IT systems. Less than a year after its IPO, USN announced a restructuring, saying that it was eliminating nearly all of its salesforce and would consolidate its offices. The company had run out of money. With a sagging stock price and a stock market now averse to investing in start-up, capital-intensive telecommunication services providers, endgame was near. By January 1999, a year after its IPO, the Nasdaq delisted the stock, effectively hammering a silver stake into the company's heart. A month later, what remained of USN was acquired for a bargain basement price of $85 million, about a fifth of its valuation at the time of the IPO.

Few start-ups succeed in competitive environments dominated by large established players where substantial capital investment is required. MCI was the exception to this rule. It successfully took on AT&T and won. But it did so with the support of the federal government and a highly charismatic chairman and CEO.

FLOP PREDICTOR 11: IF IT DOESN'T WORK ON LAND, WHY WILL IT FLOAT AT SEA?

We will examine the Internet stocks in the next chapter, but this chapter would not be complete without mentioning one of the many failed e-tailers that went public at the height of the Internet frenzy. Value America, a cyber retailer of everything from computers to cosmetics, represents much of what was wrong with these tiny Internet retailers with overly grand schemes.

Value America tried to debut in late 1998, with a proposed valuation of nearly $500 million. But the global equity markets were roiling in the wakes of the crises in Indonesia and Japan. The U.S. IPO market had shut down to all but the best deals. Microsoft cofounder Paul Allen was a 19 percent owner. FedEx founder Fred Smith was on the board.

Value America went public at the beginning of the second quarter of 1999, when spirits were flying high. The wait was worth it. Investors who had turned up their noses when Value America was a mere $500 million company now accorded it a $1 billion valuation. Priced at $23, it quickly jumped to the low seventies, which gave it a $3 billion valuation.

The company would need every bit of the $127 million it raised to execute on its grandiose strategy to create the leading online store for technology, office, and consumer products. Founder and CEO Craig Winn wanted it to become the Wal*Mart or Costco of the Net, overnight.

With a razor-thin gross margin of a tenth of a percent, Winn offered customers a 5 percent discount on already low prices. Buyers could also direct 1 percent of the purchase price to their favorite charity. Visitors to fundamentalist preacher Jerry Falwell's Web site could tell Value America to send 1 percent of the gross cost of their purchase to his ministry.

All well and good. But then reality bit. Value America was a mess. It was trying to do too much too fast. In the prospectus, its accountants identified weak financial reporting and inventory tracking. Specifically, the accountants said that there were significant deficiencies in internal controls that prevented Value America from figuring out when to ship products to customers. Its automated systems for taking and tracking orders were poor. It needed to include vendors in the electronic data interchange, the way all big-time retailers track customer orders and inventory and give purchase orders to suppliers.

Value America was also spending like crazy. When it went public, it had already lost $65 million, more than its revenues since inception. And Value America continued to spend at a heavy clip. How soon do you think the money would run out?

By November, the grim reaper was at the door. The board of directors ousted Winn. In December, Value America laid off half of its staff, one of the first major layoffs of the dot.coms. It changed its business model from selling everything from eyeliner to modems to a focus on computers, office supplies, and entertainment. By first quarter 2000, its accounting firm said it doubted the company would survive. It filed for chapter 11 in August 2000 and has since been delisted.

FLOP PREDICTOR 12: TRYING TO WED A LAND-BASED BUSINESS TO THE NET

In the scramble to build Internet businesses in 1999, imaginative entrepreneurs hatched a number of business plans and threw them at the Web to see if they would stick. Many of the companies were like May-December marriages. Emerge was one of those companies.

Emerge's plan was to take the cattle auction business bellowing and mooing into the twenty-first century. Management built a Web site on which livestock buyers could make bids on cattle without going to the actual stockyard. The Renaissance analyst checked out the Web site. "Here it is," she said, "except it has no auctions, just a demo." Hmmmm. That certainly raised a lot of questions about where the revenues were coming from if it didn't have any online auctions.

We also thought about how important it is for buyers of cattle to actually see the animals because animals can become diseased and lose weight when they are shipped from the ranches to the stockyards.

Thinking we had a sure thing, soon after the IPO we called our sales trader at Bear Stearns. "Hey," we said, "how much 'Edgar Mary Roger George' can I borrow?" We were seeing if Bear could short the stock to us.

"Sure thing," he answered, "what does it do?"

"They sell cows and steers on the net," we explained. "You can now buy beef online."

"Too bad Valentine's Day just passed," he joked. "I could have bought a heifer."

Moooooo! After we stopped laughing, the trader found some stock for us. Problem was, the short started to go against us. Propelled by aggressive Web room chat, online investors were predicting that the stock would go to $150. Arggh! We visited the Web site again. Only one cattle sale scheduled. How was this company making money?

The answer came soon enough. An analyst writing the first research report on the company defended its business model. Then he mentioned that only 30 percent of the business was being done online. Lightbulb! That was it. The company was portraying itself as a Web-based company when it was anything but that. We hadn't seen the revenue breakdown in the prospectus. We shorted some more at a higher price. The stock price started to crack.

Then, one Saturday morning, we opened *Barron's* and saw that one of their columnists had written a long article about Emerge (we called it Emoo), hoisting it on its own petard and making a number of bovine jokes. The stock got slammed. Then all of the e-tailing and business-to-business (B2B) companies were hit in a severe market downdraft; and before you knew it, Emerge was in the low teens. We covered. Although the stock price recovered somewhat, we still believe in our initial premise. We don't think that a business where physical presence is so crucial can translate to the Web.

THE FIVE PHASES OF BAD IPOs

A pattern emerges with bad IPOs. They seem to go through five phases. The first is the exuberance associated with going public and having lots of money to burn. The second is when reality hits. Then management is worried about executing on their game plan, if there is one. The third is the frenzied effort to stave off disaster. In the third phase, company managements and their employees are running in circles and putting out fires. A flurry of press releases ensues, trying to put a positive spin on the lack of accomplishment. Some companies issue press releases for the most trival company events. One company even issued a press release when the local congressman visited the headquarters.

This is when the IPO cascades headlong into phase four, which is endgame or figures out a survival strategy. But by this time, few are able to marshal their limited resources and move the company forward. At this phase, some companies have nearly run out of money. But with their stock on the skids, they can't milk the public equity markets. A London-based seller of discounted airline tickets, Ebookers, resorted to financing by insiders to save the company.

However, if the IPO is in its death spiral, you can recognize phase four when top executives start bailing out. We call this the flight of the top dogs. And phase five is, of course, the punishment of the innocent, those employees who no longer have jobs and the shareholders whose holdings are now close to valueless.

Naysayers of IPOs point to the duds mentioned in this chapter as examples of why the IPO market is a bad place to invest. On the contrary, the IPO market practices the most efficient form of financial Darwinism of any capital market. Investors are unforgiving. If an IPO hasn't proven itself within six to nine months after its debut, it's all over.

What becomes of these failed IPOs? A new business has arisen. Like insects and maggots on the forest floor picking over the carcasses of dead animals, Internet online auction houses have emerged, specializing in disposing of the assets of the failed IPOs. The end for these companies is the opposite of their overly optimistic starts with high valuations. Most of the companies sell their remaining assets for pennies on the dollar. A recent article in *The Daily Deal*, a newspaper specializing in deals, told the sad tale of Value America's funeral, in which the going-out-of-business liquidation produced a mere $132,000 in cash for the remaining investors. One of the reasons for the dramatic difference between the hundreds of millions for which these Internet companies were once valued and the $100,000 liquidation is that so much of the value of Internet companies is intellectual capital, hopes, and dreams. When those are debunked, the Internet companies are worth only what a liquidator can get for the Herman Miller work stations.

The IPO market is the financial equivalent of evolution. Market forces seek out and destroy bad business models. For example, it eventually dawned on Internet investors that e-tailers like pets.com were spending more to acquire customers than the customers spent at the Web site. When the market figured that out, additional capital funding dried up as quickly as water evaporates in the Gobi Desert. The bad genes were banned from the market place. It's not so much "survival of the fittest" but the failure of companies to exploit the market opportunity they are seeking.

Nothing is preordained. A company funded by respected pros can turn out to be a black hole for capital, a complete disaster. Witness Boston Chicken, Einstein Noah, Discovery Zone, and Iridium. Strong financial backing can prolong life, but it cannot ensure success. That is why identifying truly bad companies can be so financially rewarding. The forces of financial Darwinism *always* prevail.

SECRET 7

Internet and Technology IPO Basics

Analyzing fast-growing young companies is one of the most difficult challenges investors face. Seeing into the future requires a vision of what a company could accomplish if it runs on all cylinders—and against all odds. Only a handful of focused early entrants in a growing market are capable of long-term survival. Established companies will eventually fight back when a flea-sized start-up takes away market share. If the fast-growing company is fortunate enough to be the first into a new technology and if the area shows any promise, other competitors will follow.

During periods of intense technological innovation, like today, venture capitalists and underwriters line up for the chance to put dollars in entrepreneurs' hands. While the initial public offering (IPO) market is generous in bestowing money on start-ups, its flip side is financial Darwinism. New companies that fail to produce quickly are brutally punished. As a result, the investment history of Internet and technology companies is cluttered with the stories of many, many failed start-ups—but only a few distinguished winners. Naysayers of IPOs point to the relatively high failure rate of IPO technology and Internet companies. However, knowledgeable investors understand that it is part of the territory.

So here you are, an individual investor seeking ways to ford the unpredictable shoals of Internet and technology investing. You want to invest in the innovations of the future, but you don't want to lose your shirt. Read on. This chapter will make some sense out of recent trends in Internet and technology investing by relating them to similar periods in the past. We will point out patterns that repeat in IPO cycle after IPO cycle. We will focus on stock valuation, looking at why these stocks can trade at sky-high prices one day and bargain basement prices the next. Throughout this chapter we will discuss our philosophy of the attractiveness of growth-stock investing. Finally, we will show you some of the patterns we have observed in Internet and technology IPOs.

TECHNOLOGY AND INTERNET IPOS DOMINATE

The IPO market has always had its share of new technology companies. In the past, technology companies ranged from 30 percent to 40 percent of all IPOs. But since 1995, technology and Internet-related IPOs have become a greater and greater part of the IPO market. Today, the IPO market is dominated by these sectors. As IPO investors, you can't ignore the trend.

Why the current great wave of innovative young technology companies? Obviously, the commercialization of the Internet, advances in telecommunications technologies, and the computerization of genomic research occuring at the same time create an intense and diverse platform for innovation. At the same time, a global conversion to market economies occurred. And, in the U.S., the wealth of individual investors was slowly unleashed on the capital markets. The surge in innovation is a function of the degree to which big government imposes itself on the economy. If governments restrict capital flow, there is little or no money available for investment in innovation. Throughout the world, the countries with the freest flows of capital have produced the most new companies. If governments tightly control technology, innovation is squelched. For example, Russia is full of highly educated people with expertise in technology and biotechnology. Russian entrepreneurs venture to the United States to create their new enterprises. Informax, a U.S. IPO providing software to make sense of the reams of genetic information being produced by the mapping of the human genome, was founded by a Russian and staffed by several others.

Throughout the history of equity investing, the convergence of opportunity and innovation attracts capital. As in the past, any time there is a revolutionary invention, the opportunity exists for new business creation. The more important the invention, the greater the number of entrants. The invention of the hearing aid created enough opportunities for only a handful of entrants. But the inventions of electricity and the microprocessor had longer reaches. The bigger the opportunity, the more capital it attracts. And more capital attracts more entrants.

The amount and availability of capital are key drivers of the success of technology and emerging growth companies. The dawn of the new era came in 1975 with the enactment of federal legislation, the Employee Retirement Income Security Act (ERISA) that set standards for governing pension plans. Money from huge corporate pension plans flowed onto Wall Street, which invested it mostly in bonds and blue-chip stocks because they were considered safe and liquid. Big pension plans began investing in technology and emerging growth companies, but these investments were limited. Although the plans had billions of dollars to put to work, it was inefficient for them to invest in many small companies.

For individuals, though, the enactment of ERISA set the stage for the shift of retirement plans from corporate to individual management. In the United States, the move away from institutionally run, bond-focused pension plans to individually controlled 401(k) plans has fueled the attention and the investment in new companies. Corporate downsizing in the 1980s showed a generation of Americans that they had better take charge of their investments. The creation of individual retirement accounts (IRAs) further interested Americans in equities. Retirement is for the future, so invest in the future.

But the availability of large amounts of capital in the pockets of investors also has its downside in providing the ingredients of violent booms and busts. Institutional investors tend to think alike. They buy the same stocks at the same time and, conversely, sell the same stocks at the same time.

The peak of the last great technology-and-emerging-growth investment cycle was in 1983. Back then, Wall Street went through exactly the same throes of wondering how to value the increasingly pricey young companies. To rationalize vaporous valuations, Wall Street concocted the "old" new paradigms of investing, by throwing out traditional price-to-earnings (P/E) ratios in favor of price-to-revenue (P/R) ratios. A young company trading at 20 times next year's estimated revenue is a lot cheaper than one trading at 200 times next year's earnings. Right? Institutional investors finally concluded that valuations of technology and emerging growth stocks were bloated. However, they all had this insight at the same time. The subsequent declines in technology and emerging growth stocks was so steep and so frightening to both institutional and individual investors that it took fully 10 years for the market to muster enthusiasm to begin to fund the large number of very young companies that are going public today.

THE VALUATION DILEMMA

Before the Internet revolutionized communication, growth-stock investing was a simpler place. Although growth-stock investing was still much riskier than analyzing blue chips or electric utilities, in the past, growth-stock investors found it easier to analyze a company's business model, and the pace of development was far slower. Business models were easier to analyze because companies usually came public only after they had commercialized their products or services and had profits. At that time, the average IPO had been in business seven years. Due to the competitive pressures and swiftly moving technology, today companies are coming public at earlier stages. With unproven track records and untested business models, investors have little to go on. Public investors—that's you—are assuming the role of venture capitalists and making the type of assessments about companies that were once only made by specialists armed with insider information about the workings and the forecasts of the companies. As you can see from Exhibit 7.1, "The Troubling Trend of Profitless IPOs," the percent of unprofitable, early-stage IPOs is growing.

The biggest problem in valuing the new technology companies is that their true potentials may not be realized for many years. Many of

Exhibit 7.1   The Troubling Trend of Profitless IPOs

Year	Percent of IPOs Losing Money	Internet as a Percent of Total IPOs
1985	15	0
1986	21	0
1987	17	0
1988	16	0
1989	21	0
1990	13	0
1991	24	0
1992	31	0
1993	29	0
1994	23	0
1995	24	0.5
1996	37	1
1997	30	1
1998	38	11
1999	74	50
2000	78	35

Source: Renaissance Capital, Greenwich, CT (IPOhome.com).

these companies are still experimenting with promising approaches to doing business on the Web or discovering new drug candidates. Therefore, investors face two challenges: (1) they have to correctly make the bets on the right companies, with the right technologies, and with the right managements, and (2) they have to grapple with nontraditional valuations.

Furthermore, although many Internet and technology companies are growing at incredible rates, they face many more risks than established companies. Armed with cash from the IPO, many new companies immediately throw money at hiring employees and equipping the offices with the latest in ergonomic furniture. In far too many cases, the IPO's management is clueless about the distinction between mindlessly adding people to the payroll and purposefully building a business. In some cases, Internet and technology companies can buy revenue growth by offering their products or services below cost. But they are not building businesses. Revenues grow at amazing rates, but in many cases, losses grow faster.

Without a doubt, some Internet companies can justify large expenditures if they are building out infrastructure or acquiring customers. Internet service provider (ISP) pioneer UUNet had to spend millions building out a network. And America Online (AOL) spent a fortune building its current subscriber base. But at some point, reality bites. Investors want profits, but the cash has been frittered away.

The new technology companies are a proving ground for financial Darwinism at its most brutal. Only the companies best adapted to their environment tend to survive. IPOs that were extolled for their plans to build for the future at the expense of current profitability in 1999 are blackballed for their lack of profitability in 2000. Companies that fail to produce results quickly are slammed. High expectations turn to going-out-of-business sales in six months. What gives?

One day, investors are willing to discount many years into the future, placing enormous value on the businesses that may be created, at the expense of current profits. They are like the Japanese managers of the 1980s, who believed that management's time horizons should be long and that current profits should be foresaken for future success. Indeed, this is the very concept that has been firmly ingrained in the current breed of top executives, many trained at first-tier business schools—*build for the future*. However, seemingly the next day, there is a sea change among investors. Time horizons collapse. Today, IPO investors want *results!* They want results *today! Now!*

Shifting of time horizons and investment expectations makes for a schizophrenic market. This explains the huge spikes in stock prices, the ridiculous valuations, the sudden downdrafts, and the lack of consistency in analyzing these new technology companies. Adding to the mix are the Wall Street analysts who love the IPOs when their prices are through the roof and hate them when they are down. It's well known among savvy buy-side analysts that Wall Street earnings estimates rise in lockstep with appreciation in a company's stock price and fall in reaction to declines in price.

Market valuations of these new technology and emerging growth companies are a tug of war between future opportunity and near-term execution, between hope and reality. Is Amazon.com worth $15 billion? By traditional standards of profitability, no. But if the company has pioneered a whole new marketplace for selling a myriad of goods, then maybe it is. The key is the duration of your investment time horizon.

It is not surprising that Internet and technology stocks are among the most volatile in the entire market. Because there is no standard method of valuing these stocks, they can trade in huge price ranges, depending on current market sentiment. Amazon.com's true value may be $5 billion or it may be $50 billion. Investors won't know for years to come. In the meantime, the company's stock may trade within a huge price range. When Internet stocks were in their honeymoon phase, investors' time horizons were limitless. But when interest rates rose, money ran out, and the layoffs started, investors took a "what did you do for me today?" approach.

To survive in this dog-eat-dog Darwinian environment, successful Internet and technology investors must be confident in their choices. The best way to gain confidence in an investment is to understand how we got to where we are. Past is prologue. The early 1980s boom in technology and emerging growth stocks offers the pattern that was repeated in a far more exuberant way on the upside and a more violent way on the downside. Why? Because the volume and velocity of capital exceeded the previous boom.

MAY 1995: FROM LITTLE SEEDS . . .

The Internet IPO phenomenon on Wall Street goes back to May 1995. In that month, two pure Internet plays went public, both ISPs—Performance Systems (now PSINet) and UUNet. At that time, only a select few Internet companies had gone public. Both Performance Systems and UUNET posted excellent returns; but of the two stocks, UUNet was the powerhouse. With backing from software powerhouse Microsoft, UUNET priced at $14 and closed its first day of trading at $26. Gains of 100 percent or more on a first day for IPOs are now commonplace, but UUNET's 86 percent gain was remarkable for its time. And that was just the beginning.

Internet browser software developer Spyglass scored another hit in June 1995. The stock priced at $17, closed its first day at $27, and ended the year at $57, a gain of 235 percent over its offer price. But for many IPO investors, Spyglass was just a warmup. Three days before Spyglass priced its IPO, Netscape Communications had filed with the Securities and Exchange Commission (SEC) to go public. In August, when Netscape had finished its preparations, institutional investors were worked up in a frenzy.

The landscape of the IPO market was changed for good. Now it was possible to make a fortune in an extraordinarily short period of time if you picked the right stocks.

Netscape originally planned to price 3.5 million shares between $12 and $14 each. Demand was so strong for the deal that Netscape ended up pricing 5.75 million at $28 each on August 8, 1995. Despite the huge increase in price, shares of the Mountain View, California, company still soared on its first day to more than $58 and surged even higher in the ensuing months.

During the first quarter of 1996, Netscape hit a split-adjusted high of $162, giving it a market cap of $6 billion, a high that the stock would never see again. Fierce competition in the browser market instigated by Microsoft eroded Netscape's leading market position. Over the next two years, Netscape's stock trended lower, finally bottoming at $15 per share. Investors learned a painful lesson. Internet stocks could fall just as far as they could climb if the company's fundamentals changed.

Following Netscape's smash debut, true to form, underwriters rushed to bring young Internet companies public. The first tidal wave of Internet IPOs was witnessed in 1996. From February through August of that year, an unprecedented 24 Internet IPOs debuted, more than 8 percent of the total deals during that time. Leading names such as search engine Yahoo!, Web-site software developer BroadVision, information technology (IT) Web-site operator C/NET, and online broker E*Trade traded for the first time during this period. These Internet IPOs were household names and were broadly understood by individual investors.

OCTOBER 1996: THE WORM TURNS

Unfortunately, in the IPO market, you can have too much of a good thing. Part of the explanation for the strong performance of Internet stocks early on lay in their relative scarcity. Demand swamped supply. If investors wanted to participate in the growth of the World Wide

Web, there were only a few stocks to own. When supply finally began to catch up to demand, thanks to the IPO market, performance began to deteriorate.

In addition to the sheer number of IPOs, underwriters began to bring public many companies that simply were not ready for prime time. This is the "when the ducks are quacking, feed them" mentality of Wall Street. Internet offerings quickly moved from household names with seemingly limitless potential to underdeveloped niche players with dubious business models. The first turning point came late in 1996.

Faced with a shortage of Internet companies with real businesses, underwriters began pushing out companies that were vaguely targeted on undeveloped areas of the Internet or were lower-tier players in large areas. IPOs tried to curry valuation points by mentioning their Web sites in the prospectus. With none of the frenetic emotion that would later mark Internet investing, potential IPO buyers recognized these companies for what they were worth—not much.

By the end of 1996, all of the Internet deals from October were trading below their offer prices. Given the glut of IPOs, investors soured on new issues in general and Internet IPOs in particular. The bad deals poisoned the IPO market. Early in 1997, underwriters couldn't give an Internet IPO away. Small-cap stocks, especially riskier technology companies, were losers. From November 1996 through April 1997, just two Internet IPOs went public: ISP Earthlink and Internet auctioneer Onsale. But in May 1997, interest in Internet IPOs rekindled, thanks to a Seattle-based online book retailer.

THE WORLD'S BIGGEST BOOKSTORE

Amazon.com went public on May 14, 1997. To say that the market had mixed feelings on the deal would be an amazing understatement. Many investors were familiar with the company and knew that it was a first mover in a new area—online retailing. In addition, revenue growth was out of sight. Amazon had practically doubled sales in every quarter leading up to its IPO.

On the other hand, many investors were turned off by the young company's big losses and its brash young founder. Many analysts felt there were extremely low barriers to entry in the online retailing market. Wall Street's take on Amazon was polarized.

Amazon's first few months of trading produced the type of fireworks everybody was expecting. After pricing at $18, $4 above the top of its initial range, Amazon opened for trading at $35. Given the uncertainty surrounding the deal and the quick profits, institutional investors sold out immediately. Within days, Amazon was trading below its offer price. But individual investors, many of them loyal Amazon customers, bought in. By the end of the year, powered by continued strong revenue growth and a growing acceptance of the Internet, Amazon began a steep rally. The stock closed 1997 at $45, rewarding the true believers.

Strong e-tailing revenue and investors' appetite for quick profits enabled underwriters to bring more Internet stocks public. Because of the long period of time without any Internet IPOs, there were many decent companies waiting in the wings. In fact, the period from July 1997 through July 1998 was arguably the strongest period ever for Internet IPOs. A veritable "who's who" of leading Internet companies came public, including cable ISP AtHome, domain name registrar Network Solutions, audio-video technology developer RealNetworks, Internet security firm Verisign, Internet ad firm Doubleclick, Web hosting firm Exodus, caching technology developer Inktomi, Internet broadcaster Broadcast.com, and Internet bank Telebanc.

In many ways, this second wave of Internet IPOs came at the perfect time. Although a number of Internet companies had come public in 1996 and early 1997, there was still a relative scarcity of pure Internet plays. And despite the cold market for Internet stocks during most of 1997, Internet stocks were seeing more and more converts. A growing number of investment professionals began to realize that Internet stocks, with their supercharged growth, could produce awesome returns. Further, many individual investors began to play a larger role in the market through online trading or discount brokerage accounts. These investors tended to be Web-savvy customers looking for fast gains through technology stocks. Finally, growth in the Internet economy was hitting an inflection point. By 1998, online Web browsing and online purchasing wasn't just for the IT crowd. Average people around the world were going online for the first time, and the pioneer companies were reaping the benefits.

The surge in the Internet stocks brought worries to more thoughtful, analytic investors. As is always the case, Wall Street sought to rationalize high valuations by inventing creative metrics. Click-throughs, eyeballs, and registered users were dreamed up to compare the new companies. One creative Wall Street Internet analyst developed the "Theoretical Earning Multiple Analysis." While institutional investors fretted about the new paradigm, online investors chased the momentum, buying freely.

THE GLOBAL FINANCIAL CRISIS

But a crisis in emerging markets put the brakes on world financial markets. In August 1998, the Russian government defaulted on debt payments, and within months, a number of other emerging Asian markets plunged into near chaos. Investors around the world panicked and pulled their money out of any risky investments. Small-cap and technology stocks, which typically have a higher-than-average risk profile, were slammed.

The Internet market momentum evaporated. Gains in newly public Internet companies evaporated in a terrifying sell-off. In particular, the newest companies with the least knowledgeable and committed investors were the hardest hit. In market corrections, investors typically sell first the stocks with which they are least familiar—their most recent purchases and their IPOs. New converts to the Internet space quickly reverted to agnosticism.

The IPO market shut down. Underwriters couldn't give away young technology companies. During the entire month of September 1998, just one IPO managed to price. That was the lowest monthly total in more than 10 years. Considering how tough the environment was, therefore, that one IPO must have been something special. Indeed, the company, Internet auctioneer eBay, had one of the most important and successful debuts of all time.

Even at the height of the market's turmoil, demand was strong enough for the company's stock that it priced at $18 per share. Fundamentally, eBay had everything going for it. It was a unique company with a proprietary electronic auction capability that had grown rapidly since inception. Unlike just about every other Internet company at the time, eBay was profitable. Still, the timing could not have been any worse, so there was some question as to how the stock would perform in the aftermarket.

After a strong opening in which eBay soared to more than $47 per share on its first day, the stock slipped back. Over the next few weeks, as the market continued to struggle with the Asian crisis, eBay traded to a low of $31. Anyone fortunate to buy the stock at this level was richly rewarded in a short period of time.

To prevent the United States from succumbing to the general global economic woes, Federal Reserve Chairman Alan Greenspan embarked on an aggressive program to lower interest rates. Small stocks, particularly those in high-growth areas, tend to perform very well in periods of falling interest rates. Investors began buying again.

By late 1998, investors had all but forgotten about the Asian crisis. Internet stocks soared to new heights. Practically any investor without exposure in the area bought Internet stocks to avoid being left behind. Online investors ruled; they pushed Internet stocks to higher and higher prices. Any trepidation evaporated with the debut of theglobe.com, the now-forgotten Internet community site. Priced at $15, it opened for trading at $87 per share, 867 percent above its offer price. A record. More important, the incredible debut set into motion a feeding frenzy for anything Internet.

Predictably, underwriters quickly moved to meet this unprecedented and unexpected demand. From mid-November through the end of the year, seven more Internet deals debuted. All of the deals generated strong investor interest, and three IPOs produced first-day gains of more than 140 percent. Online auctioneer uBid soared 220 percent Ticketmaster Citysearch, a combination ticket retailer and local city guide, gained 188 percent; and online community XOOM.com jumped 146 percent.

The standards by which IPO success was judged had changed. A 25 percent jump in price, which would have been deemed a major success pre-Internet frenzy, was now regarded as a nothing, a failure. A 100 percent gain, which was once astronomical, was par for the course.

THE FEEDING FRENZY

If you had to pick a deal that was the poster child of the excesses of the Internet craze, it was MarketWatch, the CBS-affiliated Web site. First, there was tremendous buzz. MarketWatch is a name many investors knew. The financial press wrote numerous stories about the IPO, generating even more interest in the deal.

MarketWatch's underwriter, DB Alex Brown, added to the anticipation by making multiple upward adjustments to the deal's terms. Initially, MarketWatch filed with a price range of $12 to $14. Institutional investors, convinced the stock was poised to take off, asked for many more shares than were actually being offered. Consequently, DB Alex Brown raised the proposed range first to $14 to $16 and then again to $16 to $17 before finally pricing the deal at $17.

The feeding frenzy started. Many big institutional investors got "blanked" (they got no stock). MarketWatch opened with a huge premium. Shares of MarketWatch changed hands for the first time in the aftermarket at $105, up 518 percent and $88 higher than its offer price. On the first day alone, MarketWatch traded within a 40-point range, hitting a high of $130 and a low of $90. Anyone could have told you that MarketWatch would trade above its offer price. But actually making money in the stock was extremely difficult unless you were among the select few buying at the IPO price or adept at trading.

Like most Internet IPOs from this period, MarketWatch's stock price generally trended down from its first-day close. Without a doubt, there were periods in which MarketWatch rallied significantly, but a chart on the stock since its IPO highlights an unmistakable downward trend. MarketWatch proved out the adage that overhyped stocks are guaranteed to produce losses for any investor who buys them on the first day of trading.

Now investors really wanted Internet companies—any Internet companies—and underwriters were more than happy to oblige. After all, the ducks were quacking! Internet deal after Internet deal during the first few months of 1999 soared in early trading. From January through April, a string of companies produced monstrous first-day gains; for example, high-speed ISP Covad Communications, Internet consultant Modem Media Poppe Tyson, healthcare Web site Healtheon, Asian ISP Pacific Internet, Internet software developer Vignette, women's Web-site operator iVillage, Internet directory The Mining Company (now About.com), business-to-business Web-site operator VerticalNet, and name-your-price retailer Priceline.com.

Gradually, however, the market's seemingly endless appetite for Internet deals began to be satisfied. Underwriters offered up a growing number of companies that were not ready to go public and companies that were second- or third-tier players in hot areas. More and more of the IPOs had little or no revenue. To buy those IPOs is the ultimate in believing in the future. First-day gains of 200 percent or 300 percent dwindled to 100 percent or 50 percent.

MAY 1999: OVERLOAD

In May 1999, it happened. An Internet company went public and failed to produce any gain whatsoever. In fact, in the span of three weeks, it happened five times. Online finance Web site Intelligent Life and online retailer Fashionmall.com finished flat with their offer prices, while ISPs Ziplink and Juno Online and online real estate site COMPS.com actually lost money for IPO investors on their first days. Even big name IPOs that would have been moonshots just a few months prior were struggling early on. Barnesandnoble.com, one of the more eagerly anticipated IPOs, managed to produce only a small gain. Clearly, the honeymoon was over.

More interesting than merely poring over the gravestones of failed IPOs is analyzing what caused the great change among both large and small investors. Once again, the investing world's time horizon, once infinite, contracted sharply. The causes of these collapses are predictable. First, supply meets demand. Underwriters get really greedy and bring to the IPO market all of the junk stored in the attic, deals they shelved or rejected months before. Even the most naïve investors, the newbies, know that these IPOs are ridiculous and refuse to buy. Bad IPOs poison the water for the good. IPO performance momentum sinks. More investors walk away. Investors now have the time to closely scrutinize other Internet and technology IPOs in their portfolios. Those that have bloated valuations or businesses that look dubious in the sobriety of the morning after are sold. Finally, investors become more analytical and picky. This cycle happens time after time.

THE TWENTY-FIRST CENTURY

The extreme volatility of Internet and technology companies exemplifies what the IPO market is likely to be like in the coming years. New technologies and new ideas have rapid cycles. Investors will pour into favored sectors until the performance of those stocks loses momentum. Then they try to exit the door all at once and, predictably, prices collapse. At the end of the day, it is only the strongest companies that will survive. Financial Darwinism.

Early on in a cycle, investors give companies the benefit of the doubt. At the first sign of problems, investors vote with their feet. There are so many new companies in the pipeline waiting for their turns to go public, it hardly makes sense to stick it out with an IPO that had its chance and blew it.

The early Internet era was particularly instructive to investors—occasionally financially painful, but instructive. If you can invest in the fast-growing Internet and technology companies, you can invest anywhere. That volatile five-year period provided investors with templates of how and how not to catch the glimmering opportunities of the future. Here are 10 strategies that IPO investors can utilize.

1. Beware the Seduction of Internet Metrics

When Internet stocks hit the market in 1995, investors were totally perplexed about placing a value on them. Institutional investors, who are analytic by nature, solved their dilemma by sitting out—at first. For the many individual investors who used the Net and knew the IPOs, valuation was not an issue. They were preoccupied with owning Internet stocks and not too concerned about valuations.

Wall Street analysts who followed the stocks came to the rescue with inventive ways to value Internet stocks. By putting the patina of an analytic approach, however dubious, on their Internet recommendations, they were able to rationalize valuations and entice institutional investors into the market. But as we all know, just because a Wall Street analyst says a stock is worth a certain amount doesn't necessarily make it so. In a few notable cases, celebrity analysts were able to move Internet stocks up by proclaiming enormously high price targets. But looking at it more cynically, with the benefit of hindsight, how much real investment experience did many of these fledgling security analysts have?

At the height of the Internet frenzy, as Internet stocks continued to climb to new heights, analysts found it increasingly difficult to justify their price targets. So they started coming up with new valuation metrics to justify stock prices. These new benchmarks ranged from unique visitors, or "eyeballs," to the number of engineers or sales people a company had. Eyeballs and other measures are used to approximate revenue, but it's a step removed from reality. Although these metrics are not necessarily irrelevant, they often lead to conflicting results. For example, an Internet stock may appear cheap on a page-view basis compared to other similar companies but expensive on a multiple-of-revenue basis.

In addition, valuing Internet companies based on these new metrics misses the basic goal of investing. You want to invest in companies that make money. Eyeballs, for example, don't make money for a company by themselves. If a Web site gives away valuable content, Internet users will visit. But monetizing those visits is another challenge.

Early on, the mantra was that increased Web traffic would lead to increased advertising. For a while, that proved to be the case. However, with a growing number of Web sites, advertisers stuck with the biggest names. Traffic at Yahoo! is much more valuable than traffic at second-tier Web sites because Yahoo! can charge advertisers more. Consequently, comparing traffic at Yahoo! to that at another Web company can produce misleading results.

Before you spend a lot of time delving into various valuation metrics, you should determine if the company's value proposition is a valid one.

Although figuring out how to commercialize the Internet is still in experimental stages, you can always use good, old common sense to figure out whether the company is producing anything of value. If, in your judgment, the fundamentals of the company are flawed, why bother figuring out what it's worth? Investors learned quickly that content sites are dubious business models. The competition for eyeballs is tremendous, and margins are nonexistent when your main source of revenue is advertising. iVillage and drkoop led an army of failed Web sites. Internet companies that save consumers and business time and money have fundamental value propositions. For example, Ariba is the leading business-to-business aggregator on the Web. Companies are saving millions of dollars by streamlining their transactions through the intermediary Ariba. The Internet is offering tremendous opportunities to marketers in enabling them to personalize their products and services to individuals. Others in the field are E.piphany, Siebel, and Kana. Look for any Internet company that helps others in reducing its overhead costs or assists in getting, keeping, and growing customers.

With the benefit of hindsight, we know that many of the young Internet stocks crashed after ascending to ridiculous valuations. But when you are out there in the trenches, you have to make investment decisions on the basis of what the companies are currently trading at. There are two methods of valuation. The first focuses on supply and demand. Analysts in this camp reason that a company is worth what it is because buyers have pushed the price up or, conversely, sellers have pushed it down. Investors who use this approach are momentum investors. They will buy a stock because it is going up. They sell it when it starts going down. This approach eliminates the troublesome questions of valuation, but it's a technique that's difficult for most people to apply.

The second basic method of valuation focuses on an IPO's economic value. Does the company address a big opportunity or a niche? Is it a leader in its field or a new entrant in a crowded field? On the simplest level you can say that Amazon is worth more than eToys. The first has built a substantial online channel to sell everything from books to handheld wireless devices and proprietary e-commerce technology. The latter is a late entrant in a crowded field. But this is big picture, it doesn't help with knowing what the company is worth.

Over the years we have developed a hybrid approach to dealing with the Internet dilemma. When we value fast-growing companies, we look at what the company is worth as a whole, its enterprise value. As we explained before, *enterprise value* is the market value of the company, plus the debt and minus the cash. This is the value that a theoretical acquirer of the company would use. To do a reality check, we try to figure out the potential size of the future market. Often the prospectus provides a forecast. If you are looking at a young Internet provider of Web-user tracking systems, you estimate that in five years, the size of the market could be $5 billion. The company is proposing a valuation of $250 million. Because the IPO is not a leader in its area, you conservatively estimate that it can grab 10 percent market share. That's $500 million in revenue. Then, you take another leap of faith and assume that the company will have operating margins of 15 percent and net margins of 10 percent. That's $75 million in operating income and $50 million in net income. The company is now posting $12 million in revenue, and it grew 25 percent over the previous year. Is it realistic to assume a growth rate of 110 percent a year? Probably not. That means you have to lower your assumptions of future revenue growth. Once you are comfortable with your revenue assumptions, you can estimate profits and discount them back to the present. In this example, not only is it ridiculous to value a company at half its projected revenues in five years, but the growth assumptions are far too high to be realistic. Further, the size of the market opportunity is too small to justify a $250 million valuation for a second-tier player.

If you have them available, use the Wall Street analyst's assumptions on revenue and earnings growth. While they represent a biased view, they have been reviewed by management and are close to what management itself is assuming. How many years will it take for the IPO to turn a profit? The farther off the profitability is, the riskier the investment.

With unprofitable Internet and technology companies, the best benchmark of comparison is revenue. It is the only objective measure of the company's accomplishments. By using your assumptions on how fast the company can grow and analysts' estimates, you can analyze the multiples of revenue and expected growth. Also compare the IPO's valuation to others in its field. If the top companies in the area have significantly higher market valuations, then you know that the IPO on which you are focusing is priced at a discount to the other companies, which is appropriate. Compare the multiples of revenue of the IPO to others in its field. Again, leading companies should have higher valuations. If relevant, compare the number of subscribers or route miles to the proposed enterprise value. Is it reasonable? How does it stack up against others?

An example of one way we value technology companies is shown in Exhibit 7.1, "How to Value a Technology Company." The graph displays three characteristics of the companies being studied: (1) the size of the bubbles relates to the relative size of revenues; (2) the *x* axis shows the expected growth rate of the company; and (3) the *y* axis shows one valuation metric—price to sales. Here we can see that Palm is almost 5 times the size of its closest competitor Handspring and about 11 times larger than Research in Motion (maker of the popular Blackberry pager). Because of its larger size, Palm is the slowest grower of the pack at 50 percent, versus Handspring at 79 percent and tiny Research in Motion at 88 percent. But also note that Palm is valued the lowest on a price-to-sales basis, with a price-to-sales of 10 times versus 18 and 21 times for Handspring and Research in Motion, respectively. It is also very important to note the relationship between the company's growth rate and its valuation, as shown by the fair value/frontier line depicted

Exhibit 7.1   How to Value a Technology Company

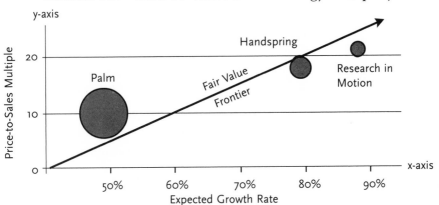

Source: Renaissance Capital, Greenwich, CT (IPOhome.com).

by the arrow on the graph. Based on this combined valuation metric, you can see that all three companies are valued pretty much the same, with Palm coming over the line (a slightly higher valuation) and Handspring and Research in Motion coming under the line (a slightly cheaper valuation). One might argue that Palm deserves the higher valuation due to its market leadership and size. When you do this type of analysis, look for companies that are significantly below the fair value frontier line to identify buy candidates and for those well over the line for shorting opportunities.

The process of valuing fast-growing Internet and technology companies is sometimes a frustrating one because of its lack of precision and lack of benchmarks. Placing a value on the first mover is particularly difficult because there are no other companies to which to compare it.

It is regrettable that in most cases we are faced with a holistic way of evaluating these fast-growing companies. Investors must take all of the pieces of the puzzle together: the size of the future opportunity, the IPO's position in its market, the size of the losses it has already accumulated, the length of time to profitability, and the valuations of other analogous companies. Then an investor must apply his or her own risk tolerance and time horizon. Because the future is far off, you can't say with certainity, "eBay is worth $10 billion today." However, you can stake out boundaries of reason for the current worth of the future economic value of the IPO.

2. Know the Flavor of the Day

It also helps to understand the current investment environment. Internet investors are trendy. They flit from Internet company to Internet company, growing tired and moving on to the next flavor. In 1997 and 1998, investors couldn't get enough of business-to-consumer Web sites. At the time, Internet analysts and industry experts proclaimed that the new breed of efficient online retailers would lead to the death of bricks-and-mortar retailing. By 2000, many of these new-style retailers were fighting just to stay alive.

Instead of analyzing the merits of individual companies, many Internet investors lump companies together by buzzword. These short-term traders buy the companies that are using the hot buzzwords and sell the companies using the wrong buzzwords. In a matter of months, top-performing Internet companies can plummet back to earth. In 1999, business-to-business e-commerce companies took center stage. By early 2000, these one-time highfliers had been grounded.

Momentum investing requires impeccable timing and trading skills that most investors don't have. Still, as an investor, you should be wary of buying into the group of the day. While it may be hard to resist buying a company that seems to be going up every day, remember, with Internet stocks, this trend can reverse itself in a heartbeat.

3. Buy the Leaders

If there is one single lesson to be learned from experience with Internet stocks it is to invest in leading companies. More than any other area, the Internet rewards early movers and companies with defensible niches. A technology lead of 6 to 12 months in a new market often proves insurmountable. Second- and third-tier names may work in the short term; but if a particular sector falls out of favor, these companies may never recover.

eBay is a perfect example. As a first mover in the Internet auction space, eBay rapidly built a network of buyers and sellers. The bigger its network became, the easier it became to attract more buyers and sellers. As the company was going public, Yahoo!, with the help of Onsale.com, made a big push to grab market share. To this day, Yahoo! is still dwarfed by eBay in Internet auctions.

Another example is Amazon. While it has taken its licks in the market, Amazon is synonymous with e-tailing, and nobody does it better. Several other e-tailing companies went public shortly after Amazon, including CDNow, Cyberian Outpost, and Cybershop. All of these companies thrived when e-tailers were the rage on Wall Street. But when the sector fell out of favor, the secondary companies were hit especially hard and never recovered.

4. Buy When Nobody Else Will

After you have done your homework, buy Internet and technology IPOs when nobody else seems to want them. The IPO market is extremely fickle and cyclical. No matter how hot or how cold the market seems at any one point, history has proven that things tend to turn around in a hurry and go to extremes. Given the fact that Internet stocks can see huge fluctuations in their valuation depending on market sentiment, the best time to buy is at the low point in the cycle.

Without a doubt, it is impossible to pick the absolute low point in any cycle. That being said, it is very easy to tell when the IPO market is out of favor. On average, there are roughly eight IPOs in a week, excluding seasonal slowdowns in August, late December, and early January. Often, the actual number of IPOs is well above eight or well below. When the number is well below eight, chances are that the IPO market is out of favor. Furthermore, when several Internet companies postpone their deals or lower the terms of their deals, it is a sign that investors simply are on strike. What most investors don't realize is that these are the best times to buy. At times like this, Internet IPOs typically price within or below their initial ranges and opening premiums tend to be much smaller. That means average investors can buy in at reasonable levels.

More important, when demand is low for Internet IPOs, underwriters are more conservative in deciding which companies to take public. Generally speaking, only the strongest Internet companies are priced in tough IPO environments. Institutions, the primary buyers of IPOs at their offer price, are extra careful in bad markets. The institutions need to be coddled and enticed. If a company does not have a sound business model and a solid outlook, institutions simply won't buy it. Therefore, any deal priced in a weak IPO market is worth investigating. It is no coincidence that the only deal to price at the height of the Asian crisis was eBay.

Aggressive buyers of high-quality Internet and technology deals during the recent corrections performed very well. It may feel extremely painful in the short-term, but when you feel like selling everything you own, it is usually a good time to buy.

5. Don't Be Afraid to Admit a Mistake

In Internet and technology investing, knowing when to sell is at least as important as knowing when to buy. Often, panicked investors will sell too early. Internet stocks are inherently volatile, and changing market sentiment can produce huge swings in their prices. A particular stock may decline as much as 80 percent only to rebound to new heights. In some cases, though, the stock never rebounds. A prudent sale can prevent a complete loss of capital on an investment.

The Internet literally moves at the speed of light. Any slip-up in execution or any fundamental change in a company's environment can lead to a rapid and dramatic decline in business. That company's stock could see a sharp decline even in a strong market. For example, in 1998 after online retailer Amazon.com announced that it would begin selling compact discs (CDs) in addition to books, the stock price of CDNow, another online CD retailer, entered a steep and prolonged decline. The market feared that Amazon would replace CDNow as the top Web retailer for CDs.

Similarly, following Netscape's debut, Microsoft made significant inroads in the browser market through aggressive marketing. Personally investors may feel that Microsoft's tactics were unfair, but an investor should never confuse personal feelings with investment judgment. Netscape was losing market share; and because the company's market cap was so big at the time, there was nowhere for Netscape to go but down. The biggest mistake made by Internet investors is holding on to beaten-down stocks too long, hoping for a recovery. It may never come.

6. Don't Believe the Hype

Once in a while, you will hear about an Internet IPO everywhere you turn. Every publication you pick up has a feature article on the company, and every financial news show mentions the deal. Financial Web sites follow the deal from the minute it files to the second it actually starts trading. Chat boards are flooded with messages talking about how hot the IPO will be. Investors can't help but get excited.

In these cases, however tempting it may be to dive in on the first day the stock opens, the best thing to do is wait. No company in the world can live up to this type of hype, and most times, early aftermarket buyers get burned. Even if the company does indeed turn out to be the next Yahoo!, excessively hyped deals invariably get ahead of themselves in early trading. There is nothing more disheartening to an investor than seeing an investment shrink in the span of days or even hours. It is very easy to become discouraged and to abandon ship before a company has the opportunity to prove itself.

TheStreet.com is a perfect example of an overhyped deal. Even before the company actually filed to go public, there were news stories about the financial Web site and its famous founder, Jim Cramer. An announcement that *The New York Times* was investing in the fledgling Internet company sparked even more interest. Add to that the fact that the company was ready to go public at the height of the Internet frenzy, and predictably the stock headed to the moon on its first day.

At the end of its first day of trading, TheStreet.com, a company with less than $5 million in sales in the year leading up to its IPO, had a market capitalization of $1.6 billion. When the buzz surrounding the deal died down, investors questioned whether that was a fair valuation for the time. Gradually, over time, TheStreet.com sank in aftermarket trading.

7. Be Sensitive to the Overall Market Environment

The IPO market is a special sector of the overall equity market. It reflects what is going on in the overall market to a large extent. Fears of interest rate rises are particularly hurtful to the valuations of pricey Internet and technology companies. However, we have noted over the years that IPO performance leads the broader market in bull markets and trails it in bear markets. The IPO market is a derivative of the broader markets and doesn't always drop when the Standard & Poor's (S&P) 500 sags or go up when the Dow Jones rallies.

You have to step back and ask yourself whether the overall quality of deals is strong or poor. Deal quality is highest during tough times in the IPO market and when the IPO market is beginning a major rally.

Deal quality is lowest when the IPO market is at its most ebullient. You don't need an exact gauge. You can simply look at the list of IPOs on IPOhome.com. If many of the deals are development stage and some are even laughable, then the IPO market and probably the Nasdaq are headed for a dive.

8. Understand Where the Company Is in Its Stage of Development

We have identified five stages of the development of Internet and technology companies from formation to being like a normal company with ongoing profits. This is diagrammed in Exhibit 7.2, "Life Cycle of Internet Companies."

1. *Market development, focus on branding.*   At this stage the IPO is totally focused on getting its name on the map. It wants visibility and traffic. It is spending like crazy to "brand" itself and to try to get market share. The dot.coms were all at this stage when they went public. With nothing to guide them, investors concocted ridiculous metrics to value the companies. How many dot.coms are around today? This is the riskiest time to invest in an IPO. Unless you are getting in for pennies a share, it's time to take a pass. You are being asked to be a public venture capitalist, without the benefit of a rock bottom price.

2. *Revenue ramp.*   At this stage the IPO has a product or a service that people are willing to pay for. The company now is focused on growing its revenue as fast as possible. It may be selling its product below cost. Internet and technology companies are very focused on having a credible revenue ramp to attract venture capitalists and public investors. This stage is still a very risky one.

3. *Years to profitability.*   Having captured revenue, the IPO now is able to better define its business model and to figure out how long it will take it to reach profitability. The longer the years to profitability, the riskier the IPO. Some IPOs never become profitable, and along the way investors begin to question the validity of their business model.

4. *Emerging Leader: The IPO has demonstrated that it can grow revenue.* This is good. You can now start to value the company in a more traditional manner by capitalizing its future stream of revenue. It is now

Exhibit 7.2 Life Cycle of Internet Companies

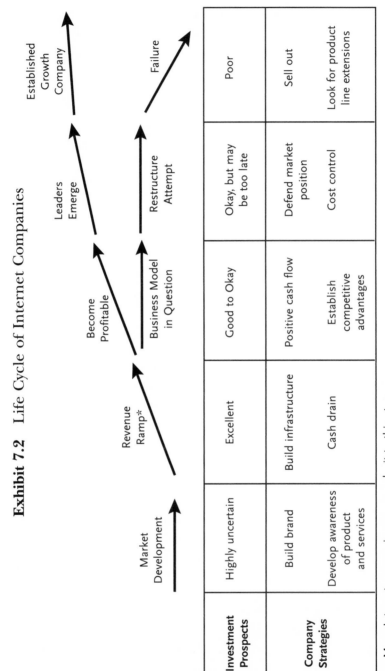

	Market Development	Revenue Ramp*	Business Model in Question	Restructure Attempt	Failure
Investment Prospects	Highly uncertain	Excellent	Good to Okay	Okay, but may be too late	Poor
Company Strategies	Build brand	Build infrastructure	Positive cash flow	Defend market position	Sell out
	Develop awareness of product and services	Cash drain	Establish competitive advantages	Cost control	Look for product line extensions

Arrows in diagram: Market Development → Become Profitable → Established Growth Company; Leaders Emerge; Business Model in Question → Restructure Attempt → Failure

*Note: Many Internet companies never make it to this stage.

Source: Renaissance Capital, Greenwich, CT (IPOhome.com).

at the emerging growth stage. How big will the company be in five years? This is the stage where laggards begin to fall away.

5. *Established growth company.*   This is now a traditional growth company. You can look to traditional cash flow and P/E ratios to value the company.

If you understand the stage of development of the company, you can better assess the timing of your investment. For example, if the IPO market is going through tough times, a "revenue ramp" stage company has a better chance of producing results for you. This is because the underwriters and private investors have thoroughly vetted the company and its management, and they have concluded that the company has a solid plan. When the IPO market is frothy, with a lot of early stage companies, stay away.

9. The Suitability of the Net to the Business Model

Internet investors learned the hard way the limitations of the Internet. Not all land-based businesses are suited for the Internet. Early on, several online grocery stores went public, for example, Peapod and then Webvan. The problem is that the grocery business itself is a low-margin business. Look at Grand Union, now in Chapter 11. Grocery stores work on razor-thin margins and sell perishable merchandise. While online shopping may be a blast at first, is it really more convenient or cheaper than picking up the telephone and ordering groceries from the local store that delivers? Webvan argued that by eliminating the fixed cost of building physical stores and substituting the variable cost of having delivery vans, they would create a better financial model. However, Webvan is also building a network of huge urban distribution centers, a fixed cost.

In analyzing business models, it helps to apply the lessons learned through common sense. Internet retailers and investors ignored the realities of inefficiences of batching small, individual orders, shipping costs, competitive pricing, lack of customer loyalty, high marketing expenses, and managing returns, just to name a few.

The lure of the Internet makes investors abandon the standards of old. There are many examples of young land-based retailers, software firms, and consultants that are profitable within a short time of their inception. However, if the company has an Internet connection, investors apply different standards. They are unwilling to own a provider of software that has low gross margins and no profits; but they fight to own the shares of a company that has a Web interface.

The Internet is a place of experimentation. Not every idea will work. The failure rates will be higher and the cost to unlucky investors in them will be more painful. Over time, however, it will become more clear which business models are adaptable to the Web. When that happens, valuations will reflect it. Investors who study success and failure will be early in figuring this out and will make money. IPOs in general and Internet IPOs in particular are works in progress. They evolve.

10. The Biotechnology Phenomenon

Biotechnology IPOs used to be the domain of highly specialized investors, many of whom were doctors or biochemists. Few laypeople strayed into the preserve. However, the enormity of the mapping of the human genome has attracted a broader range of investors. The payoff for successful biotechs is enormous. The computer-aided tools and gene databases that are being developed are changing the process of drug discovery from a hit-or-miss approach to a highly automated, structured process that will almost certainly produce drugs that are customized to the individual.

Researchers have decoded the entire human genome. Biotechnology companies, which had a brief run in 1991, came back. During the mid-1990s there had been a handful of companies involved in developing genomic tools, like Affymetrix, and genetic databases, like Qiagen. However, these IPOs were largely bought by very knowledgeable investors. This time, the prospects of genomics revolutionizing drug discovery entranced a far broader group of investors. They envisioned novel drugs being created to replace existing antibiotics, which are threatened by antibiotic-resistant bacteria. They envisioned cancer drugs being tweaked so that they are customized for the precise type of tumor with which an individual is afflicted.

Not many of us have doctorates in biochemistry. So how do you approach this area? At the early stages of exploiting the human genome, it's really anyone's guess as to which companies are going to be successful. A degree in biochemistry helps, yes. But there are other factors that are equally important. The company's access to capital and the ability of management to marshal that capital and commercialize the drug or gene information system are equally important. It will be many years before you can discern who the winners are.

Just as with the Internet stocks in the beginning of the cycle, early on, investors don't discriminate among the companies. Institutional investors are buying portfolios of biotech companies, knowing that some will be winners. Individual investors don't have the luxury of owning 20 or 30 biotech companies. Rather, you must go through the laborious process of analyzing every single one. As you do this, you will realize that the four-step approach to analyzing IPOs holds. You can compare and contrast the companies. The tenth IPO to offer a genetic database is probably a wanna-be. The biotech IPO should have experienced management and strong enough financial backing to get it to profitability. In two or three years, as these companies move to commercializing their products, investors will be able to clearly distinguish amongst the biotechs.

CONCLUSION

Unlike traditional, old-economy companies that have tangible assets, the most valuable assets for the majority of Internet companies are brands, intangible intellectual capital, market position, relationships with other companies, and timing. Valuing these intangible assets is extremely difficult. It's far easier to place a value on an electric power facility or the number of cookies that Keebler is able to pump out of its manufacturing facilities. But placing a value on an idea, the skills of a programmer, or the determination of management is hard.

We've concluded that trying to concoct "new paradigm" metrics is a fool's solution. Investors want to count dollars produced by a company, not "eyeballs." The only meaningful metrics for Internet and technology companies are revenue and losses (or in rare cases, profits).

An Internet or technology company's revenue base gives investors an idea of just how significant the company is. The size and the growth of a company's revenues are the direct product of how successful and sustainable it's intellectual capital is. For unprofitable Internet infrastructure companies, it is meaningful to look at the hard assets. For example, providers of broadband wireless backbone have a critical asset with a lot of value: the route miles of fiber laid.

The investment climate is a critical factor to invention. The free movement of capital to the most attractive returns is an important element to creating wealth. The amount of capital in individually directed retirement funds is fueling the interest in investing in innovative new companies. This is also beginning to happen in Europe, where huge corporate pension plans have long dominated the capital markets. Individual European investors are beginning to take more responsibility for their investments.

Knowing the investment cycle is key. It's a boom-bust pendulum. At its most violent, the entire IPO market can rise to great heights and then crash violently. Far more common are the mini booms and busts that occur on a rolling basis, industry by industry. E-tailers rise and fall, to be followed by business-to-business contenders, and then by the biotechs. These cycles occur because when a new IPO investment pays off, investors become increasingly confident in funding more new companies at a younger and younger stage and at higher and higher valuations. As competition heats up and too many companies with the same idea get funded or bad companies get funded, returns decline, capital flees, and more disciplined investing takes over. Then, only new companies with track records, solid business models, and experienced management can raise money.

Awareness of the rate of new invention, the capital markets climate, and where we are in the IPO cycle will make you a sharper investor.

SECRET 8

The Potential of Global IPOs

"Do You Speak English?" challenges the bright orange advertisement on the Paris Metro. If you don't, all you need to do is call the Wall Street Institute, symbolized by the Statue of Liberty. It went on to talk about the opportunities in new companies. The advertisement might as well have had dollar signs and the word "IPO" tattooed on it. The message is clear. English is the universal business language. If you want to get in on the payloads of money being made in the initial public offering (IPO) market, you need to speak the language of Wall Street.

While London, Paris, Frankfurt, Tokyo, and Hong Kong all have active stock exchanges or bourses, the king of global capital is still Wall Street with its New York Stock Exchange (NYSE) and over-the-counter (OTC) market. The ascendency of Wall Street is a post–World War I phenomenon. Wall Street came into its own after the war as the need for capital by the emerging automobile, airline, and rubber industries resulted in the IPOs of General Motors, TWA, and Goodyear. The electric utility industry took off, too, as electrification spread across the United States. Meantime, Europe was recovering from the ravages of World War I and was largely using its resources primarily for reconstruction.

Ironically, the Great Depression enabled the crowning of Wall Street as the leading global stock marketplace. The Securities Act of 1933, the Securities and Exchange Act of 1934, and the creation of the Securities and Exchange Commission (SEC) in 1934 provided much needed protections for investors. By requiring public corporations to report their financial and operational results to shareholders on a regular basis and by requiring brokerage firms to treat investors fairly and honestly, the U.S. government created the most highly regulated and shareholder-friendly market in the world. The standards for being a public company were higher and more consistent in the United States than anywhere else. Moreover, the SEC was given the power to inflict painful punishments on transgressors.

To be sure, this is a simplification of events. There were a host of other economic and political factors (including another world war) that resulted in Wall Street's predominance as the money-raising capital of the world. But, simply put, it was the economic growth of the United States and the creation of a consistent set of standards by which capital is raised and securities are traded that put Wall Street on the map.

The United States is the entrepreneurial king of capital. According to John Micklethwait and Adrian Wooldridge in a *Wall Street Journal* editorial (June 6, 2000), the United States produces four times as many start-ups per capita as Europe. Although things are changing in Europe and Asia, without a doubt the United States has the most business-friendly culture, laws, and taxes. The U.S. markets, unlike other markets, are not dominated by a handful of powerful investors.

U.S. individual investors are among the world's most knowledgeable. The long history of pension plans and then mutual funds acclimated Americans to investing in stocks and bonds. The growth of the mutual fund industry also made Americans familiar with the distinctions between aggressive growth equity funds and income funds. Americans are comfortable with both direct ownership of stocks and indirect investing through a mutual or pension fund. But it was the advent of the individual retirement account (IRA) that made Americans realize that it is they, not their employer or the government, who are responsible for long-term investment success. The decision by many large corporations to reduce retirement costs by eliminating corporate-controlled pension plans and creating self-directed defined contribution programs known as 401(k)s convinced Americans that as far as investments were concerned, you're on your own. Low-cost online trading also lowered barriers. Cynicism among middle-aged and young Americans about ever getting Social Security benefits sealed the deal.

The objective of the chapter is to give readers an understanding of both the opportunities and the risks of investing in foreign IPOs trading in the U.S. markets and in the home country markets. This chapter will describe the globalization of the IPO market, the way it has changed over recent years, and likely future developments. The chapter will also focus on the major non-U.S. bourses and how they are encouraging emerging growth companies in their countries to raise capital by going public on their domestic bourses.

THE BASICS

When a non-U.S. based company decides to go public in the United States, it must file what's called a form F-1 with the SEC. The F-1 is the non-U.S. equivalent of the S-1 filed by U.S. companies. The "F" stands for foreign. Regrettably, at this writing, F-1s are not available on EDGAR, which puts individual investors at a bit of a disadvantage in getting early information on non-U.S. IPOs. (IPOhome.com is one of the few places where individuals can access non-U.S. IPO profiles.) Additionally, non-U.S. companies must comply with SEC financial reporting and auditing requirements. Together, these requirements protect U.S. investors.

Why do non-U.S. companies want to take advantage of the U.S. IPO market? The reasons are many. Because the U.S. capital markets are the biggest and most developed in the world, non-U.S. companies can raise more capital in the United States than they can in their own countries. Could the Chinese Internet service provider (ISP) China Unicom or its Korean counterpart Korea Thrunet raise sufficient capital in their own countries to build out their businesses? No. A non-U.S. company may also regard entering the U.S. IPO market as a way to develop its global corporate presence. For example, the IPO of Germany's Deutsche Telekom at first looked like a humdrum privatization of a sleepy giant. But when Deutsche Telekom showed its cards by seeking to acquire VoiceStream, the tiny wireless telecom carrier, it showed its intention to grow beyond German borders. Companies also raise capital in the United States simply to show that they can. Trading on the NYSE or OTC lends a certain cachet and credibility to a start-up.

U.S. investors should be aware that new entrants to the U.S. markets aren't always IPOs. Sometimes non-U.S. companies are already trading on their domestic exchanges. When they trade on the U.S. stock markets, these companies usually trade at the same price (but in dollars, of course) as they do on their local exchanges. In rare instances, a non-U.S. company may have extremely limited trading on a local exchange. We consider that company an IPO if the proposed valuation is different from its current trading.

WHY BUY INTERNATIONAL IPOS?

Why would an investor want to buy the securities of a company that is based in a foreign country? Opportunity and diversification. Non-U.S. investors want to ride the economic growth and innovation of the U.S. economy. They may also want to diversify beyond investments in domestic stocks and bonds. For their part, U.S. investors may see greater opportunities in the emerging economies of Russia, China. and South America. They also saw opportunity in Europe as the European Monetary Union (EMU) took shape, particularly in the fast growing economies of Spain, Portugal, and Ireland.

As ever, with opportunity comes risk. Investing beyond your home country's borders means taking on the risk of the other country's currency devaluing in comparison with your own. The poor performance of the Euro certainly hurt American investors in European stocks. In emerging countries, inflation and political risks abound. American and European owners of Russian wireless service provider Vimpel got a wild ride every time Boris Yeltsin staggered off the political stage to recuperate from his occcasional bouts with "heart" trouble, and they got their own heart-stopping plunge during the Russian currency crisis.

However, these risks are obvious to most investors. Venturing beyond your own territory is inherently scary. The biggest practical hurdle that investors face in buying non-U.S. companies is lack of information. Despite the SEC reporting requirements for all U.S.-traded securities, there are cultural and political barriers to the relatively free dissemination of corporate information. Chinese- and Indonesian-based IPOs are particularly prone to cultural secrecy. Although the IPOs of Huaneng Power, an electric generating company, and Indosat, an Indonesian satellite company, were successful at first, their stock prices drifted down as investors realized that it was difficult—no, impossible—to get information on the companies beyond their semiannual reports of results to the SEC. The former government officials who ran the companies did not see the need to communicate with investors. Most of these companies didn't even bother to maintain a U.S.- or London-based investor relations firm. And when we tried to call headquarters, no one spoke English.

In contrast, most of the European and South American IPO managements understand that their stocks' performance is partly a function of how well they communicate with investors. Many hire U.S.-based investor relations firms to handle the responsibilities of sending out press releases and setting up investor conference calls. More and more, even start-up IPOs are savvy about making sure that institutional and individual investors can get a line into the company, either by a direct call to investor relations or via their Web sites.

THE IMPORTANCE OF REGULATION

Another risk is that European prospectuses may not contain the same level of disclosure as that required when a company files to trade on a U.S. exchange. The terminology and layout of European prospectuses are different than that of U.S. prospectuses: U.S. companies produce revenues; U.K. companies produce turnover. Vital pieces of information appear in different places. For example, on page 30 of the prospectus for easyJet (a Bedfordshire, U.K.–based, low-fare, no-frills airline), the company describes its 33-year-old chairman and founder Stelios Haji-Ioannou—he is also the founder of Stelmar Tankers, a shipping company, and the creator of such ventures as easyEverything (a chain of Internet cafes) and easyRentacar (a budget rental car business). Sounds like an entrepreneurial young man, right? Well, if you were diligent or lucky enough to land on footnote 15.5.4 on page 139 of easyJet's prospectus, you would find Mr. Haji-Ioannou portrayed in a different light. In 1991 an oil tanker owned by Haji-Ioannou's father exploded. In the aftermath, civil and criminal actions were brought against Haji-Ioannou, his father, and others for pollution, manslaughter, shipwreck, and bribery. The prospectus stated that the

civil charges were largely settled and that a court acquitted the men of
the criminal charges. However, the public prosecutor is still appealing
to pursue man-slaughter and shipwreck charges. And in further footnotes, there were other curious items. Haji-Ioannou may face criminal
charges for running an ad in an Athens (Greece) newspaper urging
voters to fly to London to "avoid the hassle" of the October 1998 election. There were two messy cases in Greece involving members of the
Haji-Ioannou family over money matters. Although Stelios Haji-Ioannou
may be as pure as snow, in the context of the other "easy" ventures he
created and the legal woes, one wonders how much time and attention
he can devote to easyJet.

In a U.S. prospectus, these legal problems would have appeared in
the management section, and probably referenced to another section
for a fuller discussion. Because of these differences, the SEC restricts to
institutional investors those sales of non-U.S. IPOs that decide against
filing with the SEC.

One thorny issue of which investors in non-U.S. IPOs need to be
aware is that most overseas stock markets are significantly less regulated
and more prone to insider shenanigans than the U.S. stock market is.
Stock market regulators in Continental Europe and Asia have far fewer
powers and resources to sniff out and punish insider trading. Corporate executives and employees regularly have knowledge about material events involving their company. The top officers of a corporation
may plan for months to target and launch a takeover of another corporation. In the United States it is illegal for the executives of the company to buy the shares of the takeover target, knowing that the share
price will rise when the takeover is announced. It is also illegal in the
U.S. to buy or to sell shares for a period of time before earnings are
reported. In the United States, the philosophy is that a level playing
field creates a healthy, solid stock market that attracts both institutional
and individual investors.

In Europe and in most large South American bourses, insider trading is illegal, but regulators lack sophisticated computer systems and
the authority to clamp down on offenders. In many countries, prosecutors cannot bring civil actions in insider trading cases, or the courts
prevent prosecutors from obtaining key information. Germany made
insider trading illegal only in 1994. The SEC itself lacks clout outside

the United States. There have been many instances when a foreign IPO suddenly moves up or down on high volume without any news. And then, weeks later, the news finally comes out that the company is making an acquisition or is reporting disappointing results. In 1996, for example, SAP AG, a German software giant which trades in the United States and Europe, suddenly fell 23 percent. Weeks later, the company announced a profit warning. According to a *Wall Street Journal* account, German investigators discovered many suspect trades by SAP employees and their families. Many trades were made at a savings bank near company headquarters. One executive's mother sold put options.

Until enforcement is heightened, individual investors are subject to being victims of insider trading and stock manipulation. As IPO fever grows in Europe, South America, and Asia, it becomes increasingly important for countries to maintain fair markets. Great Britain, which has one of the most active in-country IPO markets, recognized this imperative and recently tightened its insider trading laws.

One of the reasons why stock markets are less highly developed outside the United States, except in Great Britain, is that most non-U.S. stock markets have a relatively limited number of companies listed for trading, lower stock ownership by individuals, shorter trading hours, and complicated rules. Also, stock trading can be dominated by an oligarchy of investors. In Germany, stock ownership by individuals in 2000 was less than 8 percent. The spread of the market economy, driven by powerful economic and technologic forces, is stimulating growth of IPOs in Europe, Asia, and South America.

The importance of regulation and investor protection is not to be minimized. The tale of World Online is instructive. World Online was the hottest pan-European Internet service provider (ISP), serving 1.5 million customers in 15 countries when it went public in March 2000 on the Amsterdam Stock Exchange. It was founded and headed by Nina Brink, who, by virtue of the IPO and her high-profile social life, was a European celebrity. But soon after the offering, she admitted to selling a substantial portion of her shares in World Online prior to the IPO. The reference to this sale in the prospectus, which was not distributed in the United States, was far from clear. The stock plunged from 43 euros (about $36) to 20 euros (about $17). She was forced to resign. But the damage was done. Many employees had purchased shares at the offer price and now had their net worths chopped in half. If World Online had offered shares in the United States, the SEC would have required Brink's sale of stock to be highlighted in the front of the prospectus, to protect potential shareholders.

THE IPO WAKE-UP CALL

The IPO phenomenon in Europe, South America, and Asia is a recent development. Exhibit 8.1 shows "The 10 Biggest Non-U.S. IPOs." Many countries in Europe labored under socialist governments. The state owned the telephone company, the electric utility, and sometimes manufacturing operations. In South America, governments imposed restrictions on foreign investment and currency in a futile attempt to stave off rampant inflation. China and Russia were controlled by communist authorities who believed ownership of property and making money were criminal offenses. Japan restricted foreign investment in its country and stifled innovation.

To best understand the global IPO phenomenon, we need to look at individual parts of the world. Each region has its own IPO market characteristics.

EUROPE

In many ways, former British Prime Minister Margaret Thatcher instigated the development of the IPO market outside the United States. To jump start *Britain* out of the death throes of inflation and recession, she ordered the sale of the state-owned postal, telegram, and telephone company British Telecom to the public. She cleverly garnered favorable public opinion and virtually prevented any future Labour government from unraveling the IPO by earmarking a significant portion of the IPO to the employees of British Telecom at a sweetheart price. Priced in 1984, British Telecom was an immediate success with British and American investors, who snapped up the shares based on promises by the new management that they would cut the workforce and increase efficiency.

Exhibit 8.1 The 10 Biggest Non-U.S. IPOs

Company	Description	Date	Offer Proceeds (billions)
ENEL SpA	Privatization of Italy's electric utility	11/1/99	$16.4
Deutsche Telekom	Germany's privatized telephone monopoly	11/17/96	13.0
France Telecom	France's privatized telephone monopoly	10/17/97	7.3
Telstra Corporation	Privatization of Australia's telecom provider	11/17/97	5.6
Swisscom	Privatization of Swiss telecom PTT	10/4/98	5.6
Infineon	Spin-off of Siemens' semiconductor division	3/12/00	5.2
China Unicom Ltd.	China's second largest telecom provider	6/16/00	4.9
China Telecom	Spin-off of Chinese coastal cellular provider	10/15/97	3.9
Telecom Eireann	Ireland's provider of fixed line and mobile telecom	7/7/99	3.7
Alstom	GEC and Alcatel spin-off of their power generation equipment division	6/19/98	3.7

Source: Renaissance Capital, Greenwich, CT (IPOhome.com).

As more European countries recognized the advantages of privatizing state assets, Spain, Portugal, France, Denmark, and Germany quickly brought their telephone behemoths to the public market. Each government received the proceeds from the sale of stock—often billions of dollars—which were then used to offset deficits or to reduce taxes. And to greater and lesser degrees, the stocks of these IPOs were successful, depending on how deeply management cut the bloated payrolls and modernized systems.

With the privatizations of the telecommunications companies complete, the next wave of IPOs addressed the Europeans' next most urgent need—good television broadcasting. British television, like British cooking, used to be bad. A typical evening selection would be a recorded Parliamentary debate, a game of snooker (billiards), and something educational and thoroughly boring. What the Europeans craved was American style television—*Dallas*, MTV, CNN. To give you a more current anecdote of how important entertainment is to people, a friend of ours who travels extensively in Russia and Central Europe describes driving into a rural Russian community and seeing a large demonstration. The villagers waved signs and chanted in angry tones. Her puzzlement over what pressing local issue would cause nearly everyone in the village to protest in front of the local government building on a cold November day ended when she got close enough to decipher the cyrillic signs. "Bring Back *Dallas!*" one sign read. "We want *Dallas!*" said another. Apparently, the local government had cancelled *Dallas* reruns in a cost-cutting effort.

Fortunately, Rupert Murdock and Ron Lauder (Estee's son) came to the rescue. Rupert Murdock's British Sky Broadcasting, a 1994 IPO, brought Britons channel upon channel of U.S. television programming via satellite. Though not a particularly successful IPO early on, it has turned out to be a major U.K. and U.S. stock. Ron Lauder put together a group of U.S. television veterans to rescue an even more television-deprived area—Central Europe. His Central European Media Enterprises brought U.S. television to the Czech Republic, parts of Germany, and Poland. Although Central European Media stumbled in large part because the advertising markets are much less developed than in the rest of Europe, it is an example of how entrepreneurs quickly address opportunities as they emerge and try to raise money via an IPO. Groupe AB SA, a French independent television producer, raised capital in 1996 to bring the French more choice in television programs.

The next wave of IPOs addressed an even more pressing need—the modernization of telecommunications infrastructure. When telecommunications was in the purview of the government, little was done to upgrade telephone service, open it up to private competitors, or make it affordable. But in the mid-1990s eleven European Union (EU) countries agreed to offer a single currency, the euro. In addition to shifting to the euro, the EU countries agreed to lift onerous prohibitions on competitive telecommunications services. This, coupled with the advent of cheap, reliable, wireless services, opened the doors to a wave of telecommunications IPOs.

Britain saw the U.S. and Canadian regional telephone companies flock to its shores to build out cable TV and telecommunications systems. Bell Cable Media, TeleWest, and Nynex Cablecom were early examples. Other examples of the rush to build out Europe were Colt, a local fiber bypass carrier in London and Frankfurt; Esprit, an international long distance operator; Equant, a Dutch operator of the world's largest data network; and Global Telesystems, a fiber-optic network and carrier.

Western Europe's early development of healthy and active IPOs was due in large part to the fact that London, Paris, Amsterdam, and Frankfurt have stock markets with long histories. Britain, France, Holland, and Germany also have the longest traditions of private enterprise and are home to large businesses. The discovery and development of the IPO market followed a similar pattern in each country. First, privatization. Then, large, established, privately owned companies went public. These were closely followed by technology companies, many addressing the need to provide advanced telecommunication systems, others involved with providing software and tools. Then, each country entered the Internet era, with portals, e-tailers, and ISPs testing the IPO waters.

Take *France* as an example. Many of its largest companies had been socialized during the 1980s. It was late to the European IPO wave. Then Prime Minister Jacques Chirac came along in 1995 and saw the wisdom of freeing France Telecom, the telephone company; then THOMSON, the state-owned consumer electronics company; and more recently Aerospatiale Matra, its aerospace defense contractor.

The number and type of IPOs are reflective of the amount of economic activity and growth. *Portugal* has a less diverse economy than some of its neighbors, and its IPOs to date have been limited to privatizations of its electric and telephone utilities. *Greek* IPOs have been largely limited to telecommunications and cable television providers in STET Hellas Telecom, a wireless GSM provider, and ANTENNA TV SA, the leading television network and program producer in Greece.

Ireland's economic boom has made it the Celtic Tiger. With a well-educated population and favorable tax laws, it has long attracted U.S. companies. It offered up Telecom Eireann, the state-owned telephone company; Esat Telecom, its second largest telecommunications firm; and Riverdeep, an educational software and systems provider.

Spain, Italy, and *Germany* have been active IPO participants. After privatizing its telephone and electric utilities, Spain produced a succession of Internet and telecommunications start-ups in Terra Networks, an ISP, and Jazztel, a telecommunications company catering to small and midsized businesses. Spain has surprised many market participants by its aggressiveness and success. Membership in the EMU gave Spain credibility. The Spanish government has lowered taxes and overhauled socialistic labor laws. And the chief executive officers (CEOs) of Spain's technology companies are young, well educated, and global thinkers.

Italy, too, has gone capitalistic. Italy privatized its electric utility, ENEL SpA, and IPO'd its largest integrated oil and gas company. But other IPOs were uniquely Italian: Gucci, the designer of personal luxury goods; De Regio, the maker of high quality sunglasses; Ducati, the high-end motorcycle maker; and Industrie Natuzzi, the maker of fashion-forward leather furniture.

In Germany stock ownership by individuals used to be among the lowest in Western Europe. Stock ownership was considered tacky. But the Deutsche Telekom IPO opened Germans' eyes. Then came the 2000 debut of Infineon Technologies AG, the semiconductor maker, being spun off by one of Germany's best-known industrial giants, Siemens. Infineon was Germany's Yahoo! Infineon defined the new German desire to be a part of the Wall Street IPO party. According to *The Wall Street*

Journal, 4 million German individual investors signed up for shares via their local savings banks, which in turn were so overwhelmed by demand that they had to hire people to take orders for the stock. Infineon itself fanned the flames by embarking on a 20 million euro advertising and branding campaign. We suspect that as with other hot IPOs, many of the buyers were clueless about Infineon's business and strategy. It didn't matter. Ignorance was bliss. Priced at $33.92 in March, it soared 95 percent in early trading.

The success of Infineon will almost certainly spur other German industrial conglomerates to spin off some of their subsidiaries. German IPOs reflect the country's developed industrial and technology infrastructures. Sauer, the maker of hydraulic systems for industrial vehicles, went public in 1998. Rofin Sinar, the industrial laser division was spun off from Siemens.

Switzerland's IPO pool reflects the country's developed fine-manufacturing businesses with its TAG Heuer watch company IPO. The Scandinavian countries' IPOs show the importance of vehicle manufacturing through Scania AB, the Swedish maker of heavy trucks, and Rauma, the Finnish maker of logging and construction equipment.

Russia is a special case. Its lack of business traditions and laws has prevented the country from participating in the IPO market. Investors so distrust the apparatchiks that Russia has not been able to fully take advantage of the privatization surge. The 1998 currency crisis, during which Russia devalued the ruble by more than a third and defaulted on its debt, further undermined Russia's nascent securities markets. The only IPOs the country has offered have been wireless telecommunications providers. Vimpel, which serves Moscow, and Golden Telecom, a competitor, would probably not have made it out the door except for the involvement of European and U.S. investors and management. A third wireless provider, Mobile TeleSystems, went public in 2000. Westerners also took some comfort in the fact that the wireless carriers' built-out networks are valuable and tangible. Although Russia has many highly educated citizens and a reputation for producing first-class information technology types, Westerners are still not willing to bet on Russia's intellectual capital. Yet.

The performance of European IPOs has been mixed. In general, the privatizations have fared well, in part because large institutional investors have flocked to the shares because of their liquid trading. The other reason is that most have fulfilled on promises to cut bloated payrolls and to increase productivity. The "old" economy companies making cars, trucks, and manufacturing equipment have not been well received. But the telecommunications and Internet players have soared.

Each of these IPOs mentioned trades on either the NYSE or the Nasdaq in addition to a European bourse. However, some European IPOs choose to trade only on a European bourse because of the heightened disclosure required by the SEC or because bankers conclude that the company would have limited appeal beyond its own borders. So, many European banks and insurance companies that operate only within one country only trade on their country's bourse. For example, British insurer Prudential PLC created a popular online bank, Egg. With Egg well known in Britain, but not across the Atlantic, Prudential opted to launch its spin-off of Egg only on the London Stock Exchange.

The story of European IPOs would not be complete without mentioning how several established stock exchanges have encouraged the development of emerging companies, particularly technology companies. In London and Frankfurt, the stock exchanges have created separate, smaller markets specifically focused on helping new companies go public. Using U.S. regulations and standards as guidelines, Deutsche Boerse officials created the Neuer Markt, which now has hundreds of listings. Unlike the traditional German stock exchanges, which have loose rules, the Neuer Markt set high standards for disclosure. Earnings must be reported in German and in English within two months after the end of the quarter. Because its rules protect investors, individual investors began to flock to the Neuer Markt. IPO activity is far greater on the Neuer Markt than on other German markets. Since starting in 1997, IPOs have raised more than 20 billion euros in capital (about $17 billion). Because these companies on the Neuer Markt probably don't trade anywhere else, investors need to thoroughly research these little companies.

London offers the Alternative Investment Market (AIM) as part of the London Stock Exchange. AIM's goal is to give investors access to small, emerging growth companies. For these companies, the listing requirements are far less onerous than on the regular exchange. The exchange's CEO Theresa Wallis calls AIM "venture capital for small investors." AIM got started with 10 companies in 1995 and now has listed over 600 companies, some of which have transferred to the London Stock Exchange. Investors should understand that many of the listings are start-ups and have market capitalizations of $50 million or less. But for investors willing to shoulder the risk of buying into small, risky companies in the hope of hitting a 10-bagger, AIM deserves a look.

London and Frankfurt are forming a new market, called the iX, just for technology stocks. The U.S. Nasdaq is joining the talks. Other exchanges for emerging growth companies are Easdaq in Brussels and the Nouveau Marche in France. Even the Celtic Tiger, Ireland, has gotten into the game. The Irish Stock Exchange launched its new market in late 2000. The new ITEQ is targeting Irish technology companies by offering a dual listing in Ireland and one of the major international exchanges.

While the European IPO markets have historically lagged those in the United States, that may not be the case in the future. First, the success of privatizations and spin-offs like Infineon are awakening giant European conglomerates to the benefits of selling off fast-growing divisions, just like their U.S. counterparts did in the 1990s. Second, stock ownership is beginning to take off in Europe. Historically, U.S. individual investors own 50 percent of the stock on the U.S. exchanges. European ownership is far lower—the figure for British stock ownership hovers around 25 percent of stock issued; Germans own less than 10 percent. Third, the technology, biotechnology, and media revolutions are active in Europe. Arguably, Europe is three to five years ahead of the United States in wireless technology. Just go to a restaurant in Paris. The waiters have small, handheld devices for you to use to charge your meal. And, last, the bourses are finally getting their act together in terms of offering well-regulated markets that are friendly to individual investors.

U.S. readers need to understand that it is currently difficult and expensive to make direct investments in companies that are traded only in local European markets. While there are no laws restricting direct investment, the SEC prohibits foreign brokers from calling U.S. citizens and soliciting an order. Over time, as the new bourses adopt new standards of reporting and lower costs, expect this to change.

Europeans do not have the same tradition of investing as do Americans. In most European countries, individuals' assets are still invested in corporate pension plans controlled by the employer. Even in Britain, where stock ownership is the highest in Europe, most investors have a saver's mentality. Wealth is invested in illiquid assets, property, and mortgages. But this is all changing.

Excitement over IPOs and the creation of the new stock exchanges have enticed Germans, the French, Italians, and Spaniards into the equity markets. Making it easier and cheaper for them to do so are the growing number of online brokers. Europeans are also embracing the benefits of online trading. The leading brokers are unfamiliar to Americans: comdirect, ConSors, and Direkt Anlage Bank.

A report by U.S. banking firm J.P. Morgan showed that German investors were leading the pack and make up about 54 percent of European online investors, with French investors a surprising second. The report predicts that by 2003, 17 million European investors will be online compared to 27 million in the United States. Online investing is growing at a particularly high rate in Italy. The J.P. Morgan report predicts that the number of Italian online investors will eclipse online investors in Britain by 2001. And if they invest the way their U.S. counterparts do, look for many young technology and Internet companies to do IPOs and for much volatility.

The attempt by Spain's Terra to acquire Lycos and Deutsche Telekom's pursuit of VoiceStream Wireless are indications that European companies intend to be at the head of the line in the technology revolution. The merger of European bourses will also go a long way to creating a seamless Pan-European securities market by eliminating confusing exchange-specific rules. The plan is to have a Pan-European platform for the trading of Europe's top stocks.

ASIA

In comparison to the returns in established markets, such as London and Germany, the highest returns come in the riskiest countries, particularly Asian countries. IPO returns in developed markets are lower due to the higher liquidity and the types of companies going public. Exhibit 8.2, "IPO Returns Across the World," shows the difference in returns.

Exhibit 8.2   IPO Returns Across the World

Country	Average Initial Return*
Australia	12%
Austria	7
Brazil	79
Canada	6
China	388
France	10
Germany	28
Greece	52
Hong Kong	16
India	35
Israel	5
Italy	24
Japan	24
Korea	74
Malaysia	104
Mexico	33
Poland	36
Singapore	33
Spain	11
Sweden	34
Taiwan	35
Thailand	47
United Kingdom	14
United States	17

*These first day returns were calculated over various long-term time periods ending in the late 1990s. These studies, performed by different authors, were combined in an article published by Tim Loughran, Jay R. Ritter, and Kristan Rydqvist in (June 1994) *Pacific-Basin Finance Journal*, 2:165–169 (updated September 23, 2000). The full study is available on Dr. Ritter's Web site, http://bear.cba.ufl.edu/ritter.

Dominating the Pacific Rim IPO activity is *China*, with its population numbering in the billions and its crying infrastructure needs. The communist backgrounds and proclivity to secrecy didn't stop the Chinese government leaders from accessing the U.S. IPO markets. Since the first opening of the Chinese market years ago, Western and Hong Kong investors have been sniffing around China for opportunities. But currency and foreign stock ownership restrictions have kept investors from taking meaningful stakes in Chinese industry and, even more important, from repatriating it, that is, getting your profits out.

The first Chinese IPOs we saw reflected the state of Chinese modernization. Ek Chor China, a leading maker of motorcycles, went public in 1993. We imagined a highly labor intensive, old fashioned factory, churning out drab scooters for Chinese workers to ride down dusty, unpaved roads. Interestingly, Ek Chor was a joint venture between CP Pokphand, an Asian industrial conglomerate, and Chinese government entities. These early joint ventures were typical due to Chinese prohibitions against foreign majority ownership. The privatizations wouldn't come until later. Brillance China Automotive, a minibus manufacturer, was the next out the door. It, too, was a joint venture between the government and Hong Kong investors.

The first Chinese IPOs were first received with much excitement. But then reality set in. Was this the best China had to offer? Or was China just throwing Western investors its worst big companies and saving the best for itself, we wondered. Since most of these companies had direct or indirect affiliations with the Chinese government, information, save the bare minimum required by the SEC, was hard to come by. Communication with the companies was nonexistent. Wall Street analysts dropped coverage. The stocks sank.

Yet needing Western capital, China persisted and IPO'd Jilin Chemical, the largest Chinese producer of basic chemicals, in 1995. Due to investor concerns about most-favored-nation status and the poor performance of the Chinese IPOs, it wasn't until 1997 that China came back with yet another chemical company, Beijing Yanhua Petrochemical, and two airlines, China Eastern and China Southern. All of these deals had dropped by year end. The first somewhat successful Chinese IPO was China Telecom Hong Kong, the state-owned Chinese cellular provider, which was up 10 percent by year end 1997—by Chinese standards, a great success.

China's desperate need for power provided the impetus for three electric utilities: Shandong Huaneng Power, an investor group that owned interests in coal-fired electric utilities; Huaneng Power, which owned five plants; and AES China, the subsidiary of American AES Power.

The Asian currency crisis in the summer of 1998 closed the door on Chinese and other Asian IPOs. So it wasn't until 2000 that Western investors were willing to chance another Chinese IPO. And the IPOs China offered were not "old" economy companies, but Internet portals and telecommunications companies. *Ahah!* investors thought, *China has changed its stripes.* It recognizes that it can't keep the rest of the world out. The debuts of China Unicom, China's second largest telecom provider, and Sina.com, an Internet portal, were well received. A third old economy Chinese IPO had a tough time. Trying to raise money for its oil industry, the Chinese government tried to sell 175 million shares of PetroChina via prominent underwriter Goldman Sachs. The deal and the road show were plagued by demonstrations by human rights activists, which scared many investors away. The jury is still out on the Chinese IPOs because the managements of the companies aren't particularly forthcoming with information and communication with investors.

The same holds true of Indonesian IPOs. Like China, *Indonesia* desperately needed infrastructure. The first IPO was a polypropylene resin producer, TriPolyta Indonesia, in 1994. Meeting with modest success on this deal, Indonesia then offered two other companies, both pulp and paper producers, which is an important industry to Indonesia. However, lack of communication and information discouraged investors, who fled the stocks. The same fate befell PT Pasifik, a private Indonesian satellite company. Although not government owned, management failed to provide Western investors with insights into the company's strategy and results.

With such disappointing investments, Western institutional investors have been unwilling to give Indonesian IPOs another chance. The plummeting currency in 1998, the overthrow of President Suharto, and the current government's inability to stop the numerous violent rebellions throughout the country have served to slam the door on accessing global capital markets.

English speaking *Australia* and *New Zealand* have offered a handful of IPOs, representing a variety of industries. New Zealand's contribution to the U.S. IPO market was TransRail, a leading railroad in New Zealand, which did surprisingly well in its debut, and SkyNetwork Television, a privatization of state assets, which was a clunker. Others included OxEmail, a provider of Internet services in Australia and New Zealand, and Barbeques Galore, an Australian retailer of barbeques, which were both disappointments.

The present IPO market for Asian companies is not dominated by a single country trying to sell state assets. Rather, the IPOs being offered are private companies focused on providing wireless and Internet services to Asians. Examples are Sohu.com, Sina.com, and Netease.com, all portals hoping to attract the huge potential Chinese Internet market. Other Internet providers are Asiacontent.com, which operates pan-Asian Web sites with local language capabilities; Korea Thrunet, a Korean ISP; and Internet Initiative Japan, Japan's largest Internet access provider.

Given the size of *Japan*'s economy and its well-developed industry, we might have expected to see more Japanese IPOs. But, the Japanese government's unwillingness to allow foreign investment and the cultural patterns favoring group effort rather than individual initiative squelched IPOs. However, that may be changing.

Japan's giant Softbank, which has far-flung operations in computer product distribution, specialized publishing, and Internet infrastructure, is well known for investing in Internet-related companies. Some of its best-known investments have been in Yahoo!, Ziff-Davis, Multex, GeoCities, TheStreet.com, E-Loan, Net2Phone, 1-800-Flowers, and Webvan. Softbank, which trades only on the Toyko Stock Exchange and is valued at nearly $5 billion, has been a prolific investor in Internet-related companies, not all of which have been successful bets.

Softbank is spearheaded by Masayoshi Son, a long-time believer in the Internet. Softbank's investments are widespread—the United States, Japan, and Europe. With more than 300 holdings today, he sees Softbank growing to 800 Internet investments in five years. Hikari Tsushin is another high-profile Internet investor and cellular phone sales agent. Softbank and Hikari Tsushin are dubbed "Net-batsu," twenty-first century versions of the old zaibatsu, pre–World War II conglomerates and powerful trading companies that were disbanded by the Americans after the war.

With Softbank's willingness to invest outside of Japan, it is ironic that until recently, there were no pure Japanese IPOs. To be sure, Japan's protracted recession and severe banking problems may have played a role in the lack of IPOs. The only activity prior to 1999 was the spin-off of U.S.-based businesses by Softbank, which spun off part of its investment in publisher Ziff-Davis and by Fuji Bank, which spun off Heller

Financial, the U.S. commercial financial services firm, in an effort to raise much-needed cash for the bank. However, both Softbank and Hikari Tshushin have suffered in the deflation of Internet stock values.

The capital requirements of launching Internet-access services propelled the first Japanese IPOs into the U.S. market. Internet Initiative Japan, the leading ISP in Japan, debuted in August 1999, rising 35 percent from its $23 offer price. In the raging bull market for Internet IPOs in late 1999, it went on to hit $132. To raise more capital, Internet Initiative Japan spun off 17 million shares of its fiber-optic backbone network, Crosswave Communications, a year later, raising another $245 million.

The most interesting and most un-Japanese-like IPO was Crayfish, which hosts e-mail services for small and midsized businesses in Japan. With Internet financier Hikari Tsushin owning 43 percent of the stock, the company is run by an entrepreneurial pair of 26-year-olds. Investors weren't bothered by the fact that it relied on Hikari's sales representatives for all of its sales or that it split the monthly service fee and paid a $30 finder's fee for each new subscriber. Priced at the height of the spring 2000 Internet madness, Crayfish rocketed 414 percent from its $24.50 offer price, making it the second best performing IPO of the year. Japanese and U.S. Internet fans eventually pushed the stock up to $166. But troubles soon befell the aggressive e-mail provider. A Japanese magazine accused its parent of questionable business practices regarding its cellular phone sales, and Hikari Tsushin's stock plumeted. Hikari Tsushin soon announced a huge loss of $109 million, and both Crayfish and Hikari Tsushin dropped further. By May 2000, Crayfish announced larger than expected losses and a corporate reorganization. By July Crayfish admitted that customer growth was down 50 percent on a month-by-month basis. By this time the stock was $5. The situation has since deteriorated further into a lawsuit.

Although shareholders left holding Crayfish are likely bemoaning their misadventure in the brave new world of Japanese dot.coms, more Japanese IPOs are on the way. Just as the European bourses are encouraging public venture capital through their junior stock exchanges, the Tokyo Stock Exchange recently created the oddly named "Mothers" exchange for young companies. With Crayfish one of the first IPOs to debut on Mothers, the goal of the new exchange is to provide easier financing for emerging companies. Mothers has minimal financial requirements for trading, asking for a minimum of 1,000 shares, and 300 shareholders. However, it is interesting that they require companies to report quarterly business results and have at least two analyst meetings a year.

As testimony to the coming importance of the Asian IPO markets, local venture capitalists Hikari Tsushin and Softbank, as well as U.S. companies have begun moving in, particularly in Japan. For example, powerful GE Capital is teaming with Daiwa Securities; Goldman Sachs and partner Kyocera raised a 30 billion yen fund. Other venture capitalists and U.S. bankers are using an unusual strategy of buying up publicly traded Hong Kong shell companies (companies that are incorporated but have few assets or operations) with the intention of using the shell company's stock to make investments in Asian Internet companies. The Crayfish IPO, while hardly a glowing success, is the tip of the Japanese entrepreneurial iceberg. There are many new ventures percolating below the surface that venture investors will help launch.

In general, we have found the Asian markets less comforting in which to invest than the European markets. Business practices in Indonesia and Hong Kong favor the locals, particularly the business leaders closely tied with government. Japan still has currency and investment restrictions on foreigners. As the numerous scandals coming out of Japan and the Philippines attest, insider trading and price manipulation are common. Enforcement is weak. Institutional investors have turned away from some of these markets. However, the opportunity that faces investors as Asian Internet activity begins is enormous; and for risk-tolerant investors, it may pay to become comfortable with the peculiarities of investing in Japan, Korea, and China so you're ready when the Asian IPO market takes off.

LATIN AMERICA

As Latin America found out, the keys to economic health are stable, market-economy goverments and currencies tied to the dollar. *Argentina* and *Mexico* were among the first large countries to elect leaders who believed in capitalism. Following the same pattern in Europe, state-owned entities were privatized. YPF Sociedad, Argentina's huge oil and gas company, was a hugely successful IPO in 1993, one that has continued to be popular with global investors.

Many of the early Latin American IPOs were industrial or basic materials companies. For example, *Brazil*'s Clark Automotive, a maker of manual transmissions, and Mexico's Durango Industrial Group, a maker of container boards, both went public in 1994. Mexico's elite and powerful families, who had been unable to liquify their long-standing holdings in Mexico's heavy industry, used the liberalization of currency restrictions to sell their holdings in the form of U.S.-traded IPOs. For example, Consortium G. Dina, nationalized in 1989 but now owned by the Gomez-Flores family, makes trucks and busses, and Grupo Radio Centio, the largest radio broadcaster owned by the Aguiere family, were opportunities to raise cash.

The American soda companies, Coca-Cola and Pepsi, participated in IPOs of their local distributor in Brazil, Argentina, Mexico, and Puerto Rico. Coca-Cola FEMSA, Pepsi Bottling PR, and Panamerican Beverages were all high-profile IPOs.

As in Europe, the newly affluent Latinos had to have their MTV: Multicanal Participancoes, TV Filme Quinenco, SA, and TV Azteca. Performance of these companies was mixed and largely dependent on the strength of the local currency. Mexico's mid-1990s currency and debt crisis squelched IPO activity. Political unrest and sporadic violence also have put a damper on entrepreneurial activity.

It was the advent of the Internet that spurred Latin American innovation—and, interestingly, with significant U.S. backing rather than local backing. Star Media Network, which offers Internet services in Latin America, has its headquarters in New York. El Sitio, which offers Spanish and Portuguese language portals, raised money with its U.S. IPO but didn't list its stock in its home city, Buenos Aires. Impsat Fiber Networks, an Argentinian telecommunications company, is based in Florida. PanAmSat, which was one of the first companies to launch television and communications satellites for Latin America, until its acquisition by Hughes was headquartered a half a block away from us in Greenwich, Connecticut.

Latin American eyes and ears are much sought after by the American and European companies. Telefonica, Spain's largest telecommunications provider, has acquired numerous telephone companies in Latin America. Its subsidiary, Terra Networks, itself an IPO, was rumored to be sniffing around StarMedia for a possible acquisition. America Online has an aggressive but only partly successful operation, Latin America Online, that is trying to sign up Latin American Internet subscribers.

To date, there has been little sign of Latin American home-grown Internet activity. This may be due in part to the fact that large Spanish and well-financed U.S.-based Internet providers are daunting competitors. The concentration of wealth in a few elite families in countries like Mexico, Brazil, and Venezuela has also slowed entrepreneurial efforts. The income gulf between the rich and the poor has spawned socialistic leaders in countries like Venezuela, whose efforts to redistribute wealth force those with financial assets to focus on protecting those assets rather than on further investment and wealth creation. The bottom line is that Latin America may well be a huge opportunity, but it is Europeans and Americans who are largely taking advantage of it.

Latin America, however, has failed to live up to its IPO potential. One key reason for this is the issue of shareholder rights. Many large corporations are either government run or controlled by powerful families. On one hand, the privatizations of state-owned assets, like YPF, have been well received by investors. This is because the newly public corporations follow a predictable pattern. They bring in professional management, reduce inefficiencies, and pay good dividends. Although the state may force the corporation to act in accordance with the government's social policies by limiting the amount of layoffs or by forcing the company to retain hefty pension and health benefits, these social policies are usually benign.

In contrast, the family-owned businesses of Mexico and Brazil have been far less well received, with good reasons. In most Latin American countries, insiders can vote themselves big dividends or otherwise feather their nests at the expense of the public shareholders. The problem is that many of these families want to liquidate part of their investments in these large enterprises, but they don't want to give up the entitlements they have as a privately held organization. To some extent, doing a U.S. American depository receipt (ADR) forces them to agree to relinquish—at least on paper—the many perks of private ownership.

However, investors don't completely trust these companies to protect the rights of the public shareholders. If they are listed in the United States, the SEC and NYSE have certain powers to force disclosure; but in the end, these companies are governed by the local laws in their own countries.

There have been a number of attempts by various governments to enact shareholder protections. But in countries like Venezuela and Colombia, which are governed by left-leaning politicians, these efforts conflict with socially oriented policies. Even in countries like Brazil, which have worked hard to bring their economies up to market economy standards, shareholder protection legislation has foundered. Regrettably, these failures have prevented Latin America from fully participating in the IPO boom. If you look at the bulk of recent IPO activity in Latin America, it is directed by U.S., Spanish, and Portuguese entrepreneurs.

ISRAEL

Given its tiny size, *Israel* has produced a disproportionate number of IPOs. With a highly educated and technologically savvy population, many of the country's IPOs have been oriented to telecommunications and the Internet. Israel's government has long-standing polices of providing tax breaks and research-and-development (R&D) grants to young companies. Recent examples of Israeli IPOs are Internet Gold, a leading ISP, and Partner Communications, the only provider of global systems mobile communications (GSM) wireless service in the country. Both have performed well.

CONCLUSION

The IPO market is steadily becoming more global. There's no doubt that IPOs are stirring global interest in equities. IPO successes stir national pride. In 10 years, the volume of non-U.S. IPOs may well surge past U.S.-based IPOs. Successful investors in IPOs will have to look beyond the boundaries of their own countries and become comfortable investing abroad. To accomplish this feat, the stock exchanges need to automate, to eliminate archaic settlement procedures, and to cut exchange fees. The brokers must cut fees that make trading unnecessarily expensive. And governments must eliminate obsolete laws that prevent cross-border purchases and sales of securities. Uniform financial reporting in multiple languages is another must.

Given the trends in online brokerage and the emergence of new exchanges, Europe will lead the way in truly global investing. While Asia will still be an active source of IPOs, corruption, the lack of financial standards, and lack of information will likely discourage all but the most sophisticated and daring.

If these things occur, New Yorkers taking the IRT downtown to Wall Street may one day hear: *"Comment! Vous ne parlez pas français? Vous risquez de ratter l'occasion de gagner un maximum de fric!"*

Or, *"Sie sprechen kein deutsch? Dadurch verpassen Sie Ihre Chance auf's grosse Geld in Deutschland!"*

In other words, if you don't speak French or German you stand to miss out on making big bucks in those countries' hot IPO markets!

SECRET 9

How Management Helps or Hurts an IPO

The importance of Wall Street's view of management is encapsulated in the story of how Capstone Turbines' chief executive officer (CEO) got a rare standing ovation at the New York road show lunch for his summer 2000 initial public offering (IPO). Management that is well regarded by Wall Street can add points to an IPO's stock price and help propel it upward. In contrast, to know how bad management can hurt an IPO's stock price, you only have to look at the army of failed Internet companies whose entrepreneurial but ultimately inept young executives are being jettisoned in favor of more experienced management veterans.

This chapter will describe the standards by which Renaissance Capital judges management. Each IPO's prospectus reveals much about its managements' backgrounds, activities, and relationships. We will show you the top 10 factors we use in evaluating managements of IPOs. We will also illustrate some negative factors that in our experience ultimately produce IPOs that turn in poor performances.

When ranking the management of an IPO, we also consider what we call *control issues*. These issues address how much stock is owned by management, what relationships exist among the key shareholders, and whether the company is structured to meet the standards of being a public company. Taken together, these factors provide a clear picture of whether the IPO's management is properly motivated and whether the company is organized to benefit you, the public shareholder. All told, the interests of the management of an IPO should be closely aligned with yours.

Just as the presence of Netscape's founder James Clark can add multiple points on an IPO, questionable backgrounds can kill deals, even in the headiest of times. It is relatively easy to to spot the future stars. But it is far harder to pick up on the negative clues left by companies whose management teams can make or break an IPO. Certainly, much can go wrong from the time a company goes public. A recession can mute demand for the IPO's products or services. Competitors can appear on the horizon offering better, cheaper products. However an investor can assure himself or herself before buying into an IPO the degree to which management's interests are aligned with the public investors' interests and management is capable of running the company.

Let's take a fairly obvious example. Aristotle, a technology company that provides information and services to political campaigns, seemed to have its timing right as it tried to debut in the weeks before the 2000 Presidential election. Aristotle counted 200 members of the House of Representatives, 45 members of the Senate, and the National Rifle Association as clients. Its losses shouldn't have troubled investors, as most IPOs during the period sported losses as badges of honor. Investors could also take in stride the fact that their independent auditor issued a "going concern" letter. After all, the money raised from the IPO would cure that problem. What killed the deal was management.

The co-founder, chairman of the board and CEO was John Aristotle Phillips, a Princeton graduate with a bachelor of science in aerospace engineering. Sounds good so far? Read on. Quoting verbatim from the prospectus, "While at Princeton, Mr. Phillips received international recognition for his design, from publicly available documents, of an atomic bomb. He is the co-author of *Mushroom: The Story of the A-Bomb Kid*, which was sold to a television network for a made-for-television movie." Kaboom. The fact that a CEO would highlight this information as his chief—in fact, only—qualification to run a public company was a red light to potential investors. Who said prospectuses can't be entertaining?

Let's go through each of the 10 key factors one by one.

1. WHO BENEFITS FROM THE IPO?

Follow the money. Tens of millions of dollars are raised by a typical IPO. Who gets it? For a public shareholder, the most advantageous use of the proceeds from an IPO is putting the money back in the business for expansion, capital expenditures, research and development (R&D), or marketing. Obviously, much depends on management's ability to derive a return on invested capital. But, for starters, you want to see the money go to growing the new company.

Any selling by insiders raises a huge negative. If the company is so good, why are the insiders bailing out? The larger the amount of shares that are being sold, the greater the reason to avoid the company. We have seen some instances of the young entrepreneurs of new companies selling a few shares. We can understand that executives in young companies who are being paid relatively low salaries may need cash for certain of life's needs—college tuition bills, for example. While we don't like to see any insider selling, as long as the executives are selling a relatively small portion of their holdings, it's okay, so long as other aspects of the IPO are favorable.

However, in too many IPOs, the money goes elsewhere, benefiting insiders. Even in Internet and technology start-ups, we have seen instances in which insiders—whether management or investors—use part of the proceeds to repay loans they made to the company or to pay loans used to fund big cash distributions. For example, cutely named WebSideStory, a Web-site-user tracking service started by a bunch of ex-Baker & McKinsey lawyers, proposed using $17 million of its IPO proceeds to redeem insider-owned preferred stock, another $20 million for a cash dividend to the founders and other executives, and $15 million to pay a dividend to the preferred holders. Paying money directly to the parent in the case of a spin-off or a tracking stock is usually a no-no for an online or technology company. In raising money for University of

Phoenix Online, parent Apollo opted to pay the proceeds of the IPO directly to itself. Only when the spin-off's balance sheet is clean is that acceptable.

Early in the current IPO cycle, we saw many young companies that paid substantial dividends to insiders at the time of the IPO. The IPOs were "S" corporations, which under the Federal tax code pay no taxes until the profits were paid to the owners. On the IPO, they converted to a tax-paying corporation. The insiders would use that event to clear out all of the accumulated profits and pay themselves a healthy dividend. In cases like these, we ask ourselves how devoted to the business the owners would be once they were multimillionaires.

One way IPOs try to disguise large insider payments is to take out a loan prior to the IPO and pay the dividends before going public. Then, the official use of proceeds is to pay down debt. Right? Obviously not. The insiders are still lining their pockets. The thin attempt to disguise it should also raise questions about management's integrity and business practices. The "Use of Proceeds" section will indicate if any bank loans were used for insider payouts.

We haven't seen too many large dividends of late, but not because the standards of IPO insiders have been raised. The dearth of insider dividends is due to the lack of profitability and negative cash flow of most Internet and technology IPOs. Even the most scurrilous underwriters and the most naïve investors wouldn't tolerate up-front cash payments for a money-losing operation.

2. OTHER BENEFITS AND FEES

As a private company, management can run the operations pretty much any way they like. But when a company decides to go down the path of an IPO, they must clean themselves up and forego the company-paid planes, cars, and apartments. While most do, it is common for insiders to be paid fees for doing consulting work, for identifying acquisition targets, or for leasing back insider-owned facilities.

The most common instances of fees going to insiders occur with acquisitive companies. In many cases, one of the underwriters or backers has also been a prime mover in identifying acquisitions, and they are often on the receiving end of a fat fee for closing the transaction. Financial backers will also try to cadge fees for consulting work. Occasionally, directors will get consulting fees. Biotechnology start-ups are prone to this type of payment. One of the directors may have been involved in developing the technology or product and is paid either an ongoing consulting fee or a royalty.

Heady IPO markets often bring out the worst in underwriters and also allow inexperienced underwriters to bring forth deals that wouldn't make it past the management committee at Goldman Sachs, even at the height of the greed cycle in IPOs. Inexperienced underwriters lack the clout with their clients to tell them what is acceptable for insiders to take out of a deal. In late 2000, for example, young underwriter Weatherly Securities tried to debut Victory Entertainment, which produces and distributes animated children's television programming, including *The Dooley & Pals Show*. The prospectus described Weatherly as having "limited experience acting as lead underwriter in underwritten public offerings."

While management possessed relevant experience in television production, there were far, far too many insider goodies being distributed. The CEO got a cool $6 million if terminated. Victory had hired the ubiquitous spokesman Ed McMahon to tout the company, paying him $500,000 per year. Other insiders were paid $2.4 million in legal and financial advisory fees. A director got $300,000 a year in consulting fees. Considering that the auditors doubted the company had the ability to continue as a going concern without completing its IPO, this was a lot of money for a "financially challenged" company to spread around. In fact, the money they were paying out to insiders completely eclipsed the paltry $310,000 in revenues the company had posted for its most recent fiscal year.

Also troubling were the financial arrangements Victory had made with South Carolina Education TV and the creator of the *Dooley* series. Victory had agreed to provide South Carolina Education TV with episodes of *Dooley* and to pay up to $250,000 in expenses. Isn't that backward? Don't television stations usually pay production companies for shows? Isn't that the way it works? And finally, under a separate agreement, they planned to pay the *Dooley* creator 8 percent of gross profits from *Dooley*.

Arrangements like these may be appropriate for a private company but they are simply unacceptable for a public company.

3. MANAGEMENT EXPERIENCE AND LONGEVITY

Investing in a young company is inherently risky, but if the CEO and CFO (chief financial officer) have a history with the company and have produced positive results, the risk is far less that the company will fail to achieve its goals. Ideally, you want to see results.

For example, years ago, we analyzed a then, new, young company called MFS Communications. Like some of the Internet start-ups of today, MFS was a pioneer in providing local-bypass telecommunications services, allowing businesses and residential customers to get their local telephone service from someone other than the giant local phone company. Although MFS was then unprofitable due to huge capital spending, its chairman and CEO James Crowe had been with MFS for six years, building the company from scratch. Peter Kiewit and Sons, an investor company with ties to Warren Buffett, owned the majority of shares. Crowe owned less than 2 percent of the shares. We thought MFS was likely to be a winner, due to fact that management had been in place since the company was founded and that they had successfully built the company to the point at which it was doing an IPO and about to turn profitable.

We were correct—MFS was a strong performer and eventually wound up being acquired by WorldCom in 1996. Crowe went on to be the president and CEO of Level Three Communications, a 1998 IPO that provides a fiber-optic network in Europe for Internet service providers (ISPs) and data-intensive carriers.

With Internet and technology start-ups, obviously longevity is not an option. The company may have been started six months ago. With a new management team, you need to be even more focused on management backgrounds. Sometimes, the venture capital backers of a new company will bring in hired guns to run the company. While this strategy sometimes pays off, the danger is that the management team hasn't worked together before. A less risky situation for a start-up is if the founders and managers have worked together before in a successful operation. At Handspring, the maker of handheld electronic devices that rivals Palm, the two top executives, Donna Dubinsky and Jeffrey Hawkins, had been the top executives at Palm.

Healtheon, the company that plans to bring doctors' practices and healthcare information to the Internet, was a wildly successful IPO because the founder and chairman of the company was James Clark, co-founder of Netscape. It also didn't hurt that the CEO had been in place for several years.

Another strong performing IPO in the hot optical-fiber area was ONI Systems, whose CEO, Hugh Martin, had been an "entrepreneur in residence" at Kleiner Perkins, one of the venture capital royalty. He had good operational experience. He had been president of 3DO, the maker of entertainment platforms. The venture capital community is starting to use the entrepreneurs-in-residence concept. Sometimes these CEOs-in-waiting have great experience, but often times they are merely former bankers or consultants who lack hands-on operating experience.

But sometimes, great pedigrees can be irrelevant to the challenge of steering a fast-growing company. Online grocery chain Webvan was an IPO that had a great pedigree due to sterling backers in Softbank, Louis Borders (who founded the bookstore chain), Sequoia Venture Capital, and Benchmark Ventures. George Shaheen, who had been an executive with Andersen, was the CEO. It was a case of overkill. The CEO had a great background, but not in starting up a new business. He was also extremely well compensated, which was inappropriate given the $50 million in losses at the time of the November 1999 offering. Having Louis Borders as chairman of the board was impressive, but not relevant to the low-margin, highly competitive grocery store business. Not only did the board lack outside directors, but it also allowed a director's firm to be used for placement services.

Although the initial offering was successful, Webvan quickly sagged into the single digits. Although the management issues weren't the primary factor in the company's downfall, questions about management were contributing factors in investors' disenchantment with the once highly touted start-up.

4. MANAGEMENT'S JUDGMENT AND
ABILITY TO WORK TOGETHER

Public shareholders depend on management to command the ship and to make judgments that are beneficial to the success of the company. Obviously, public shareholders aren't able to follow the day-to-day or even month-to-month progress of the IPO, but they need to trust that the management is acting in the shareholders' best interests.

Clues to whether management should be entrusted with IPO proceeds of tens of millions of dollars are often found in the prospectus. The Value America example is particularly enlightening because investors totally ignored the many warning signs in the prospectus. Value America, as you recall, was the once high-flying Internet retailer of technology, office, and consumer products. The entrepreneurial chairman and founder, Craig Winn, had previously started Dynasty Classics Corporation, a manufacturer and distributor of decorative and fixture lighting. The first problem was that Dynasty had filed a petition for relief under Chapter 11 of the United States Bankruptcy Code. Incredibly, the prospectus stated, "Relying on his experience with Dynasty Mr. Winn sought to develop a new low-cost high-value business model that reduces the risks associated with inventory, customer concentration, and reliance upon debt." That's the ultimate in turning lemons into lemonade. Talk about learning from your mistakes.

While Winn's biography raised questions about his judgment under fire, there were clues elsewhere about trustworthiness. Prior to filing the IPO with the Securities and Exchange Commission (SEC), a senior member of management blabbed at a meeting of hosiery manufacturers that Value America was contemplating an imminent IPO. This is an absolute no-no. The Dow Jones Online News Service ran statements implying that Value America had filed a registration statement with the SEC. Since Value America hadn't filed with the SEC, the SEC required them to disclose the gaffe in the prospectus. At about the same time, *Chief Executive* magazine ran a story about Value America attributing a statement to Winn that Value America was working with General Electric to create a customer store. The SEC required Value America to retract that and to say that a customer store with GE may not be implemented. The SEC also required Value America to disclose that erroneous statements were made by Winn and the general counsel that Frederick W. Smith, the founder of Federal Express, was a current member of Value America's board of directors, when in fact, he planned to stand for election at a later date.

During the period prior to an IPO, there are strict rules regarding statements made to the press and public. By law, officers of a pending IPO are limited to the material disclosed in the prospectus. And, if the prospectus hasn't been filed with the SEC yet, they should say nothing about the company or its prospects. Touting an IPO prior to its debut is highly questionable behavior. The fact that the SEC forced Value America and its officers to retract these and other statements favorable to Value America was a highly visible punishment. Executives of public companies know that they shouldn't portray initiatives in progress as done deals. Every time an initiative fails to come to fruition, credibility is lost. Further touting a company prior to its IPO by dropping hints of favorable events that might happen is an indication of how the management would conduct themselves once the company was public. In fact, during its chaotic decline, little information about the company's troubles was issued by Value America.

The behavior by Value America's management prior to the IPO was entirely predictive of their future performance. It showed a track record of painting the best picture of the company, even when the facts didn't support it.

In addition to judgment, the ability to work together is a highly underrated management attribute. To be sure, many start-up companies, by definition, have management teams that are new. That is one of the inherent risks of start-ups. However, even with relatively new companies there are clues to whether the shoe fits.

One danger signal about an IPO is turnover among its management team. High turnover can reflect personal disputes, a lack of agreement over strategy and execution, or the inability of its CEO to provide leadership. Or all of the above.

Take the story of iVillage, the first online women's community. With backing from America Online (AOL) and NBC, many investors thought the company was a winner, and the stock surged from its $24 offering price in the spring of 1999, at the height of the dot.com rage, to $113.75. The company had been founded by Nancy Evans and Candice Carpenter in 1995. But the prospectus revealed that the company had a new CFO, a new chief operating officer (COO), and several new vice presidents. That's a lot of executive change in a four-year-old company. Also, the company was involved in a sexual discrimination suit by a former vice president. This was not a big, happy family.

We had the opportunity to meet one-on-one with Carpenter soon after the IPO. She had taken umbrage at some of the criticism in our IPO Intelligence take on iVillage. We were curious to meet her, partly because we wanted to understand if we had erred in our skeptical view of Internet "community" companies and partly because she had a reputation of being an aggressive CEO with a highly personal style.

We were unimpressed with her strategy. Internet communities like iVillage have to spend a lot of money on content to bring visitors to their sites; the sources of revenue, advertising, and e-commerce are not enough to create a profitable business model. Carpenter also came across to us as intelligent, marketing oriented, and a strong deal maker. But we wondered about her management skills.

It soon came to light that there was, in fact, significant management turmoil. The front page of *The Wall Street Journal* carried a lead story reporting that iVillage's chief of sales had been booted out after conflicts with Carpenter. The story also mentioned that the former CFO had left after four months. The two then sued for luring them to iVillage by deceptive practices. The former general counsel left after nine weeks and was suing to regain stock options. Months later its next CFO resigned.

Bleeding cash, iVillage altered course and sold its iBaby e-commerce unit, which had been a key part of its e-commerce strategy. Finally, in the summer of 2000, with its stock below $5 a share, its employees deserting ship, Carpenter resigned.

5. INDEPENDENCE FROM CONTROLLING SHAREHOLDERS

Not all shareholders of IPOs are alike. Some shareholders are more than shareholders. They are also suppliers, customers, or former controlling owners. These special shareholders should not stand in the way of the new company's potential for success. You have to make sure that the new company is not dependent on these special shareholders for sales or supplies. Also, make sure these special shareholders do not restrict the new company's corporate opportunities.

Some shareholders are corporations who made an investment in the IPO and, as part of the deal, are suppliers of goods and services or are purchasers of the company's products. In a hot IPO market when pre-IPO shares are good currency, many tech companies issue IPO shares to suppliers and customers as an incentive to reduce the cost of purchased goods or to get orders. Take a look at drugstore.com, a July 1999 IPO. The good news was that Amazon, its 27 percent shareholder, permitted it to advertise heavily on the Amazon site. The bad news was that drugstore.com was restricted from advertising on other competing sites such as barnesandnoble.com. This may be a way to reduce costs or obtain orders, but these deals can have a negative effect. These shareholders have another agenda. They discourage the company from doing wiser transactions with nonshareholder suppliers or customers. New investors should be aware of the agenda of these types of shareholders and how they might limit the company's opportunities.

Special shareholders, such as the parent company of a business taken public through a partial spin-off, may continue to have ongoing relationships with the spin-off. Some of these relationships may be valuable and at arm's length; however, most often these relationships limit the independence of the new IPO. We have seen large investors provide office space and tax and accounting services. That may be okay. Some provide more significant services such as manufacturing, sales, or management. Others provide significant components or sales. Take a look at the May 1999 IPO of Time Warner's fiber-optic telephone operation Time Warner Telecom. Time Warner, its 51 percent shareholder, provided all its fiber capacity, and Time Warner restricted it from offering residential services or content. Ask yourself the question, if you take away the transactions of these special shareholders, would the new company have a greater opportunity to achieve success?

6. HIGH SHARE OWNERSHIP BY MANAGEMENT

As we've said before, a top executive who has a significant amount of personal assets tied up in shares of the IPO is highly motivated to produce good results that translate into strong stock market performance.

The CEO and president should have stakes worth at least 3 percent each. In the case of iVillage, the two cofounders owned 1 percent or less each.

The exceptions to this general rule are spin-offs and privatizations. With a spin-off, management has not yet had the opportunity to own shares of the new company. Management probably owns shares and options on the parent. In the best of circumstances, parent shares and options will be converted to shares of the newly spun-off company. Other incentives will be tied to shares of the spin-off, not the parent. In the case of privatizations, the IPO is a state-owned asset. Some IPO privatizations put in place options on the new company. But it is not unusual to see management owning no stock and having no options in the IPO. To assess the fire in managements' bellies, you will have to depend more on their backgrounds and other financial incentives.

7. REASONABLE AND INCENTIVE-PROVIDING COMPENSATION

Stock options are the rage. After reading newspapers and magazines, you could have the impression that the currency of Internet start-ups is options. That might be close to the truth. When a company is losing money, it can't afford to pay big salaries to its management. Ideally, management should be issued stock options at fair market value. Then, management and the public shareholders are on a level playing field. If the stock options are issued at very low prices, which is common now with technology and Internet companies, executives already have a large built-in profit. For example, if management was issued shares at $.50 and the IPO price is $15, they can still make money if the stock falls to $5.

Cheap options inflate the value of the company. To figure out what a company is valued at, you must include the cheap options in the number of shares outstanding. When a young company has been overly generous in handing out cheap options, those securities can increase the capitalization by huge amounts. One consequence of having many cheap options is that the company may be priced much higher than it deserves to be. Smart investors pay attention to the total value of an

IPO, including options, not just to the per share stock price. The other disadvantage to public shareholders is the future dilution of those cheap securities. Options dilute the ownership of the public shareholders.

The cash compensation, including bonuses and benefits, of management should be reasonable. Anything over $1 million a year begins to be excessive. Think of it this way, if you had a guaranteed annual compensation package of more than $1 million, where would you be likely to be found on a sunny summer afternoon—at the local golf course or on the factory floor? As mentioned in Secret 4, "Mining the Prospectus," these details must be disclosed in the prospectus.

Bloated salaries are found in the most unlikely places. Internet grocery retailer Webvan boasted of top executives with impressive backgrounds and high compensation. The compensation packages were well beyond what you would expect of a start-up, even a well-financed one. You want executives who have more of a financial stake in the company. Someone who knows that a formidable portion of their net worth is represented in company stock is going to be more motivated than a richly compensated executive who can already afford the best things in life.

It is also useful to relate cash compensation to the size and the profitability of the company. A company with revenues of over $50 million and operating profit margins of over 10 percent can afford to pay its CEO and president a half a million dollars. But a puny company with revenues of less than $5 million or perhaps no revenues and reams of losses can ill afford to pay princely cash salaries. In the case of start-ups or profitless companies, any cash salary over $250,000 should be scrutinized closely.

8. INDEPENDENT DIRECTORS SKILLED IN FINANCE, MARKETING, OR CUSTOMER CONNECTIONS

The company should have a board consisting of several independent directors. One role of the independent director is to look out for the interests of the public shareholders. Among developed countries, the United States is unique in requiring independent corporate governance. The SEC routinely issues directives detailing the appropriate role of independent directors. Venture capitalists or leveraged buyout (LBO) investors sitting on the board with cheap stock pass the SEC's test, but they are not independent. They think like management, not shareholders.

Still, there is much positive to be said about good venture capital (VC) investors. Remember that their investment strategy is to find promising young companies, invest at low prices, take the company public, and sell out. Good VC firms can help realize value through their connections to underwriters and other sources of capital. Although they may think like management, the only way they can successfully achieve their goal is to hold management's feet to the fire and demand the achievement of certain objectives.

The backgrounds of the outside board members should be relevant to the IPO's business and strategy. Look for a board consisting of experienced business executives with value-added skills in marketing or finance or with customer connections. It is common to see retired executives serving on the board. New companies can derive great benefits from having a few grey beards on their boards. Directors whose backgrounds are unimpressive, irrelevant, or nonexistent are probably on board because they are buddies of the CEO, chairman, or president. They are not looking out for you. They are probably looking forward to the post–board meeting golf outing with management.

The cash compensation of directors should be reasonable. Cash compensation over $20,000 per year motivates directors to rubber-stamp management decisions. Agricultural chemical giant Monsanto was spun off by parent Pharmacia in late 2000. Monsanto had attracted an all-star group of independent directors, including Mickey Kantor, former U.S. secretary of commerce; Steven McMillan, president and CEO of Sara Lee Corporation; and John S. Reed, the former chairman and co-CEO of Citigroup. How had Monsanto attracted such an illustrious lineup? The answer was money. In addition to getting options to purchase 10,000 shares of stock, each outside director gets a "retainer" of $110,000 a year, half paid in deferred stock (meaning stock delivered at some point in the future) and the rest paid in cash at the director's option. Heads of committees get another $10,000. The chairman of the board of directors gets another $40,000. The chairman of the board of directors, who is the retired president of American Cyanamid Company, is paid a consulting fee of $400,000. These fees are the highest we've ever seen in an IPO and certainly rival the fees paid to directors of Fortune 100 companies.

The problem we have with high directors fees is that the amount of money paid is so significant that it can motivate even the most ethical individual to vote the management line and not rock the boat. Even for multimillionaires, the loss of a $110,000-a-year gig that requires attendance at the four quarterly board meetings and the occasional committee meeting can be a bummer.

Getting a bead on the boards of directors of non-U.S. IPOs is a bit trickier. Toughest to evaluate are the IPOs coming out of Asia. Virtually all IPOs coming out of China and Indonesia have some connections to the governments of each country. Even though they must disclose the backgrounds of the officers and directors, this is often not much help in deciphering their ability to lead. For example, China Petroleum & Chemical Corporation is the leading petroleum and petrochemical company in the People's Republic of China (PRC). It was formed by the Chinese government in 1998 when the government decided to restructure its energy and petrochemical businesses. Although the Chinese government is not a direct owner of China Petroleum, it has indirect control through China Petroleum's parent Sinopec Group Company, which owns 55 percent of China Petroleum. The Chinese government directly owns and regulates Sinopec.

Because of the indirect ownership, investors should assume that the officers and directors of China Petroleum are handpicked by the PRC government. The president of China Petroleum is Wang Jiming, age 58. The prospectus dutifully discloses that he graduated from China Eastern Petrochemical Institute in 1964 and was a "professor-level" senior engineer for 30 years. He moved up the ladder at Shanghai Petrochemical General Plant, finally serving as president. Then he job hopped over to the predecessor of China Petroleum as a vice president. From this you can deduce that he has a lot of petroleum experience and is either an able administrator or has solid PRC political connections, or probably both. But the vast majority of people know nothing about the China Eastern Petrochemical Institute or Shanghai Petroleum. So an investor doesn't know whether Wang went to the Chinese equivalent of the Massachusetts Institute of Technology or Northwest Arkansas Junior

College. Similarly, Shanghai Petroleum could be the peer of Mobil or a one-well oil wildcatter in Shanghai. But, from having read numerous Chinese prospectuses, we concluded that at worst he is a politically well connected administrator with many years of relevant experience.

With Chinese and Indonesian IPOs, it is safe to assume that there are no outside directors on the board and that government functionaries will be involved in corporate decision making, directly or indirectly. Your decision on whether to invest in one of these companies will depend on your willingness to assume the risks of being a minority shareholder in a company whose controlling shareholders are related to a corrupt government.

The officers and directors of European based IPOs are similar to U.S. IPOs. If the company is large, it is usually a spin-off from a European conglomerate, as Infineon was from Siemens, or a privatization, as in the case of France Telecom. In these cases, expect cushy board compensation and a lack of independent directors. The smaller, faster growing companies are similar in their makeup and structure to their U.S. peers.

9. FULL-TIME, INDEPENDENT EXECUTIVES

It stands to reason that public shareholders expect management to devote their full time to running the company. Any outside or conflicting corporate interests are highly suspect. Time and time again, we have come across IPOs where the top executives also own consulting or banking firms that receive fees from the company. Although it's not uncommon to find IPOs in which the company leases its headquarters or manufacturing plant from top executives, any transactions that go beyond straightforward leases should be examined closely.

One of the troubling things about some entrepreneurs is that they have their hands in many pies. That's *their* business when the company is private. But it's *your* business when the company wants to do an IPO. A top executive should devote all of his or her professional time to running your business. That's what you are paying him or her to do. If an executive has other businesses to run, there is always the danger that there may be economic, personal, or legal reasons for the executive to devote most of his or her time and attention to the other businesses. For example, both the CEO and CFO of IPO Viasystems, a circuit board contract manufacturer owned by investor Hicks Muse, were also the CEO and CFO, respectively, of another Hicks Muse–controlled company, International Wire. Both men were also very highly compensated.

Another danger of a top executive having outside interests is that these enterprises may conflict with the interests of the IPO. For example, if the CEO of a hotel chain also owns other real estate interests, he may be tempted to make acquisitions that only benefit his private real estate business at the expense of the public company.

10. A FAMILY-RUN BUSINESS WITH PROFESSIONAL MANAGERS AND A SHAREHOLDER-FRIENDLY OUTLOOK

Family-run businesses entering the IPO market should be carefully scrutinized. Although the family may have done a good job in growing the company, family-owned enterprises have a tough time meeting the standards of public companies. Decisions are typically made to benefit the family members, not the public shareholders. Sometimes the payroll is loaded with cousins, siblings, and spouses. The likelihood that they all were selected on the basis of merit is remote.

Family-run businesses that try to do IPOs are plagued by a number of obstacles that prevent them from being successful public companies. In addition to nepotism, issues that turn off public investors are succession problems, cozy insider transactions, small size, and insider selling. The stock of Columbia Sportswear, a well-known maker of quality sportswear, suffered because of initial insider selling and lack of comfort in management. Aristotle, which was mentioned previously, is run by two brothers, John and Dean Phillips, who serve as CEO and president, respectively.

Few family-run businesses transition smoothly to the public marketplace. Federated Investors, a large mutual fund manager, was an exception. Because Federated is an SEC-regulated mutual fund family with $96 billion in assets, it was already structured like a public company. Its board of directors had independent members. It had over two thousand employees. It had outside investors. In other ways, Federated fit the pattern of many family-owned businesses. The 73-year-old founder and chairman John Donahue's son Christopher was CEO and president. As is usual with an elderly founder, the family was using the IPO to liquidate some of its holdings. And, the family retained voting control of the company. However, the family had a solid management team in place and had an admirable track record of growth.

Manhattan Associates, an Atlanta-based provider of distribution center management software, is a good example of a family-controlled company that got its act together after it went public, not before. The company's failure to cede control to professional managers and to remove many private company perks nearly killed the company. When it went public in the spring of 1998 at $15, founder, chairman, and CEO Alan Dabbiere was at the helm. His three brothers were all executives with cheap stock. Nearly one-third of the IPO proceeds went to pay a dividend to insiders and to repay money Dabbiere had loaned the company. Many of the nonfamily executives had recently joined the company. Although the company was highly profitable, the new management team was a bust; and in late 1999, the company reorganized. The CFO resigned, Dabbiere stepped down, and a new CEO was hired. Since then the company has rebounded due to the experienced management team and its new strategy.

CONCLUSION

These are the top-10 attributes of a solid company. As with everything else with IPOs, there is no black and white. Negative issues associated with management need to be balanced against positive attributes in fundamentals or valuation. But if there are truly egregious issues associated with management—really high salaries, rampant nepotism, sales of stock, and large distributions of cash to insiders—you can be sure that the IPO will be run without the public shareholder in mind.

When you evaluate a company, use Renaissance Capital's Management and Control Checklist shown in Exhibit 9.1. When reading through an IPO's prospectus, look for the positive and the negative cues. In the plus column are executives with relevant background and histories of success, independent boards of directors with connections that can help

Exhibit 9.1   Renaissance Capital's Management and Control Checklist

		Yes	No
1	**Who receives IPO proceeds?**		
	Proceeds from the IPO go to the company, not to founders, officers, or investors.	☐	☐
	Proceeds are not used to pay off debt that was incurred to pay insiders.	☐	☐
2	**Are there management perks and fees?**		
	Fees (e.g., rents, royalties, commissions, mergers and acquisitions, consulting) are not paid to insiders.	☐	☐
	Perks such as boats, planes, and home mortgages do not exist.	☐	☐
3	**Is management experienced and able to work together?**		
	Backgrounds of management are relevant to their job title and to the industry.	☐	☐
	Management has a history of working together.	☐	☐
4	**Does management have a record of good judgment?**		
	Prior companies run by management have not gone bankrupt.	☐	☐
	Management has no pattern of litigation or credit problems.	☐	☐
5	**Can the company succeed independently of controlling shareholders?**		
	The company is not dependent on controlling shareholders for sales or services.	☐	☐
	The company's corporate opportunity is not limited by controlling shareholders.	☐	☐
	Entities controlled by insiders are not customers or suppliers.	☐	☐
6	**Does management own enough shares?**		
	Top officers (e.g., CEO) each own over 3 percent of shares.	☐	☐
7	**Is the management compensation package reasonable and motivating?**		
	Modest cash salaries are paid to management.	☐	☐
	Recently issued cheap shares are not the key holdings of insiders.	☐	☐
8	**Is the board of directors independent?**		
	Several independent directors serve on the board.	☐	☐
	Director compensation is reasonable (less than $20,000 per year).	☐	☐
	Directors are not paid consulting fees.	☐	☐
9	**Does management devote full time to the company?**		
	Full-time attention is given by management to the IPO and no other entity.	☐	☐
	Management does not have outside interests in other entities.	☐	☐
	Management is not on the payroll or on the benefit plan of another company.	☐	☐
10	**Is the management of a family business professional?**		
	Board positions and management jobs are not stacked with family members.	☐	☐
	Management is on your side (if you checked "yes" multiple times)	☑	☐
	Watch your wallet! (if you checked "no" multiple times)	☐	☑

Source: Renaissance Capital, Greenwich, CT (IPOhome.com).

the IPO, and incentives that focus the management team on performance. In the negative column are executives with histories of bankruptcy, lack of relevant experience, and cushy salaries. Other turnoffs
are obvious, like insider selling and consulting fees. But other warning
signs are more subtle, like a history of job hopping or recent departures from the management team. Regard the prospectus as a story to
be pieced together from the clues the company is forced to reveal in
the process of going public. As a public investor, your bottom line is to
ensure that management's interests are aligned with yours. You want a
stock that goes up in price because management is capable of and
motivated to deliver solid performance.

SECRET 10

How to Trade IPOs

Initial public offerings (IPOs) are different from other stocks. The unique process of selling a portion of its shares to public investors in the event of an IPO sets it apart from stocks in the Standard & Poor's (S&P) 500 and the Dow Jones averages. The event of an IPO not only produces trading patterns and shareholder turnover on the day of its debut, but also has effects that reverberate for months. On an ongoing basis, the amount and quality of information are different. The shareholders and their behavior are different. Except for the few extremely large IPOs, the liquidity is significantly less than that of established stocks.

Each of these factors plays a role in how an IPO trades. Successful IPO investing involves more than analyzing the fundamentals of the company and getting a grip on its valuation; you also need to understand the ins and outs of trading. This chapter will explore some of the trading patterns we have observed in IPOs over the years. It will also point out common mistakes that investors make when they buy IPOs both on the offering and in the aftermarket. It will provide you with rules that help reduce risk in this volatile terrain.

The starting point for understanding an IPO's trading comes before the deal ever gets priced. During the road show, everything that management says and does is closely observed by the underwriters' sales force, the bankers, and investors. Strong road show attendance, credible presentations by management, and positive reactions from investors help ensure that a deal gets priced at the upper end of its proposed range or even above it. In contrast, spotty road show attendance, poor management presentations, and negative feedback from analysts can doom a potential IPO.

During the road show preliminaries, the underwriter's top sales executives are on the phone with the leading buy-side players, asking them for feedback on management and valuation. They also want to know how much stock the institutional investor wants to "circle" (order) on the IPO. The investor may indicate the amount of an aftermarket order, usually placing a caveat on price levels. For example, the investor may say that he or she is in for another 100,000 shares up to a limit of $50.

With that valuable market information in hand from key investors, the capital markets desk, which is the first market maker, can better judge how much demand there is for the IPO and at what price levels. This "price talk" continues up until the day the deal is priced. A hot IPO may find its price raised more than once during this dialogue between underwriters and investors. During the frenzied Internet IPO market in 1999, a number of the hottest IPOs had their offering prices double from the original price stated in the prospectus.

The goal of the capital markets desk is to get the highest price for the IPO, while ensuring that demand is still strong enough in aftermarket trading to produce positive returns for investors who buy in subsequent trading. If they keep the price too low, management is dissatisfied and investors may conclude that the deal is cold and stay away. Pricing a hot IPO at a price that satisfies all demand would have the same effect. Institutional investors would walk away because they don't see any returns in the aftermarket. To price an IPO, the capital markets desk employs supply-demand information gleaned from investors, valuation benchmarks of similar publicly traded companies, and psychology.

So, it's late afternoon on the day before the IPO starts trading, the markets are closed, and the IPO management and capital markets chieftains sit in an office on the underwriter's trading floor. It's sweat-in-the-armpits time. It's time to pin the price on the IPO and decide who gets shares. The capital markets desk shows the chief executive officer (CEO) and the chief financial officer (CFO) the books on how many orders there are for the IPO. If demand for the IPO has been poor, there have already been frantic calls among the bankers, management, and key institutional investors. The IPO's size and price have been cut. But the question remains, is there still enough demand for the deal? In a hot market, if the deal is only two or three times oversubscribed, the IPO will probably be priced in the midpoint of its price range because institutional investors routinely put in for several times more shares than they expect to get. In a weak market, two to three times might warrant the top of the range. And in any market, if the deal is many, many times oversubscribed, the IPO's price will be pumped up.

Once the price is set, the group moves on to deciding who gets what. There are three pots of shares: (1) the institutional pot, which is the biggest by far; (2) shares intended for small institutional, high-net-worth and retail investors; and (3) friends and family. Each underwriter has policies on allocations, but as previously explained, the bulk of the shares go to the most active investors in each of the first two categories. As far as friends and family are concerned, the size of the allocations depends on how strongly the company's management goes to bat for each individual.

By this time, it is usually early evening. If the deal is hot, many salespeople are still waiting around anxiously for the capital markets desk to announce price and allocations. They want to call their biggest clients with the news. The rest of the investors will learn the verdict in the morning.

However, knowing that you are unlikely to get shares on a hot IPO or will only get a few shares, your strategy must be focused on the aftermarket. Of course, the underwriter doesn't control buying and selling in the aftermarket. But they do know where they placed the stock, and they want to see investors to whom they gave good allocations come back with strong aftermarket orders. And, they can ask the IPO to issue another 15 percent of stock in what's called the "overallotment" to stabilize supply and demand. Extremely strong Internet feeding-frenzy types of first-day returns are actually an underwriter's nightmare. The institutional investors who got good allocations are looking at the high valuation of the stock, and instead of saying "Buy," they say "Sell." Often, they'll put the stock back to the underwriter, who parcels out those shares to individual investors with buy orders.

To figure out your IPO tactics in the aftermarket, you must first figure out what type of a deal it is. You've already decided you want to buy the shares. You know your price limit or lack thereof. Let's look at four common scenarios.

SCENARIO 1: HOT IPOs

First, the white hot IPO. Of late, most have been Internet related, but they can come in all shapes and sizes. Let's focus on common trading patterns of two types of hot IPOs.

Look at the *first mover in a new sector*. Yahoo! and Sycamore Networks are two good examples. Although the early buzz on the IPOs was loud, it was deserved. Each company had pioneered a new technology, established a solid management team, and faced a large opportunity. Institutional and individual investors understood that. They wanted to have the companies in their portfolios because they could clearly see each company becoming the industry leader in the years to come. Each stock opened up with a then-record-setting first-day return, 154 percent for Yahoo! and 386 percent for Sycamore. Institutional and individual investors wanted to have the stocks in their portfolios.

The trading pattern for IPOs like these is that *the opening trade is significantly above the IPO price and then rises higher.* High-demand IPOs can take hours to open, as the capital markets desk polls institutional investors on their aftermarket orders. Invariably some of the stock will have gone to short-term traders or institutional investors who think the valuation is too high and flip the stock, hoping it will trade off so they can come back in. This places pressure on the stock price. Trading on the IPO's debut is volatile and heavy, as market makers process the ton of orders. The prices can differ by $5 or $10 because of the intense demand and the flipping activity.

In our long bull market, the best strategy for individual investors with white hot first movers is to wait for the second or third day of trading when trading has settled down. The reasons for this are several. You aren't glued to a quote machine. You don't know when or at what price the IPO will open. If you put in a limit order, you risk not getting any stock. But if you put in a market order you absolutely, positively guarantee that you will get hosed. By the second day, the flippers are out, and the price has settled down. The difference between the bid and the ask has narrowed. You have enough information to put in a limit order, and you are far less likely to pay a huge amount over the last trade if you place a market order.

Let's contrast this with a *momentum driven hot IPO*. In cases of momentum driven hot IPOs, several IPO successes in the same category have preceded this IPO. Let's take a business-to-business (B2B) example. ONVIA.com, a B2B e-marketplace for small businesses, was late in taking advantage of the IPO market's love affair with B2B. It had been preceded by Ariba, CommerceOne, Neoforma, and Chemdex. Priced in March 2000 at $21, which was nearly twice its original price range, it soared to $78 on the first day of trading. ONVIA.com quickly swooned, closing at about $21 at the end of March and was a single-digit stock by year end.

The same pattern occurred with Caldera, a Linux-based software developer. Investors had a field day with companies that were involved with the Linux operating system. Never mind that profits—if any—were far off and that aficionados could download the Linux software for free. Investors pushed the first group of Linux-based companies up to ridiculous valuations. RedHat, VA Linux, and Andover all soared. Then came Caldera. The momentum investors had moved on. Priced at $14, nearly twice its original $7 to $9 range, it barreled up to $33 on its initial day of trading. Then it slowly cracked and is now trading in the single digits.

With these types of stocks, it is better to take a pass. If you buy on the first day of trading, you are almost certain to get burned. Most of the aftermarket investors are momentum players. They don't know the company. In fact, they could care less about the company. Their strategy is to buy IPOs in the aftermarket until the strategy stops working. Then they stop doing it. It is far better to let a late entrant into the IPO market get some seasoning. Study the trading, wait for the analyst's reports. If the company is going to be a leader in its field, the stock price will slowly respond to positive earnings or to other corporate news after the initial sell-off. The volatile markets show that it is always better to do your research and *wait* for a buying opportunity.

SCENARIO 2: PRICEY MERCHANDISE

And finally, there is the long-awaited hot stock that gets priced at a premium and flops on its face in the aftermarket. Planet Hollywood and Ralph Lauren fell into this category. Both IPOs were hyped for months. Both were priced at significant premiums to peers. There was no money left on the table. To justify the valuations, each company would have to produce results that were significantly superior to expectations, which were already high. But investors clamored for shares because it was a point of prestige to receive shares in the IPOs, even a few. Individual investors wanted to own shares so badly that they forgot all about valuation. They just wanted to be able tell their friends they owned the shares.

So stockbrokers gladly obliged the eager buyers with shares of Planet Hollywood and Polo Ralph Lauren on the first day of trading at prices that neither stock ever saw again. The shares were willingly provided by savvy institutional investors who flipped the shares on the first day of trading. Then, knowing that Polo Ralph Lauren was still overpriced, they shorted the stock as soon as they could. The best thing individual investors can do in the case of overhyped consumer products companies is wait before buying. By waiting you remove yourself from the frenzy of the IPO's debut and place yourself more firmly in the more objective role of assessing investments with a cool eye.

SCENARIO 3: IPOs ON FIRE SALE

There are circumstances in which the management of an IPO is so desperate to get the deal done that they will dramatically cut the price of the IPO, putting it on sale. When that happens, because of market conditions or a psychological shift in the investment popularity of a particular industry group, it is often an excellent buying opportunity. However, when the deal is pushed through at bargain prices due to investor indifference to the company itself, then the IPO is likely to trade poorly.

The mapping of the human genome has created great opportunities for small biotech companies. Whether the company is involved in drug discovery, mapping proteins, or providing tools to researchers, time is of the essence because research and development (R&D) is moving rapidly and there are many competitors. In early 2000 many biotechs were queued up waiting to go public. But then the Nasdaq market started to quake, and investor interest in emerging growth companies evaporated. The biotech sector, because many of the companies lacked revenue streams from product sales, was among the first to get thrown overboard by institutional investors looking to raise cash.

Several of the companies in this sector didn't want to risk waiting for the emerging growth stocks to regain popularity. Orchid Bioscience, which is developing genetic diversity technologies for drug development, was slated to go public at $11 to $13 in May 2000. But faced with a bad market for emerging growth companies, it had to slash its price nearly in half to $8 to pull off its deal. By month-end, it was up 50 percent. Paradigm Genetics had a similar experience. It cut its offer price by more than half, to $7 a share, during the same time period; and by month-end, it returned 57 percent for investors. Individual investors can use occasions like this to get ahold of IPO shares in companies they have researched and do well.

However, if the difficulty in getting the deal done is company related, the performance of the cut-rate IPO is likely to be poor. The underwriter's salesforce has been told to get the IPO sold. Rebuffed by institutional investors, they will often then turn to individual investors, hoping to find them more credulous and naïve. Coolsavings.com, which provides online and offline incentive marketing services, couldn't get its IPO done at its original price of $11 to $13, so it cut its price to $7. Investors weren't buying it, and the price fell. If you are a regular investor and get a call from a Wall Street broker offering you shares in an IPO, be immediately on warning that the deal is a dud.

SCENARIO 4: DEALS THAT DON'T TRADE WELL

Sometimes, IPOs just don't trade well. Normally, institutional investors get fractions of the amount of shares they said they want. So, when they get large allocations, they get suspicious. They are like Groucho Marx remarking about country clubs—if they want me to join, it can't be any good. So, they sell regardless of the quality of the deal. Other institutions, seeing the selling, start selling themselves, often creating a tidal wave of shares. This happened in the case of Neff, a company that is a lessor of industrial equipment. The fundamentals were solid. The management was experienced. General Electric was an investor. It had the right pedigree. Demand for the deal wasn't up to expectations, so the underwriter decided to give very large allocations to a small number of institutions. In doing so, they decided against the normal strategy of allocating few shares among the many. The underwriters mistakenly thought this was a better way of insuring a successful IPO.

They were wrong. With allocations well over what they expected, the institutional investors assumed something was wrong with Neff. They thought that they were being "stuffed," a term of art referring to getting large allocations of a bad deal. And they sold and sold and sold. With the stock price pushed down into the single digits, the company never really recovered. Its key strategy had been to make acquisitions through stock and debt. Lacking a robust stock price, it was limited in its ability to grow.

How can you tell if an IPO trades down because institutions are getting stuffed? The IPO will have been issued by a major underwriter used to dealing mostly with large institutional investors. The volume will be extremely large blocks of stock, and the drop in stock price on the first day of trading will exceed 15 percent to 20 percent.

ONLINE TRADING

As online trading has taken hold, it has become clear that the new, powerful force driving IPOs at certain times are online and day traders, not institutional investors. Many online traders and all day traders transact quickly, moving in and out of positions. Further, these investors are not buying on the offering, but in the aftermarket. One reason why online traders were aggressive in late 1999 and early 2000 in the aftermarket is that the Internet stocks, and then the biotechs, have traded well. It is interesting that it is the institutions who are selling the eBays and the uBids after strong initial run-ups. Individual investors still believe in the Internet more than the institutions do.

As we've seen, the IPO market rotates from sector to sector, inflating the valuations and then letting the air out in a great whoosh. First it was the online communities, then e-tailers, then business-to-consumer (B2C), infrastructure, Linux, fiber, gene tools, . . . the favorite sectors go on and on. At first, there is minimal selectivity. When the returns and the valuations of the first to market and leading companies are clearly higher than their lesser brethren, valuations for all can be abnormally high. Institutions, which are analytic in their approach to stock valuation, try to rationalize these prices by force ranking the Internet companies by looking at price-to-sales, price-to-eyeballs, or far-off future profitability. But, in fact, the prices of Internet and biotech stocks are at times being driven by the new paradigm of online investors who don't rely on or believe in traditional assessments of enterprise value.

The stocks of many Internet and biotech companies were driven up on the first day of trading by naïve online investors who assumed that they'd pay the offering price for an IPO. They put in market orders for the IPOs, and given the huge run-ups, these orders were executed at the high prices. It was these 100- and 200-share buy orders that drove up the prices for uBid and Sycamore Networks and other hot IPOs. For a while, the online and day traders knew that stock momentum was at their backs. Putting in market orders on hot IPOs worked. When it stopped working, the day traders were gone, and naïve online investors were left holding stock for which they'd paid top dollar and that was now worth a fraction of the cost.

The Internet stocks, helped by the legions of online traders, changed the entire risk profile of the IPO market and created a sense of frenzy for both Internet and technology IPOs. Much of this may be attributed to demand/supply imbalances, which will eventually be equalized as more Internet and technology companies come to market. But when the IPO market gets hot, it is dominated by its riskiest sectors and least well informed investors.

So how should you, the individual investor, cope with the brave new world? Simply by understanding the dynamics. If the IPO market is hot, the momentum investors are in there. They will continue to buy until this strategy stops working. Some of them will short stock until that, too, stops working. Those are the smart ones. The dumb ones will lose reams of money and be forced out of the market. During periods like these, if you are a risk taker you need to be a short-term thinker. Take profits and losses quickly. Risk-averse investors should take a seat and wait for the next market downturn. During slower and down IPO times, it pays to be analytical and to look for the best companies at bargain basement prices. We've learned that bad IPO markets produce the best long-term buying opportunities.

HOLDING PERIODS

With all of this hurried activity, it should come as no surprise that holding periods for stock are at their lowest point since the 1920s. A recent study by well-known brokerage research firm Sanford C. Bernstein & Company showed that 1999 share turnover among New York Stock Exchange (NYSE)–listed stocks was 79 percent, which means that 79 percent of the stocks on the NYSE charged hands in 1999. In contrast, in 1990, the figure was 50 percent, and in 1940 it was 9 percent. However, turnover on the Nasdaq was a mind-boggling 221 percent in 1999.

For years, professors of finance have produced studies showing that long-term holders of securities produce better returns than quick-draw investors. However, let us point out a nonobvious fallacy of this point of view. Those studies were done on the performance of established, seasoned companies, like those in the S&P 500. Studies indeed support that you can make more money and can avoid paying taxes by hanging on to your IBM and GE for long periods of time. But we aren't talking about GE. We're talking about IPOs. We're talking about stocks that can trade at $100 on one day, $125 the next, and $30 the day after. We're talking volatility.

While we haven't done any comparable studies, we argue that, save for the industry leaders like British Sky Broadcasting, Yahoo!, Sycamore Networks, and Genentech, at times it indeed pays to be short-term in investing in IPOs. If you are lucky and get IPO shares that go up several hundred percent on the first day of trading, what should you do? Given the size of the gain, it may make sense to protect that gain by flipping the shares, if you can. If you got your shares through an online broker, consider shorting the shares through a regular brokerage account to lock in your gains. The same goes for buying in the aftermarket. If you are in a hectic, momentum driven market, look for signs of slowing momentum and sell.

In extremely hot markets, even the underwriters don't mind if the institutional investors flip their IPO shares back to them. Most hot deals are relatively small in size, and the underwriters can use the shares for other investors.

To use a housing analogy, sometimes the IPO market is a buyer's market and you have "keepers" in your portfolio. But if valuations are sky high and the pace is frenzied, it may be a better choice to rent.

LOCK-UP PERIOD

In every IPO there is a time when the insiders agree not to sell their shares in the open market. This period is called the *Lock-up Period* and usually lasts about 180 days from the pricing of the offering. The reason the underwriters insist on this concession from the insiders is that the investment banker knows that excessive selling of shares early in the life of a new IPO can have disastrous effects on the successful aftermarket trading of the stock. The 180-day time frame is a general benchmark and it can be shorter. Shorter time cutoffs are sometimes described in the prospectus where the company's insiders are permitted to sell earlier under certain circumstances, such as the share price appreciating over 100% from the offer price. The underwriter also has discretion to shorten the lock-up period if they determine the sale of the insider shares would not be harmful to the trading activity.

What does this mean to individual investors and why is everyone so interested in knowing when the lock-up period expires? The common wisdom is that all things being equal, the price of the new company's shares will decline when the insiders are allowed to finally get liquidity and sell their large stock holdings. Therefore, many investors closely track lock-up expirations, hoping to sell their own shares before the insiders are allowed to. You can track all IPO lock-up expirations at our IPOhome.com site. While lock-up expirations put pressure on a company's stock, the effect may only be temporary. Look at other factors such as the fundamentals of the IPO. Are they meeting their business plan objectives? How has the company been trading recently? How many shares are already trading? What is the daily float? Many companies can blast through the extra supply of lock-up shares on the market, so make sure you look at the complete picture.

MARGIN CALLS

Another contributing factor to IPO market volatility is *margin*. Both traditional brokerage houses and online brokers allow customers to borrow money to buy securities. Federal rules require you to maintain equity (securities less the debt owed) equal to 25 percent of the portfolio's value. Brokerage firms usually require higher amounts. In a market decline, investors will be asked to provide more cash in the account to cover margin calls. Brokerage firms love margin accounts because they can borrow the money from one customer, paying a low rate, and lend the money to a margin customer at a much higher rate.

However, several of the recent market declines in Nasdaq stocks were exacerbated by margin calls on ultra-aggressive online individual and small institutional investors. The big brokerage houses knew that margin calls had gone out to weaker players, some of which had to liquidate entire portfolios. Because margin debt tends to increase during hot stock markets, it pays to keep that in the back of your head when corrections start. The best performers among Internet and technology stocks tend to be the worst hit, as forced liquidations start.

QUIET PERIOD

Companies like IBM have armies of Wall Street security analysts watching over every move IBM makes. In contrast, there is no research published on pending IPOs and for a "quiet" period following the IPOs debut. When the research is published 25 days after the IPO, it is invariably bullish. And because everyone knows that the research will be positive, as far as its analytic value is concerned, it is of little value. It may take months for a newly IPO'd company to establish itself among

Wall Street analysts. In some instances, research coverage is fleeting. An IPO that stumbles early in its career is likely to be quickly abandoned by analysts. The IPO research at IPOhome.com is available before the deal is priced. IPOhome also has a list of quiet period dates.

IMPACT OF CHAT

The Internet has not only brought individual investors access to a myriad of valuable, timely information they previously could not get, but it also has foisted on them loads of worthless disinformation. *Chat rooms* on Yahoo!, Raging Bull, and IPOhome.com allow investors to trade tips and to ask questions about why an IPO is going up or down. The same chat rooms are home to hucksters and investors trying to pump up and dump out of IPO shares.

Do chat rooms influence IPO stock prices? Probably not. But, they very much reflect the sentiments of the online traders, which we previously discussed. Chat room talk needs to be accepted for what it is— a collection of investors reaching out to each other for information, shills hyping stocks, short sellers creating rumors, and investors looking for romance. On IPOhome.com's chat board, we recently had our first IPO date.

The Internet, because of its transparency in accepting information, has created the perfect spawning grounds for online fraud. Phony press releases on Emulex, a maker of fiber-channel adapters, caused the stock to drop intraday by as much as 60 percent. Because of the competitive time bind of journalism, a number of reporters repeated the rumor as truth. It took several hours for company management to figure out the cause for the stock price drop and to take corrective action.

While the SEC is trying to be a watchdog against phony press releases and to nail Internet "pump and dump" hucksters, the very nature of the Internet is an obstacle to effective enforcement. Techno-savvy crooks have been known to create Web sites that look like a real news site. The safest course for individual investors to follow is to rely on their own judgments and corporate information filed with the SEC and on the company's Web site.

CONCLUSION

While there are no cast-iron rules to trading success, it helps to understand the jungle out there. The IPO market is a derivative of the overall stock market, and its upturns and downturns are more steep. Volatility in the IPO market necessitates more rapid reactions on the part of investors. It is not good enough to use a buy-and-hold strategy. By their nature, IPOs experience much more volatility than established publicly traded companies because investors show less patience with stocks that lack track records demonstrating resilience in the face of adversity.

What then is the answer? The answer is to make buy decisions with an eye toward long-term fundamentals, without ignoring practical concerns like profit protection and loss control. The fundamentals guide the decision whether to buy, but trading performance should dictate entry and exit points in a way that protects gains and mitigates downside risk. For this reason, once individuals make the decision to buy or sell, it is wise to set disciplined stop-out levels that lock in gains and limit losses in IPO investments.

SECRET 11

The Sustainability of IPOs

When we first meet with new people to discuss Renaissance IPO research or the IPO+ Fund, they always ask us what we're going to do when the initial public offering (IPO) market dries up. It's a good and serious question. The press has predicted the death of the IPO market seven times over the last ten years. Before we launched Renaissance Capital's IPO business, we studied the IPO market thoroughly. We discovered that breaks in IPO volume over the past 50 years were few and, except for the Great Depression years, relatively brief. Even the stock market crash in October 1987 had fleeting negative effects. The IPO market was hushed for all of six weeks. The longest IPO drought we've lived through was in the summer of 1998 during the global currency crisis.

While IPOs may be relatively new to the broad investing public, IPOs have been around as long as equity investing. You can make the case that the first IPO was the Dutch East India Company in 1602. It was a joint stock company founded in Amsterdam by a number of small, independent trading companies operating out of Amsterdam in the Netherlands. Just as today's IPOs exploit the resources of the Internet, the Dutch East India Company's goal was to promote trade with Asia, which they did for over a hundred years.

The IPO market is here to stay. The number of new companies that come to market is driven by the strength of the world economy, by intellectual capital, by human creativity, and by the burning desire to be wealthy. At times, the IPO market is driven to excess. But for the most part it is a healthy reflection of economic growth and innovation. In the coming years, the market sectors that we expect to be the most active are business commerce via the Internet, Internet infrastructure, biotechnology, and alternative energy. We also expect to see "old" economy companies shedding their traditional skins to offer new ways of doing business. The break-up of AT&T is a good example of this trend. As another example, electric utilities are selling or spinning off their power generation facilities in response to state energy deregulation. Other old economy industries will be performing similar financial re-engineering to reshape themselves to be competitive in the twenty-first century. And the IPO market will be where the action will take place.

IPOs thrive during periods when people have money to invest, investors are optimistic, technological innovation is rapid, commerce is changing, interest rates are low, and governments encourage the free flow of capital. Although there have been interruptions, we are in such a period. The main reason why the IPO market has been so active and high profile is that all of these factors have converged. Simply put, entrepreneurs in every developed country in the world have unprecedented access to capital markets. In London, Paris, Frankfurt, Madrid, New York, Chicago, and San Francisco, it's apparent that prosperity is in the air. Commerce is streamlining, thanks to the Internet and to the liberalization of fusty old constraints on telecommunications. A tourist in New York can find hotels in Ireland by trolling the Internet and booking the room direct, without the added expense of a travel agent, a major change from five years ago. IPO activity spread to Europe precisely because there were and are innovative companies deserving of capital. And the governments of European countries realized that selling the shares of their old-line telephone and electric utilities accomplished a number of objectives: raising money for the never-sated state budgets, modernizing the business at someone else's expense, and satisfying the populace. Smart governments from Brussels to Mexico City figured out that relaxing antiquated laws on currency and cross-border movements of capital could make their countries richer.

Eyeing the IPO and capital-raising activity, less well developed countries like China are virtually being forced to move toward market economies. All the diplomacy in the world is no match for the human desire to be rich. China and the rest of the Pacific Rim will eventually move toward having Western-style laws on investment, and notoriously corrupt countries like Indonesia will eventually reform their governments and capital markets to keep up with everyone else. If they don't, they will be left out of the technologic revolution. Just as television allowed people in communist countries to glimpse a little bit of the way the rest of world lives, the access provided to the rest of the world by the Internet and improved telecommunications means that the emerging middle classes in developing countries will not tolerate being left out of the economic largesse being enjoyed by the rest of the world.

In these ways IPOs have been a force that moves the world economy. In both developed and emerging nations, the need to raise capital by governments and enterprises alike has forced change. China presently restricts foreign ownership of its companies. Most of its IPOs have some type of government involvement and ownership, to the detriment of the public investor. In South America, many of the public companies are family-owned or closely held, with laws that allow these majority shareholders to benefit at the expense of the public shareholders. The desire to participate in the IPO market will force countries to liberalize their financial regulations. Shareholders' rights must be protected. Otherwise, foreign investors will shun these countries and their attempts to enter the U.S. and European IPO markets. These emerging countries will eventually capitulate and adopt the standards of financial ownership and regulation that are demanded by the powerful U.S. and European investors.

In developed nations a constant flow of innovative companies will provide fodder for the continuing IPO market. The Internet is challenging entrepreneurs to experiment with new ways of doing business. The revolution in biotechnology has only just begun. The retreat of socialism in Europe has freed intellectual capital. The changes being made in the European bourses to protect shareholders will entice more individuals into the IPO market.

All of this will continue to fuel and to sustain the IPO market. There will be hiccups along the way, of course, that will scare investors off—

but only temporarily. Investors' desire to make money in innovative new companies will eventually win out. As we have seen, it takes a major cataclysmic event like the collapse of several countries' currencies to stop the IPO train, but, even then, only for a short period of time.

Another reason why IPOs are here to stay is the arrival of the individual investor. At the same time that the general public realized the power and fascination of the IPO market, a number of favorable things happened, making the public's access to information and IPOs easier. The advent of the Internet, online trading, and new regulations put in place by the Securities and Exchange Commission (SEC) have considerably leveled the playing field for individual investors. Individuals can download financial information from the SEC's EDGAR and from the many financial Web sites. Online trading not only made buying and selling stock much cheaper, but a number of e-brokers realized that they could attract more investors by offering them democratic access to IPOs. The SEC made individual investors a priority and issued rules for fair disclosure. No more can companies whisper about material changes in their enterprises to a few favored security analysts. They now must widely disseminate information at the same time to investors big and small.

Institutional investors will continue to get the bulk of IPO shares. However, the rules of the game have improved somewhat as far as individual investors are concerned.

Investors in the United States and Europe have been drawn to their IPO markets in part because of their interest in innovative young companies. It's a lot more fun learning about and owning the gene chip business of Affymetrix than the tobacco business of Philip Morris. By drawing more individuals into the market to actively participate in IPOs through direct ownership and through investing in the IPO+ Fund, the importance of the individual investor is far greater now than it used to be. Laslo Birinyi, a friend of ours and a regular on the television show *Wall Street Week*, commented several years ago that his research was showing far more trades being done in smaller amounts of stock, an indication of more individual stock ownership. The growth of individually managed individual retirement accounts (IRAs) and 401(k) plans has continued that trend.

The presence of the individual investor in the equity markets is misunderstood by many. Some pundits mistakenly think that when individual investors get in the market, it's time for the really smart folks to abandon ship. That's just arrogance. There is the old story about how investment tycoons in the 1920s on hearing cabbies or shoeshine boys talk about the stock market and what they are buying, would take that as an indication of a precipitous market downturn—if the news of the stock market rally had reached the hoi polloi, then the cognoscenti ought to run in the opposite direction, fast. That indeed was true back then. Individual investors were not well informed. Many companies didn't even deign to release financial or operating information to the public. Powerful brokers had inside information, which they used to make money at the expense of the uninformed and naïve. Insiders could and did manipulate stock.

But, today, with a far more level playing field, ready access to information, and a vigilant SEC, the presence of the individual investor in the broad stock market and in the IPO market, in particular, is a sign of the vitality of our economy. The fact that individual investors are participating in equity ownership should be a source of comfort to institutional investors. Diverse stock ownership is a favorable portent for the overall equity market.

However it is a more level playing field only if you do your homework. Reading the prospectus and closely analyzing each IPO of interest will place you ahead of most of the pack. Armed with information, individual investors have the ammunition to know more about IPOs than institutional investors and are thus able to outsmart the smart money. The Web is a wonderful tool in your quest for information on IPOs. Not only can you obtain the SEC filings, but most IPOs have their own Web sites. It's particularly informative to go to an IPO's Web site and see if reality is in line with what it advertises in the prospectus. When we shorted Emerge right after the online auctioneer of cattle did its IPO, we discovered that the cattle auctions were few and far between. We concluded that the main source of their revenue couldn't be online auctions. It had to be traditional cattle sales. The company finally admitted that most of its business, at least initially, was offline, and the stock plummeted. By searching for and obtaining information on IPOs, you can avoid expensive mistakes.

Discount heavily the value of chat on the Web. Most of it is there for a reason: to promote a stock or to trash a stock. There have been numerous examples of stock promoters, some of them teenagers, who use "pump and dump" techniques on the Web to push penny stocks up in price and then to sell their own stock to unsuspecting buyers. The Internet is a great place to get information, but you have to be suspicious of what is real and what is air. To be cynical, the Web allows more false information to be passed along more efficiently. The Web has unleashed a torrent of amateur gurus and swindlers. The Internet makes it easier for these frauds to reach more prey. The flip side, however, is that the technology of the Internet makes it easier for the SEC and the FBI to track these guys down.

The Internet will also play a more important role in the future. Online trading by the customers of discount brokers will spread because it is efficient and cheap. Online and day traders have already impacted the IPO market. The rapid-fire behavior of day traders has affected the behavior of other investors, including institutions. Holding periods for IPOs are shorter and shorter. Trading in these companies is heavy. Although many studies have shown that rapid trading produces lower performance, in a volatile market, rapid turnover can lock in profits and curtail losses. Individual investors will also become more sophisticated in their use of financial tools to reduce risk. For example, to get around the ban on flipping IPOs, individual investors can and are setting up separate margin accounts at other brokers and shorting the stock of IPOs they obtained through their online broker IPO program.

Individual investors, as they become more sophisticated about the IPO market, will participate in it more and more. And they will demand more shares of IPOs. A typical trading pattern for IPOs, as we discussed, is for institutional investors to place an order for IPO shares and then buy additional shares in the aftermarket as long as the price is within their price target. However, if the IPO shoots way up in price, the institutional investor will immediately sell those shares, sometimes back to the underwriter or sometimes through a broker that makes a market in post-IPO shares. The buyers of these shares are usually individual investors. As individual investors participate more in online discount-broker programs, they will be able to use their collective power to get more IPOs.

The online discount brokers are trying to use the power of their growing numbers to convince companies going public to include them on the list of underwriters. In calmer IPO markets expect companies going public to see the wisdom of allocating more shares to individual investors, particularly if the online brokers can show a more stable pattern of ownership and longer holding periods.

We believe that IPOs have a place in the portfolio of a risk-tolerant investor. Because individuals are directly managing more and more of their own money in IRAs and 401(k) plans, it makes sense to figure out what percent of your portfolio should be allocated to this special sector of the equity market. By limiting risk through research and focusing on the best IPOs, you can build a portfolio of promising young companies for the future. Because the time horizon for your retirement assets is probably long, IPOs make sense for a certain portion of your portfolio. How large a portion depends on the risk tolerance of the investor, the size of the portfolio, and the number of years left until the funds are taken out of the portfolio. An investor close to retirement might want to set aside only 5 percent to 10 percent of his or her portfolio for IPOs. A younger person with a higher tolerance of risk might want to devote as much as 25 percent of his or her portfolio to IPOs.

We advocate investing in a portfolio of at least 10 IPOs to achieve a minimum level of diversification. By comparison, the IPO+ Fund has positions in at least 50 IPOs. By developing a portfolio of companies, you increase the probability that one or more of your investments will prove to be a real winner and you reduce the damage that a mistake can cause. A diverse portfolio should also have different types of IPOs. A portfolio of 10 enterprise-level software providers would not be diversified. The stocks would likely all trade in a similar pattern. They would all rise together, which is good. However, when the group fell from favor, they would all fall together.

Consider only a few of the stocks as long-term core holdings. These would be IPOs like Genentech or Sycamore Networks, which are clear industry leaders. These are the keepers, the long-term holds. The other IPOs in your portfolio should be watched like a hawk. IPOs are not the one-decision stocks of the 1960s that you could put in your portfolio and forget about. Expect turnover. As we've mentioned before, IPOs try to pretty themselves up as much as possible to lock in one or two quarters of financial performance. After holding an IPO for three or four months, do an objective assessment of progress. If you have any lingering questions about the investment, sell it and move on. The greatest risk that an IPO will fail occurs after the six-month mark of being a public company. Any financial chestnuts that the chief financial officer (CFO) squirreled away before the IPO are probably used up. The lockup period is over, and insiders may start selling. If you do get shares of an IPO that moves up hundreds of percent, you should consider selling because the probability of its dropping and then retracing its rise is high.

Investing in IPOs is a high-maintenance activity. Direct investment in these companies demands that you stay on top of industry developments and news releases from the company. Most of this information can be readily obtained from the company's Web site. You should regularly track quarterly filings with the SEC. Read the company's quarterly filings, called 10Qs, and look for any 8K filings, which are required if the company has any material news outside the regular quarterly filings. In response to the SEC's full disclosure ruling, more and more companies are reaching out to individual investors in their conference calls.

The late 1990s were a period of such extremes, even excesses, for IPOs that we learned our lessons well. The IPO market is always going to be a financial experiment. It's not only the place where innovative young companies raise money to commercialize new technologies; it's also the place where older, established companies spin off assets or undo a leveraged buyout (LBO). Because the IPO market is an ever changing experiment, expect the IPO market to continue to run through phases. The early 1990s brought a flood of biotechnology companies, followed by medical device companies. Then with the enactment of gambling legislation up and down the Mississippi River came a raft of riverboat gambling IPOs. The retail "category killer" phase produced Baby Superstore; Bed, Bath and Beyond; and Petsmart. Another phase was roll-ups. And then the e-tailers, business-to-business (B2B), business-to-consumer (B2C), Internet infrastructure, and enterprise-level software.

Every time the IPO market goes through a phase favoring a particular industry, it always, always gets overdone. The first riverboat gaming

IPOs did very well. That encouraged others to follow the same path. In the end, the category gets overcrowded with substandard IPO merchandise, and the stocks collapse. And, as we saw with the Internet IPOs, different sectors go in and out of fashion with astonishing rapidity. This is yet another reason why IPO investing is a high-maintenance activity. Expect to experience more of this in the years to come.

If there is one concept you should take away from this book, it is that the Wall Street IPO game doesn't change. The IPO market repeats itself over and over again. The reason why the IPO game is so difficult to master is that human nature doesn't change either. So the IPO market will continue to move through its inevitable fear-and-greed cycles.

The newness of the companies, the brashness of some of their business plans, and the diversity of the companies make the IPO market one of the most fascinating in which to invest. The best approach to take when grappling with IPOs is to view the IPO market as the financial equivalent of evolution. The development of the Internet is a perfect example. The first pure plays were the Internet service providers (ISPs), the companies that provide access to the Web for businesses. Uunet and PSI had relatively simple business models. Companies pay them not only to get on the Web, but also to maintain the servers and e-commerce connections. As in the beginning stages of developing a new technology, the first to exploit it do it in a basic way, as in providing access to the technology. These ISPs were quickly followed by other basic providers of Internet access and manipulation. These were the Web browser Netscape and then the portal Yahoo! As is always the case in experimentation, some business models work and others don't. While Yahoo! used its IPO proceeds to move from being a basic utility to being a provider of enhanced services and content, Netscape struggled. Yahoo!'s business model evolved from the time of the IPO to today. However, Netscape was unable to get out from under the crushing competition from Microsoft. And PSI, too, has had a number of problems.

These IPOs were followed by the software developers and then by the e-commerce companies, who used the new technology, the access to the Web, to try to create a new retail channel. Already, entrepreneurs were trying to find ways to further exploit the new technology. And, their ever changing business models reflected the lack of direction and the high degree of experimentation. Developing e-commerce, as we saw, was a lot like exploring the wilderness without a map, hiking boots, or a compass.

The downfall of the e-tailers in late 1999 was an example of IPO evolution at work. The IPO market efficiently and quickly eliminates inferior companies. At first it gives them a chance to thrive, but if success is not soon in coming, the stocks gets punished. While they can linger for years as $3 and $4 stocks, accessing the IPO market for additional money is not an option. Just like mother nature systematically weeds out genes that prevent organisms from being best of the breed, financial Darwinism eliminates losing IPOs by cutting off their life source—money. A good many little e-tailers tried to survive by merging with each other or by seeking private funds. London-based Ebookers, having spent millions on branding itself as the premier online airline-ticketing source, couldn't access the public markets again because it had burned through its cash too quickly and the stock price was low. They arranged private financing, and the executives threw in some money, as well. But to no avail; the time it would take to reach profitability was too far in the future.

As we recounted in the sixth chapter (Secret 6) on truly bad IPOs, it is not so much a case of survival of the fittest but that companies will fail if they are unequipped to exploit the opportunities they are seeking. Sometimes the failures are spectacular. IPO Iridium planned to offer the first global wireless service, leapfrogging over all of the incompatible wireless services offered in the United States and Europe. Its equipment and some financing came from Motorola, itself no slouch in the technology arena. It had global agreements with service providers lined up. Management was experienced. Yet, within a few years it had filed for bankruptcy. What happened? Everything seemed to be in place: a large opportunity, strong partners, solid management, a plan. As it developed, Iridium had bitten off far more than it could handle. Customers were unwilling to wait years for Iridium to offer its expensive service. They signed up with competitors that offered an acceptable service when they needed it. With fewer customers than they had projected and capital expenditures piling up, Iridium ran out of money. They couldn't access the public market again, and lenders refused to throw good money after bad. In retrospect, you can figure out why companies fail to thrive in a particular period of time under the circumstances they were dealt.

With IPOs, nothing is predetermined. A company founded by respected pros can turn out to be a complete disaster. Witness Boston Chicken, Einstein Noah, and Webvan. Strong backing, deep-pocketed venture capitalists, and prestigious investment-banking ties can prolong survival, but cannot ensure success.

As we develop and exploit the Internet, we will eventually come across strategies that make e-tailing and other kinds of e-commerce profitable. Until that time, expect more experimentation, some spectacular successes, and many failures.

It's the investor's goal to pick as many future winners as possible and to avoid the companies that won't make the grade. One of the other challenges that IPO investors face is the issue of valuation. Market capitalizations can move up or down by 50 percent or more simply because investors expand or shrink their time horizons. As we discussed in the chapter on Internet and technology IPOs (Secret 7), if you study the IPO environment, you will be able to discern whether valuation is a function of supply and demand or based on future fundamentals.

Because the methods of valuing fast-growing, innovative companies are so ephemeral, investors must understand the market conditions at the time and the rationale behind the valuations. We regard investing in Internet, technology, and biotechnology companies as akin to having an option on the future. If the company's management is experienced, the product is in demand, and the future market is sizeable, we ask ourselves, "What if it hits on all cylinders?" and conversely, "What if the projections are off?" We project way into the future and discount the projected earnings from there. We try to assess the company's future economic worth. If our assumptions have to be overly aggressive and rosy, then we know that the valuation is bloated. In the long run, the most important determinant of value is fundamentals.

Any Internet, technology, or biotechnology analyst who says that there is a fireprooof methodology to valuing these fast-growing companies is being intellectually dishonest. The only way to be certain is to take a time machine and go five or ten years into the future. If you accept the limitations of placing certain values on Internet companies, you are on your way to being a more discerning investor in this area. Since most individual and institutional investors in this area make their decisions based on price momentum, even with a few tools at hand, you will be more knowledgeable.

IPOs are for everyone. With the United States and much of the rest of the world in a once-in-a-generation period of growth, individual portfolios should be structured to capture some of that bounty. IPOs, because they represent the forces of economic activity and development, are the way to make direct investments in the future.

Although the IPO spotlight has been on Internet and technology companies, the IPO market is a diverse place. As we've discussed in *IPOs for Everyone*, IPOs are a special sector of the equity market. They are different from other stocks. Investing in IPOs requires different tools and knowledge than investing in blue-chip stocks.

We hope *IPOs for Everyone* has given you a greater understanding of the inner workings of the IPO market and a greater comfort level in investing in IPOs. Renaissance Capital is a firm believer in giving individual investors the ammunition and the information they need to make intelligent decisions. The IPO market is where great companies get their starts. Every year, it produces a Microsoft, an EMC, or a Sycamore Networks. With the tools we have given you in *IPOs for Everyone*, you now have the ability to venture into the IPO market and look for the gems that can make a real difference in your portfolio.

SECRET 12

Finding the Right Resources

Before an individual investor decides to invest in an initial public offering (IPO) or to make any investment decisions, we recommend going to the best sources. We have compiled a resource guide of some of the best Web sites for investors.

IPO Information

IPOhome.com (www.IPOhome.com). Renaissance Capital offers the most comprehensive Web site for IPO information. The content on the Web site is written by experienced IPO research analysts who share their expertise and insights on the market and on upcoming IPOs. The site offers many helpful free features, including IPO News, the IPO Pick of the Week, a Weekly Market Commentary, Best and Worst Performers, IPO Calendars, an IPO Glossary, links to IPOs' corporate websites, and an IPO course from IPO Homeroom. In addition, users may access descriptions of the companies going public, their competitors, financial information, and underwriter information. The site was recently named in *Forbes* as "Best of the Web" for IPO information. This site will provide a complete education for novice IPO investors and up-to-the-minute information on IPOs, priced deals, research, and performance. In addition, our IPO chat board is one of the most popular chat boards for IPOs, where individual investors will share their top picks and voice their opinions about upcoming and priced IPOs.

IPOhome.com also gives investors access to Renaissance IPO research which is the leading source for independent, timely, and opinionated research on every IPO. It has been used by major financial institutions and individuals, since 1992, to determine if they should buy an IPO on the offering or in the aftermarket.

IPO Mutual Funds

IPO Plus Fund (Nasdaq: IPOSX).   The first mutual fund to focus on the IPO market. The IPO+ Fund was founded in 1997 by Renaissance Capital and uses its proprietary fundamental research that covers every IPO, to determine which IPOs it invests in. The IPO+ Fund is designed for investors who want an alternative to direct IPO investment by investing in a diversified portfolio of IPOs that is professionally managed. The IPO+ Fund carries no sales load.

Hambrecht & Quist IPO & Emerging Company Fund (Nasdaq: HIPOX).   Founded in late 1999, this Fund uses a quantitative model developed by Symphony Asset Management, the Fund's subadvisor, to decide which issues to buy and sell. Hambrecht & Quist was acquired by Chase in 2000. The Fund carries a sales load of 5% to 5.5%.

MetaMarkets IPO & New Era Fund (no symbol).   Founded in late 2000 by Internet firm MetaMarkets, it focuses on businesses that are connected to or benefit from the New Economy. It posts updates of its holdings on its web site in real time. It does not carry a load.

Market News

Yahoo!Finance (www.finance.yahoo.com).   Yahoo!Finance is a good starting site where investors can find stock quotes, business descriptions, links to the company Web sites, consensus EPS estimates, insider selling information, and historical quotes. In addition, this site offers general market news, index performance, and daily highest volume and biggest gainers and losers. An added benefit for investors is the MyYahoo! account (www.my.yahoo.com), which enables users to create a personalized start page. Investors can create customizable portfolios and can view the latest stories about their portfolio companies on the start page.

Bloomberg Online (www.bloomberg.com). Bloomberg.com offers a simple navigation tool for investors who want briefings on the market and companies. The Bloomberg home page is well organized and offers financial and world headline news, after-hours trading recap, top stock movers (updated throughout the day), and technology stock news. In addition, the site offers information about mutual funds.

CBS MarketWatch (www.marketwatch.com). MarketWatch offers in-depth news and frequently updated coverage headline news on the economy, stocks, bonds, and IPOs and offers 20-minute delayed stock quotes. In addition, it offers features on personal finance, portfolio tracking, taxes, and mutual funds.

USA Today (www.usatoday.com). *USA Today* maintains a dedicated Money section that offers business headlines, economic news, features on companies and personal investing tools, and articles. *USA Today* also has international business headline news and a calendar of economic events. The Web site also has a weekly calendar of upcoming IPOs, provided to USA Today by IPOhome.com.

Message Boards

Silicon Investor (www.siliconinvestor.com). Silicon Investor's chat board is one of the most populated on the Web. Investors can look up threads (conversations) on a company or can browse through threads organized according to industry. Comments are made by mostly serious investors who often give insights on hot and cold stocks, the latest industry buzz, technology news, and so on. Browsing the threads does not require registration, but participation in discussion does. Reading discussions on stocks on the Silicon Investor is a good way to gain extra insight about stocks for both novice and experienced investors.

Raging Bull (www.ragingbull.com). The Raging Bull maintains a popular chat board for investors. Visitors can search for threads by ticker or by industry groupings and can participate in discussion after completing a registration form. The site also offers the ability to create portfolios of stocks to keep up on the latest buzz about the companies they are interested in.

Firms Offering IPOs Online

E*Trade (www.etrade.com).   E*Trade is an online broker and offers trading in stocks, bonds, options, and mutual funds. Trades may be placed for a fee, and discounts are offered after a certain number of trades are made on a quarterly basis. E*Trade offers research, portfolio tracking, online access to accounts, and online banking. Individuals can invest in IPOs via E*Trade but must complete an eligibility profile and must agree to have first read the offering prospectus. Investors should carefully consider the IPO before investing in it because E*Trade would prefer investors to hold their IPO shares for a 30-day period. Flipping IPO shares allocated by E*Trade may be detrimental to getting shares in future IPOs.

DLJdirect (www.dljdirect.com).   This online broker offers strong research capability. DLJdirect offers investors institutional research reports and daily morning notes. The site also features headline news and market data (quotes, charts, company profiles), real-time quotes (for a fee), e-mail alerts on portfolio companies, and streaming news. Other interesting features of DLJdirect are its portfolio tools, such as asset allocation, portfolio evaluation, and cash flow tracker. Account holders may participate in IPOs in which DLJdirect is an underwriter.

Datek (www.datek.com).   Datek focuses on quick execution and low-cost trading, at $10 per trade. The site offers free, streaming, real-time quotes; low margin rates; after-hours trading; and quick trade confirmations.

Fidelity (www.fidelity.com).   Fidelity, one of the largest mutual funds, offers a one-stop shop for the individual investor. Fidelity offers a customizable "My Fidelity" start page for investors to track their portfolios, stock quotes and charts, stock and market news, and political and world news. The site offers excellent financial planning and retirement planning tools, such as an overview of basic investing knowledge, tips for investing in volatile markets, and points to consider when designing an investing strategy. Another strong suit of this site is its comprehensive mutual fund section. It offers mutual fund information on Fidelity funds and features a mutual fund network, where investors can find information on other funds, including performance and fund manager information. Finally, for customers who have Fidelity accounts, the Web site also serves as an online brokerage for stocks, bonds, options, and mutual funds.

Charles Schwab (www.schwab.com).   Charles Schwab offers brokerage and aggregates news and research tools from other sites. While the price per transaction is a bit higher than other online brokers, Schwab offers many useful investment-planning tools to novice investors and allows users to customize a MySchwab home page.

Picking Stocks

TheStreet.com (www.thestreet.com).   TheStreet.com offers comprehensive market news coverage and colorful features written by James Cramer and Herb Greenberg. The site offers latest news on the economy, breaking news on companies, analyst upgrades/downgrades, interviews with mutual fund managers, Wall Street analyst rankings, and personal finance advice. TheStreet.com is a good site for updated news coverage and interesting stock ideas.

Motley Fool (www.fool.com).   Motley Fool offers irreverent investing advice for individual investors. This site requires a free registration for news and feature stories, a chat room, stock quotes, a customizable portfolio tracker, and pay-per-report Motley Fool proprietary research. Motley Fool also offers good articles and tips on managing your money, including areas on investing strategies, retirement, personal finance, and a basic investing guide. The site has regular feature profiles on strong or poor investments geared to individual investors.

Worldlyinvestor.com (www.worldlyinvestor.com).   This site is focused on international investing and is geared toward individual investors. Worldly-investor offers proprietary stories on industry sectors, stocks, mutual funds, and bonds. The site is updated every day with new feature articles on companies that investors can use to generate stock ideas. Columnists focus on telecommunications, computer, semi-conductor, and biotechnology stocks from the United States, Asia, and Europe.

IPO Registration Statements

IPOhome.com (www.IPOhome.com). The IPOhome.com Web site also has links to every IPO's registration statement. Just get to the link at the bottom of each IPO profile to get the registration statement quickly.

U.S. Securities and Exchange Commission (www.sec.gov). This is the official Securities and Exchange Commission site. Users can search by company name for all types of domestic filings, including initial public offering S-1 filings, annual and quarterly financial statements, insider stock sale registrations, and so forth.

EDGAR Online (www.edgaronline.com) and *Freeedgar.com* (www.freeedgar.com). EDGAR Online offers real-time filings for a fee. The site's best feature is the ability to search filings using text. Freeedgar.com, a free service from EDGAR Online, offers online registration statements searchable by date, ticker, and company name. The site also has a link to today's filings and offers an e-mail watchlist, which sends an e-mail to you if a company on your watchlist has filed a statement.

10kwizard.com (www.10kwizard.com). This site features the ability to view all SEC filings, to conduct text searches, and to export financial information to Excel spreadsheets.

Aftermarket Research Reports

First Call Web (www.firstcall.com). First Call, owned by Thomson Financial, offers Wall Street analyst research for a monthly subscription fee. These reports are invaluable for investors as they are a gauge of Wall Street's opinion on a stock. First Call notes are written by sell-side analysts who closely follow several companies in a specific industry. However, it is important to keep in mind that the brokerage firms where these analysts are employed often have a vested interest in the company and may sometimes paint a slightly rosier picture than reality. If you are willing to pay for this service, it is an indispensable resource.

Multex (www.multex.com). Multex is an aggregator of research written by brokerages and independent research providers (i.e., Renaissance

Capital, Market Guide, etc.). Reports can be obtained by individual investors on a per report basis for fees ranging from $4 to $150.

Search Engines

Google (www.google.com). Oftentimes in conducting fundamental research, investors need to dig a little deeper to understand a new technology (e.g., optical networking) or a new area (e.g., genomics). Google.com is one of the best search engines available for conducting general Web searches. This search engine's hit rate (successful Web sites returned) is very high, and its search capability is very flexible.

AskJeeves (www.ask.com). Users type in a question, for example, "What is a gigabit Ethernet router?" AskJeeves returns links to specific sites and offers links to other portals that contain relevant information on your selected topic.

Specific Tools

Wall Street Research Network (www.wsrn.com). Although many parts of the site are subscriber-only areas, this site has many excellent features for serious investors. In addition to offering headline market and company news, the site offers a comprehensive calendar of companies' earnings releases, earnings conference calls, board meetings, and stock splits.

Zacks (www.zacks.com). Zacks offers analysts' quarterly and annual earnings per share (EPS) estimates, overall analyst ratings, analyst consensus estimates (average estimates), a brief company profile, stock performance charts, and quarterly and annual financial data. Other features include personalizable portfolios, news articles, and 20-minute-delayed stock quotes. This site's best feature is its compilation of analyst EPS estimates for each company. Investors can view the number of buy, hold, or sell ratings a company has and the range of analyst estimates.

BigCharts (www.bigcharts.com). This site offers free easy-to-use charting tools, quotes, and news (provided by CBS MarketWatch, its parent company). The strongest features of this Web site are the industry performance charts and the customizable charts, which allow investors to compare several stocks and several indices on the same grid.

MarketGuide (www.marketguide.com).   This site is one of the best aggregators of information. In addition, affiliate sites like Telecom Investor, Internet Investor, and Biotech Guru are good ways for an individual investor to begin understanding the major trends affecting these sectors, not to mention ways to generate some stock ideas.

Stock Exchanges—Domestic

New York Stock Exchange (www.nyse.com).   The official Web site for the New York Stock Exchange contains NYSE news, regulations, calendars, updates on accounting and policy changes, and updates on newly listed and delisted companies. Also the site lists most-recent disciplinary actions taken against companies, trading halt criteria, market news and an investor education area.

Nasdaq (www.nasdaq.com).   This site contains NASD-sponsored conferences and events, a calendar for market closings, NASD policies, and news. In addition, the site offers general market and stock data, academic papers, and guidance regarding decimalization, margin accounts, and Nasdaq dispute resolution.

Stock Exchanges—Foreign for New Companies

London Stock Exchange's Alternative Investment Market (AIM) (www.londonstockexchange.com).   Launched in 1995, AIM is the London Stock Exchange's alternative investment market for new and fledgling companies. This stock exchange was created to meet the needs of younger companies by loosening listing requirements. The companies that trade on this market range in industry sector, size, and maturity. This site contains a list of companies listed on AIM, stock quotes, and links to company Web sites.

Neuer Markt (www.neuer-markt.de).   The Neuer Markt is the Deutsche Boerse's segment for high-growth companies. The site offers a list of companies traded on the Neuer exchange, stock quotes, daily winners and losers, most actively traded, new issues, and the latest news on European exchanges.

Tokyo Stock Exchange (www.tse.or.jp) and *Tokyo Mothers Market.* The official site for the Tokyo Stock Exchange offers a list of companies traded on all Japanese exchanges, including the new Mothers market. The Mothers market is for younger and earlier stage companies and has less strict listing requirements. The site offers recent Tokyo market news, recent listed and delisted companies, stock quotes, daily advancers and decliners, most actives, market statistics, and bond and option information.

APPENDIX A

Directory of Underwriters

This directory of underwriters was compiled by Renaissance Capital Corporation. Inclusion on this list is not an endorsement of the underwriter or of its initial public offerings.

ABN AMRO
Foppingadreef 22
NN-1102 BS Amsterdam
The Netherlands
31-20-628-9898
www.abnamro.com

Adams, Harkness & Hill
60 State St.
Boston, MA 02109
617-371-3900
www.ahh.com

The Advest Group, Inc.
90 State House Square
Hartford, CT 06103
860-509-1000
www.advest.com

A. G. Edwards, Inc.
One N. Jefferson Ave.
St. Louis, MO 63103
314-955-3000
www.agedwards.com

AXA Financial, Inc.
1290 Avenue of the Americas
New York, NY 10104
212-554-1234
www.axa-financial.com

Barington Capital Group
888 7th Ave.
New York, NY 10019
212-974-5700
www.barington.com

Banc of America Securities LLC
600 Montgomery St.
San Francisco, CA 94111
415-627-2000
www.bofasecurities.com

Bear Stearns & Co. Inc.
245 Park Ave.
New York, NY 10167
212-272-2000
www.bearstearns.com

C.E. Unterberg, Towbin
Four Embarcadero Center
San Francisco, CA 94111
415-659-2222
www.unterberg.com

Chase H&Q
One Bush St.
San Francisco, CA 94104
415-439-3000
www.hamquist.com

CIBC World Markets
200 Liberty St.
New York, NY 10281
212-667-7400
www.cibcwm.com

Commonwealth Associates
830 Third Ave.
New York, NY 10022
212-829-5800
www.comw.com

Credit Suisse First Boston
  Corporation
11 Madison Ave.
New York, NY 10010-3629
212-325-2000
www.csfb.com

Dain Rauscher Corporation
Dain Rauscher Plaza
60 S. 6th St.
Minneapolis, MN 55402-4422
612-371-2711
www.dainrauscher.com

Daiwa Securities Group Inc.
6-4, Otemachi 2-chome, Chiyoda-ku
Tokyo 100-8101
Japan
81-3-3243-2111
www.daiwa.co.jp/index-e.html

Deutsche Banc Alex. Brown
1 South St.
Baltimore, MD 21202
410-727-1700
www.alexbrown.db.com

Deutsche Bank AG
Taunusanlage 12
60325 Frankfurt
Germany
49-69-910-91000
www.deutsche-bank.de

E*TRADE Group, Inc.
4500 Bohannon Drive
Menlo Park, CA 94025
650-331-6000
www.etrade.com

Fahnestock Viner Holdings Inc.
20 Eglinton Ave. W.
PO Box 2015
Toronto, Ontario M4R 1K8, Canada
416-322-1515

Fechtor, Detwiler & Co., Inc.
225 Franklin St.
Boston, MA 02110
617-747-0100 or
800-451-0100
www.fede.com

Ferris, Baker Watts Incorporated
100 Light St.
Baltimore, MD 21202
800-436-2000
www.fbw.com

First Albany Companies Inc.
30 S. Pearl St.
Albany, NY 12201-0052
800-462-6242 or
518-447-8500
www.fac.com

First Analysis Securities Corporation
The Sears Tower
233 S. Wacker Drive
Chicago, IL 60606
312-258-1400
www.firstanalysis.com

First Union Securities, Inc.
River Front Plaza
901 E. Byrd St.
Richmond, VA 23219
800-999-4328 or
804-782-3278
www.firstunionsec.com

FleetBoston Robertson Stephens
555 California St.
San Francisco, CA 94104
415-781-9700
www.rsco.com

Friedman, Billings, Ramsey Group
1001 19th St. N.
Potomac Tower
Arlington, VA 22209
888-200-4350 or
703-312-9500
www.fbr.com

Gerard Klauer Mattison & Co., Inc.
529 Fifth Ave.
New York, NY 10017
800-309-1371 or
212-885-4000
www.gkm.com

GKN Holding Corp.
61 Broadway
New York, NY 10006
800-338-8964 or
212-509-3800
www.gknholding.com

The Goldman Sachs Group, Inc.
85 Broad St.
New York, NY 10004
212-902-1000
www.gs.com

Hanifen, Imhoff Inc.
1125 17th St.
Denver, CO 80202
303-296-2300
www.hanifen.com

HSBC Holdings plc
Thames Exchange
10 Queen Street Place
London EC4R 1BL,
United Kingdom
44-22-7260-9000
www.hsbc.com

ING Barings
350 Park Ave.
New York, NY 10022
800-838-6096 or
212-251-3403
www.ingbarings.com

InvemedAssociates Inc.
375 Park Ave.
New York, NY 10152
212-421-2500

Janney Montgomery Scott LLC
1801 Market St.
Philadelphia, PA 19103-1675
800-526-6397 or
215-665-6000
www.janneys.com

Jefferies & Company, Inc.
11100 Santa Monica Blvd.
Los Angeles, CA 90025
310-445-1199
www.jefco.com

John G. Kinnard & Co.
920 Second Ave.
Minneapolis, MN 55402
612-370-2844
www.kinninvest.com

Josepthal Lyon & Ross
200 Park Ave.
New York, NY 10166
212-859-9200
1-800-836-4639

J.P. Morgan & Co. Incorporated
60 Wall St.
New York, NY 10260-0060
212-483-2323
www.jpmorgan.com

Ladenburg Thalmann
590 Madison Ave.
New York, NY 10022
212-409-2000
www.ladenburg.com

Laidlaw Holding
100 Park Ave.
New York, NY 10017
212-376-8800

Lazard Frères
30 Rockefeller Plaza
New York, NY 10020
212-632-6000
www.Lazard.com

Legg Mason Wood Walker, Inc.
100 Light St.
Baltimore, MD 21202
410-539-0000 or
800-368-2558
www.leggmason.com

Lehman Brothers Holdings Inc.
3 World Financial Center
New York, NY 10285
212-526-7000
www.lehman.com

McDonald Investments, Inc.
800 Superior Ave.
Cleveland, OH 44114
216-443-2300
www.mcdonaldinvest.com

Merrill Lynch & Co., Inc.
4 World Financial Center
New York, NY 10281-1332
212-449-1000
www.ml.com

Mesirow Financial Holdings Inc.
350 N. Clark St.
Chicago, IL 60610
312-595-6000
www.mesirowfinancial.com

Morgan Keegan, Inc.
Morgan Keegan Tower
50 Front St.
Memphis, TN 38103
901-524-4100
www.morgankeegan.com

Morgan Stanley Dean Witter & Co.
1585 Broadway
New York, NY 10036
212-761-4000
www.msdw.com

National Securities Corporation
1001 Fourth Ave.
Seattle, WA 98154
206-622-7200
www.nationalsecurities.com

The National Security Group, Inc.
661 E. Davis St.
Elba, AL 36323
334-897-2273

Needham & Company, Inc.
445 Park Ave.
New York, NY 10022
212-371-8300
www.needhamco.com

The Nomura Securities Co., Ltd.
1-9-1, Nihonbashi, Chuo-ku
Tokyo 103
Japan
81-3-3211-1811
www.nomura.com

Pacific Growth Equities, Inc.
4 Maritime Plaza
San Francisco, CA 94111
415-274-6800
www.pacgrow.com

Paine Webber Group Inc.
1285 Avenue of the Americas
New York, NY 10019
212-713-7800
www.painewebber.com

Parker/Hunter Incorporated
600 Grant St.
Pittsburgh, PA 15219
800-441-1514 or
412-562-8222
www.parkerhunter.com

Paulson Investment Company, Inc.
811 SW Naito Pkwy.
Portland, OR 97204-3332
503-243-6000
www.paulsoninvestment.com

PMG Capital Group
Four Falls Corporate Center
Conshohocken, PA 19428
610-260-6200
www.pennmerchant.com

The Principal Financial Group
711 High St.
Des Moines, IA 50392-0001
800-986-3343 or
515-247-5111
www.principal.com

Prudential Securities Incorporated
1 New York Plaza
New York, NY 10292
800-368-8654 or
212-214-1000
www.prusec.com

Punk, Ziegel & Company
520 Madison Ave.
New York, NY 10022
212-308-9494
www.pzk.com

Ragen MacKenzie Incorporated
999 Third Ave.
Seattle, WA 98104
206-343-5000
www.ragen-mackenzie.com

Raymond James Financial, Inc.
880 Carillon Pkwy.
St. Petersburg, FL 33716
727-573-3800
www.rjf.com

R.J. Steichen & Company
One Financial Plaza
120 S. 6th St.
Minneapolis, MN 55402
800-328-4836 or
612-341-6200
www.rjsteichen.com

Roth Capital Partners, Inc.
24 Corporate Plaza
Newport Beach, CA 92660
800-678-9147 or
949-720-5700
www.crut.com

Salomon Smith Barney Inc.
388 Greenwich St.
New York, NY 10013
212-816-6000
www.smithbarney.com

Scott & Stringfellow, Inc.
909 E. Main St.
Richmond, VA 23219
800-552-7757 or
804-643-1811
www.scottstringfellow.com

SG Cowen Securities Corporation
Financial Square
New York, NY 10005
800-221-5616 or
212-495-6000
www.cowen.com

Simmons & Company International
700 Louisiana
Houston, TX 77002
713-236-9999
www.simmonsco-intl.com

Stephens, Inc.
111 Center St.
Little Rock, AR 72201
800-643-9691 or
501-377-2000
www.stephens.com

Sutro & Co. Incorporated
201 California St.
San Francisco, CA 94111
800-557-8876 or
415-445-8323
www.sutro.com

Thomas Weisel Partners LLC
Pacific Telesis Tower
One Montgomery St.
San Francisco, CA 94104
415-364-2500
www.tweisel.com

Tucker Anthony Incorporated
One Beacon St.
Boston, MA 02108
617-725-2000
www.tucker-anthony.com

U.S. Bancorp Piper Jaffray Inc.
Piper Jaffray Tower
222 S. 9th St.
Minneapolis, MN 55402
612-342-6000
www.piperjaffray.com

UBS Warburg LLC
299 Park Ave.
New York, NY 10171-0026
212-821-3000
www.ubswarburg.com

Wasserstein Perella & Co., Inc.
31 W. 52nd St.
New York, NY 10019
212-969-2700
www.wasserella.com

Wessels, Arnold & Henderson
901 Marquette Ave.
Minneapolis, MN 55402
612-373-6100

William Blair & Company, L.L.C.
222 W. Adams St.
Chicago, IL 60606
312-236-1600
www.wmblair.com

Wit Sound View Corporation
826 Broadway
New York, NY 10003
212-253-4400
www.witsoundview.com

WR Hambrecht + Co.
539 Bryant St.
San Francisco, CA 94107
415-551-8600
877-673-6476
www.wrhambrecht.com

APPENDIX B

Top 25 IPO Underwriters

(Ranked by Number of IPOs Over 5 Years)

Ranking	Company Name
1	CS First Boston
2	Goldman Sachs
3	Morgan Stanley Dean Witter
4	DB Alex Brown
5	Robertson Stephens
6	Salomon Smith Barney
7	Merrill Lynch
8	Chase H&Q
9	Lehman Brothers
10	Banc of America Securities
11	Bear Stearns
12	UBS Warburg Dillon Read
13	CIBC World Markets
14	SG Cowen
15	Prudential Securities
16	J. P. Morgan
17	William Blair
18	PaineWebber
19	Volpe Brown Whelan & Company
20	Dain Rauscher
21	USB Piper Jaffray
22	ING Barings Furman
23	Needham & Company
24	A.G. Edwards
25	Morgan Keegan

APPENDIX C

A Short History of IPOs

This short history of IPOs, starting with the first joint stock companies that financed trading and ending with the slew of Internet-related companies four hundred years later, shows that time after time, the IPO cycle repeats itself over and over again: Early investors profit from a new invention or a way of conducting commerce. Later, me-too investors lose money because they ignore warning signals and bloated valuations. In the eighteenth century, British investors were easily duped by dubious companies that proposed to privatize the national debt and to salvage Spanish shipwrecks for gold. American investors were likewise bamboozled two hundred years later by companies proposing to develop cyberspace, financed by the proceeds from IPOs.

1602   Amsterdam merchants fund a joint stock company called the **Dutch East India Company** to exploit the tea and spice trade in the Far East. This was one of the first attempts to organize a joint stock offering and float shares.

1621   Amsterdam merchants fund another joint stock company called the **Dutch West India Company**, first to exploit Spanish colo-

Sources: Renaissance Capital, the New York Stock Exchange, *Devil Take the Hindmost* by Edward Chancellor (Farrar Straus & Giroux, 1999), *The Great Game* by John Gordon Steele (Orion Business, 1999), *The Big Board* by Robert Sobel (The Free Press, 1965).

nies, but wind up founding New Amsterdam in 1626 strictly for trading the riches of the upper Hudson River Valley.

1680   Not to be outdone, the British Government charters three companies that raise money on Britain's stock exchange, the **East India Company**, the **Royal African Company**, and **Hudson's Bay Company**. All are investment favorites for years.

1697   Stocks collapse in London. Only thirty percent of the 140 companies traded in London survive. In a panic that would be repeated numerous times on the London and U.S. stock markets, some of the bellwether companies lost 70 to 80 percent of their values.

1710   **Sun Fire**, Britain's first insurance company, goes public.

1718   North America becomes the target of IPO madness when John Law induces French investors into the **Louisiana Company**, which had rights to develop areas in the Mississippi Valley. Like the Internet IPOs of 1999, the Louisiana Company lacked revenue and earnings and couldn't pay the promised dividends. It imploded in 1720 in the "Mississippi Bubble." The word *millionaire* is coined.

1720   IPO madness reaches Great Britain, with British investors flocking to buy shares of the **South Sea Company**, which was formed to privatize the national debt. Britain's love for the IPO began before the offering, and it was snapped up in hours. Everyone from the king to shopkeepers goes in on the action.

1791   New York's first "hot issue," the **Bank of the United States**, sells out in an hour and a half. It is followed by the Million Bank of the State of New York and Tammany Bank in the first IPO frenzy.

1792   The **Bank of New York** debuts on the New York Stock Exchange.

1799   The predecessor of **Chase Manhattan Bank** starts off its public existence as a water company.

1812   **Citigroup's** predecessor, City Bank, raises capital two days before the outbreak of war between the United States and Great Britain.

1817   Construction begins on the **Erie Canal**, enabling easier transport between East and West and marking the beginning of feverish demand for canal construction.

1824   **Consolidated Edison's** predecessor, New York Gaslight Company, goes public. Scores of soon-to-be defunct canal companies sell shares.

1827   Infatuation with railroads gets rolling. The **Baltimore & Ohio Railroad** sells shares at $100.

1834   **Erie Railroad** raises $10 million at the height of railroad fever. It would take 17 years and $24 million to complete.

1844   Samuel Morse founds the **Magnetic Telegraph Company** to build a telegraph line between New York City and Philadelphia. **American Express** and **Wells Fargo** get their starts.

1849   The California Gold Rush begins.

1850   During the 1850s, nearly 360 railroad stocks raise money on Wall Street, along with 985 bank stocks and 75 insurance companies.

1860   The Civil War puts a damper on IPO issuance.

1878   **Bell Telephone Company** is sold to a group of investors.

1881   **Philip Morris** goes public in London. It later moves its offices and incorporates in New York City in 1919.

1884   **Eastman Kodak** goes public with 14 shareholders.

1891   After over 60 years as a partnership, **Procter & Gamble** lists on the New York Stock Exchange on June 11. It sells stock in blocks of 100 shares and has a single-share price of $100.

1892   Edison Electric Light Company and the Thomson-Houston Company merge, forming **General Electric**, which today has the world's highest market capitalization. It is the only company that was in the original Dow Jones Industrial Average and still is today.

1896   The Klondike Gold Rush starts.

1901   **American Telephone & Telegraph (AT&T)** and **Eastman Kodak** list on the New York Stock Exchange. **U.S. Steel** is formed.

1903   The so-called "Rich Man's Panic" hits the stock markets. The Wright Brothers take their first flight.

1906   Founded in 1886 as the R. W. Sears Watch Company in Minneapolis, **Sears, Roebuck**, moves to Chicago and expands into the mail order business. In 1906, to raise capital, Sears offers common and preferred stock to the public.

1911   The U.S. Supreme Court orders the dissolution of **Standard Oil**, resulting in the spin-off of 34 companies. Among these companies are the predecessors of **Exxon/Mobil**, **Chevron**, **ARCO**, **BP Amoco**, and **Penzoil**.

1914   World War I interrupts commerce, but in its wake a flood of new companies come to market. The stock market closes. The Federal Reserve is established.

1919   **Coca-Cola** is sold to a group of Atlanta investors for $25 million. According to the Coca-Cola Web site, the same investors take the company public later in the same year at $40 a share. Today, those original shares are worth $6.7 million each. Other notable debuts during this time period include: **General Motors**, **Honeywell**, **International Paper**, **Merck**, **Mobil**, **Pacific Gas & Electric**, and **Philip Morris**. The Nineteenth Amendment passes, marking the beginning of Prohibition.

1929   **Caterpillar Tractor** goes public. The stock market crashes.

1930   **North American Aviation (Rockwell International)** lists on the New York Stock Exchange.

1933   The U.S. Congress passes the Securities Act of 1933, which establishes rules regarding fraudulent misstatements of information and mandates minimum standards of disclosure by new issuers of securities in an offering prospectus. Out of this legislation springs the modern form of preliminary prospectus known as the Red Herring.

1934   The Securities Exchange Act of 1934 codifies many of the regulatory financial disclosure requirements that distinguish private companies from publicly traded companies. Before 1934, the main differentiation between private and publicly traded firms was whether such companies were listed for trading on a recognized exchange.

It also requires brokers and stock exchanges to follow rules established by the Securities and Exchange Commission (SEC).

In the same year, **Boeing** goes public.

1940   **Walt Disney Productions** offers 600,000 shares of common stock at $5 plus preferred, raising $3.5 million. *Pinocchio* and *Fantasia* premiere.

Investment Company Act of 1940 establishes laws governing mutual funds. Mutual funds become the top target of investment banks peddling initial public offerings.

1941   The United States enters World War II.

1942   **J.P. Morgan**, one of the nation's leading banks, offers stock. **Pfizer**, founded in 1852 and now one of the world's largest pharmaceutical companies, debuts with 240,000 shares offered.

1943   **Motorola**, in its IPO, encourages employees to buy shares at the $8.50 offer price.

1944   **Johnson & Johnson** goes public, offering shares at $34.75. Not accounting for splits, today, one share would be worth $108,000.

1945   **Corning Glass Company** debuts on the New York Stock Exchange. Japan surrenders. World War II ends.

1956   **Ford Motor Company** offers shares in what was at the time the largest public offering ever. The 10.2 million shares, which made up 22 percent of the family-owned concern, raised a record $643 million.

1957   **Hewlett-Packard**, the legendary technology company, debuts.

1966   **McDonald's** does its IPO. According to the company, 100 shares purchased in the offering at a cost of $2,250 have multiplied through stock splits into 74,360 shares today, worth over $2 million.

1968   Shoemaker **Dexter**, the oldest continuously operating company in the United States, founded in 1767, lists on the New York Stock Exchange. Berkshire Hathaway later acquires it.

1969   Initially founded in 1919 by C.V. Starr as American Asiatic Underwriters, insurer **AIG** relocates to New York from Shanghai and goes public.

1970   **Donaldson, Lufkin & Jenrette** becomes the first member firm of the New York Stock Exchange to go public. Thirty years later, it is acquired by CS First Boston.

1971   Sam Walton opened his first Wal-Mart discount store in 1962. Nine years later, **Wal-Mart** offers its first shares to the public. It eventually grew to be the largest retailer in the United States.

1980   **Apple Computer** kicks off the personal computing boom, going
       public in December at $22 a share.

       Genentech becomes the first biotechnology company to go
       public, offering 1.1 million shares at $35 and jumping to $71.25
       on its first day.

1981   After losing his job at the age of 49, Bernie Marcus, along with
       friend Arthur Blank, founds home improvement retailer **Home
       Depot** in 1979. In its IPO, Home Depot raises $4 million. It lists
       on the New York Stock Exchange in 1984.

1986   **Microsoft** and **Home Shopping Network** go public, both more
       than doubling. **EMC**, a maker of computer memory and stor-
       age products for corporate computing environments was taken
       public by one of **Renaissance Capital**'s founders, Kathleen Smith,
       while an investment banker at Merrill Lynch. From January 1,
       1990, to December 31, 1999, EMC's stock rose 80,575 percent.
       It went on to achieve the highest single-decade performance of
       any listed stock in the history of the New York Stock Exchange.

1987   The stock market has its historic October crash. The IPO mar-
       ket is flattened until the end of the year.

1990   The initial public offering of **Cisco Systems** is a precursor to the
       explosion of demand for Internet infrastructure equipment.

1991   **Renaissance Capital**, the first IPO research firm is formed.

1992   **America Online**, the preeminent provider of online services,
       offers shares to the public at $11.50. This offering precedes the
       explosion of Internet-related business in the coming year. One
       hundred shares purchased at this offering would now be worth
       nearly $600,000.

1993   The hot **Boston Chicken** at first more than doubled. Later, it
       would prove to be a turkey.

1995   Marks the debut of Web browser **Netscape**, which rose from $28
       to $58.

1996   **Yahoo!** becomes the hottest of the hot, nearly tripling. Investor
       attention is now Web centric.

       Vimpel Communications becomes the first Russian IPO on the
       New York Stock Exchange.

1997 **Amazon's** IPO marks the beginning of the craze for online retailers.

1997 **Renaissance Capital** starts the first ever mutual fund solely devoted to IPOs, the IPO+ Fund (IPOSX).

1998 In August, the near global financial implosion puts the damper
on IPOs. But that doesn't deter Internet community **Geocities**
from its debut, nor **eBay** a month later. In November,
theglobe.com breaks the 600 percent barrier for the first time.

1999 The greed cycle of the IPO market sets in early in the year. This
is the midpoint of the great bull run in IPOs. There isn't a
dot.com that investors don't like. **MarketWatch.com, Healtheon,
Pacific Internet, pcOrder, Multex.com, Cheap Tickets, iVillage,**
and **Priceline.com** were members of the Class of Spring 1999.
Where are they now?

1999 is also the year of records. The largest non-U.S. IPO is
priced—**ENEL SpA** raises $16.5 billion. **United Parcel Service**
becomes the largest U.S. IPO, raising $5.5 billion. And **VA Linux**
produces the biggest first-day return.

This year was also notable for the explosion in demand for fi-
ber-optics equipment makers. Companies such as **Juniper Networks** and **Sycamore Networks** go public at this time, taking
advantage of interest in next-generation telecommunications
networks.

What goes around comes around. After being acquired by Roche,
biopharmaceutical company **Genentech** goes public again.

Venerable Wall Street icon **Goldman Sachs** becomes the last of
the bulge-bracket investment banks to go public.

2000 More IPOs soar through a 100 percent gain on the first day of
trading than in IPO history. However, it is a time when only a
few notable IPOs are able to sustain their first-day pricing gains.
Rising oil prices, tightening by the Federal Reserve, presidential election uncertainties, and mid-East conflicts conspire to produce a sell off in stocks, particularly new issues. Memorable IPOs
include **Palm, Capstone Turbine,** and **Krispy Kreme Donuts.** In
fact, as the new century begins, only one-third of all Internet-
related IPOs are above their original IPO prices.

Glossary of IPO Terms

Renaissance Capital is dedicated to educating individual investors about the IPO market. We hope that this glossary of common IPO terms will help you feel more comfortable with IPO investing and more confident when talking with your broker or investment adviser. (Italicized terms are defined in this glossary.)

Allocation: The amount of stock in an initial public offering (IPO) granted by the underwriter to an investor. For most IPOs, the allocation is significantly less than the *indication of interest*. The allocations are meted out based on commission volume, trading history, and type of investor. IPO allocations are normally communicated to investors the morning after the pricing.

Aftermarket: Trading in the IPO subsequent to its offering. Trading volume in IPOs is extremely high on the first day because of *flipping* and *aftermarket orders*. Trading volume can decline precipitously in the following days.

Aftermarket orders: Buying IPO stock in the days after the IPO first goes public. Underwriters look favorably on investors who place aftermarket orders. Although underwriters cannot solicit aftermarket orders, some expect investors to purchase two or three times their IPO allocation in the aftermarket.

Aftermarket performance: The price appreciation (or depreciation) in IPOs as measured from the offering price and going forward. However, to obtain a better benchmark of IPO aftermarket performance, some investors track performance from the *first day close*.

American Depository Receipts (ADRs)/American Depository Shares (ADSs): A certificate issued by a U.S. bank for a share or shares of a non-U.S. company. Non-U.S. companies that wish to list on a U.S. exchange must abide by the regulatory and reporting standards of the Securities and Exchange Commission (SEC). These securities are called receipts because they represent a certain amount of the company's actual shares. Examples of ADRs are France Telecom, British Sky Broadcasting, and Equant.

Beauty contest: The process by which the executives of a company that is considering doing an IPO interview a number of investment banks to determine which ones would do the best job of managing the offering and providing ongoing research reports once the company is public. The parade of investment bankers through a company's offices is known as the beauty contest.

Blanked: The term given to the situation when an investor places an *indication of interest* for shares in an IPO and receives no shares.

Blue sky laws: State securities laws designed to protect individual investors. The phrase purportedly originated from a state judge who said that the securities of a particular company had all the value of a patch of blue sky. Both companies and mutual funds are affected by state blue sky laws. However, the SEC and Congress have superseded these rules because the rules in some states are obsolete, arbitrary, and poorly enforced.

Board of directors: The group of people who oversee the executives of a company. The composition of the board of directors is particularly critical for an IPO. Typically, a board is composed of both inside and outside directors. Inside directors could be management, significant shareholders, venture capitalists, vendors, or relatives. Outside directors have no underlying financial or personal relationship with the company that could create a conflict of interest and are on the board for their experience, business judgment, and contacts. Outside directors may own stock but are not large shareholders. Investors should look for a board that has at least two outside directors. Typically, IPOs add their first outside directors at or immediately after the offering.

Breaking issue price: When an IPO's trading price in the aftermarket is less than its IPO price. This is not a good thing. Regardless of fundamentals, investors regard breaking issue price as a bad omen. In the old days of Wall Street, *syndicates* of underwriters would prop up the IPO price with a *stabilizing bid,* often for days. Due to profit considerations, the *lead manager* may disband the syndicate even if the IPO is cratering.

Bucket shop: Brokerage firms with dubious reputations. Many of these are fly-by-night operations, consisting of many brokers making cold calls to investors. These shops specialize in low priced "penny stocks," which they sell to one fool and then to a greater fool. The brokers may hop from shop to shop, just ahead of federal regulators.

Buy-side: Term that describes institutional investors and members of the professional investment community including mutual funds, hedge funds, trusts, and financial advisers.

Calendar: Refers to upcoming IPOs and *secondary* offerings. Brokerage houses have equity calendars, bond calendars, and municipal calendars. (See IPOhome.com for IPO calendars.)

Capital markets: Another label for the potential investing pool made up of money managers and investment firms that buy into *initial public offerings* of new stocks or bonds.

Carve-out: A specific type of *spin-off* in which the corporate parent consolidates a particular line of business (e.g., Cantor Fitzgerald's combination of its electronic bond trading units into one subsidiary) and then sells that newly created subsidiary to investors. In essence, the company is "carving out" a piece of its business with a specific business focus and selling it to the public to highlight the value of niche business operations within the larger company. It is usually done in the form of a true spin-off with an independent board and separate financial statements, but heavy cross ownership by parent. Sometimes it is done in the form of a tracking stock structure (e.g., AT&T Wireless).

Class action suit: Litigation undertaken on behalf of shareholders against companies whose shares have declined in price, alleging misstatements or omissions in the *preliminary prospectus* or other material communicated to the public. These lawsuits, now harder to mount due to federal legislation, are spearheaded by a handful of law firms specializing in this area and are focused on recent IPOs and technology companies.

Clearing price: The lowest price at which all shares of an IPO can be sold to investors in a *Dutch auction*. Sometimes referred to as the "market clearing price."

Commissions: The money paid to brokers for buying or selling stock; ranges from 3 to 5 cents a share for institutions to 15 cents a share for discount brokers. But when investors purchase an IPO at the *offering price*, they pay no commission. Instead, the underwriter charges the issuing company a *gross spread*, which is the difference between the public offering price and what the issuing company received. Typically, this spread is 5 percent to 7 percent of the IPO's offering price. The high profitability of doing IPOs is one important reason why investment banks focus on developing this business.

Comparables: Similar, already public companies of which investment bankers study the valuations to decide how to price an IPO. The pricing range indicated in the registration statement or in the prospectus reflects the proposed valuation of the IPO relative to the comparables. It is critical to select good comparables. Bankers sometimes lean toward comparables with high valuations, but knowledgeable investors do their own homework. Sometimes, an IPO may be the first company in its industry to go public. Then there are no comparables. In those cases, investors look to analogous companies on which to base a valuation. Companies that had no direct comparables at the time they went public include Yahoo!, Amazon, and MFS (now Worldcom).

Contrarian investing: The opposite of *momentum investing*. Contrarians stress taking long positions in stocks that are out of favor or short positions in stocks that are in favor. Contrarians seek to build positions before a price trend develops.

Covering: The process of unwinding a short position by purchasing shares of the company sold short and returning them to the entity from which the short seller borrowed.

Day-to-day (DTD): A term used to describe an IPO listed on the offering calendar; indicates that the lead underwriter does not have sufficient orders in the book. IPOs listed as DTD are likely to be *postponed.*

Dead cat bounce: The brief rebound a stock makes after it has dropped significantly in price. It is likely caused by short sellers closing out positions rather than by real buying.

Depositary Trust Company (DTC): Essentially a clearinghouse between institutional buyers and sellers of securities and brokers. It allows institutional investors to seamlessly buy and sell stock using multiple brokers.

Direct public offering (DPO): The process by which some companies try to go it alone by selling their shares directly to the public to avoid the cost of expensive lawyers and investment bankers. This has been used by small consumer products companies with loyal customers. These offerings are usually extremely small and highly illiquid.

Due diligence: An in-depth examination of a proposed IPO that the investment bankers and lawyers for the underwriters conduct as part of the process of taking a company public. They speak with management about the company's prospects, strategy, competitors, and financial statements. Information that is material to the company's prospects must be disclosed in the prospectus.

Dutch auction: An alternative to the traditional *negotiated pricing* process used by underwriters to set IPO prices. This method requires the underwriter to solicit bids from potential investors. Investors indicate the number of shares that they want and the price that they are willing to pay per share. Shares are then priced at the lowest *clearing price.* Allocations are made with priority given to the highest bidders, first with regard to bid price and then according to bidded share size. Because the only considerations taken into consideration for allocating shares are the bid price and shares, this pricing method does not discriminate between institutions and individuals with regard to allocations. W. R. Hambrecht is the only investment bank to employ this method and does so only through the use of an online bidding platform.

EDGAR: Established by the SEC, the system used by companies and mutual funds to file documents electronically. It is significant to individual investors because they can directly access the EDGAR filing room on the Internet (www.edgar.gov) and retrieve IPO prospectuses, annual reports, and quarterly filings.

Event-driven investing: A strategy that emphasizes investing in companies whose stock prices are likely to be strongly affected by an anticipated significant news event or circumstance.

Fallen angel: Stocks that were once high fliers that fell out of favor with investors and experienced a precipitous decline in price.

Fast money: Derogatory term often used to describe short-term investors and frequent traders. Also called *hot money*.

Fast track: The accelerated course toward an IPO taken by some companies that are extremely confident that their registration statements will pass SEC review with no changes. They print the *preliminary prospectus* immediately and begin the *road show* process. It usually takes eight weeks for an IPO to complete the offering process, which begins with the filing of the *registration statement* with the SEC and ends with the pricing of the IPO.

Final prospectus: The prospectus that a company prints and distributes to buyers of its IPO after the IPO has been priced. The final prospectus contains the information presented to the public in the *preliminary prospectus*, printed before the offering plus the actual offering price and number of shares.

First-day close: The closing price at the end of the first day of trading. It reflects not only how well the *lead manager* priced and placed the deal, but also what the near-term trading is likely to be. For example, IPOs that shoot up 300 percent or 400 percent on their first day of trading are likely to fall back in price on subsequent days due to profit taking. Conversely, IPOs that break offer price immediately are likely to drop further as institutions bail out. *Breaking issue price* right out of the box is a poor reflection on the lead manager's pricing and placement.

Flipping: The immediate selling in the *aftermarket* of shares of stock that were bought at the IPO price. While many flippers are small players looking for a point or two of quick profit, large, well-known mutual funds also practice flipping. It is a controversial practice because the underwriters want to control the trading in the IPO immediately after it goes public and the company wants their shares placed with long-term investors. However, flipping also provides liquidity for additional purchases of stock. The underwriters try to discourage flipping by placing stock in the hands of long-term investors. Nevertheless, flippers who are identified by underwriters move on to flip again by setting up new firms. Brokerage firms try to curb flipping by individual investors by imposing waiting periods and fees on sellers and a *penalty bid* on the individual's broker. However, the largest institutional investors and mutual funds continue to flip with impunity because of their great size and influence.

Float: The volume of a company's shares held by the general public. When a company is publicly traded, a distinction is made between the total number of shares outstanding and the number of shares in circulation. For example, if a company offers 2 million shares to the public in an IPO and has 20 million shares outstanding, its float is 2 million shares.

Friends and family: IPO shares set aside by underwriters to be allocated, at the behest of the issuer, to individuals and entities that have a close working or familial relationship with the issuer. These shares are sold at the IPO price. Examples include suppliers, top customers, consultants, and employee relatives.

GARP: An acronym that stands for "growth at reasonable prices." This is a popular investment style that blends elements of growth and value investing. The goal of GARP investing is to buy fast-growing companies and market leaders at valuation levels that can be justified by company fundamentals and expected future returns.

Going with the "Mo": Trading slang describing a strategy for buying stocks when a security has a strong trend of price appreciation and selling them when the price appreciation trend weakens. The strategy is also used to short stocks that show a strong trend of falling prices. "Mo" is short for momentum.

Green shoe: A typical underwriter agreement that allows the underwriters to buy up to 15 percent more shares at the offering price for a period of several weeks after the offering. This option, also called the *overallotment,* may be exercised if the deal is oversubscribed. The ability to buy additional shares also allows the underwriter to manage the aftermarket trading by meeting additional demand. The term comes from the Green Shoe Company, which was the first to have this option.

Gross spread: The difference between the public offering price and what the issuing company received. When you purchase an IPO at the offer price, you pay no *commission.* Instead, the underwriter charges the issuing company a gross spread. Typically, this spread is 5 percent to 7 percent of the IPO's offering price. The profitability of doing IPOs is one important reason why investment banks focus on developing this business.

Group sale: The allocation by the underwriters of the overwhelming bulk of IPO shares to a small group of large investors or an investment bank's best clients. Usually indicative of both high demand from big investors and the desire by the issuer and the banker to restrict distribution to a more knowledgeable and stable investor base.

Hot deal: An IPO for which there is significantly more demand than supply. The term *hot deal* has particular significance to the SEC because federal law prevents hot IPOs from being sold to owners or employees of broker-dealers and other industry insiders.

Hot money: Derogatory term often used to describe short-term investors and frequent traders. Synonymous with *fast money.*

Indication of interest: An order for a specific amount of stock given to the lead manager by an investor interested in buying an IPO. Since most IPOs are oversubscribed, indications of interest are usually for several times what the investor really wants. On some deals, the valuation of the IPO may be an issue. In this case an investor might give a limit order for the IPO. For example, the investor might say, "I'm in up to $15," meaning that he or she will take shares if they are priced at $15 or less.

Initial public offering: The event of a company first selling its shares to the public. Due to unseasoned trading and lack of information, equities are often referred to as IPOs for months, if not years, following their debuts.

Insiders: Individuals privy to information about the operations of a company not known to the general public. Management, directors, and significant stockholders are regarded as insiders. Insiders are restricted in the timing and manner in which they can dispose of shares. (See Lockup Period.)

IPO+ Fund: The first mutual fund to specialize in investing in IPOs. The IPO+ Fund is managed by Renaissance Capital.

IPO Research: A research report that an underwriter is allowed to issue after an IPO. These research reports are invariably positive. Prior to the offering, the underwriters involved in the IPO are prohibited from issuing research or recommendations. Renaissance Capital, through our IPO Intelligence research service, provides independent analyses of these companies. Renaissance Capital is the leading provider of this specialized research to prominent institutional investors. This research is available at IPOhome.com.

Keeper: A stock with compelling investment fundamentals based on industry, product, or technology leadership, growth potential, developing market trends, and strong management team. These are stocks that investors are inclined to "buy and hold" and to accumulate during corrections and brief down-ticks. Sometimes referred to as "best idea" stocks because of their inclusion in focused funds that only contain money managers' top ideas.

Lead manager: The underwriter who has ultimate control of an *initial public offering*. Other underwriters are called co-managers. The names of the managers appear on the bottom of the front page of the prospectus, with the lead manager's name on the uppermost left. The lead manager controls all aspects of the offering, from how many shares of stock the co-managers get to sell, to the timing of the *road show*, to the ultimate pricing of the deal.

Leveraged buyout (LBO):   When a public company goes private by issuing a lot of debt to buy out insiders. By definition, LBOs are highly leveraged. Management is counting on improved margins through cost cutting or revenue growth to generate cash flow, which will enable them to pay down the debt. Given the chance, LBOs will do a reverse LBO by selling stock in the public market by doing an IPO to raise cash to pay down the debt.

Lockup period: The period of time—usually 180 days—for which *insiders* are restricted from selling their IPO shares. However, the lead underwriter has the option of lifting the lockup period earlier. Knowledgeable investors track the termination of lockup periods, knowing that stocks may weaken at about the six-month mark. (See IPOhome.com.)

Market capitalization: The total market value of a firm. It is defined as the product of the company's stock price per share and the total number of shares outstanding. The market cap should not be confused with the *float*, which is the amount of shares in circulation. A company's total market cap can greatly exceed the market cap of floated shares, especially in the case of a new publicly traded company, because many of the outstanding shares are held by insiders and not floated.

Momentum investing: An investment style that emphasizes buying stocks with the strongest price appreciation trend or shorting stocks with the strongest price depreciation trend. Momentum investors are often unconcerned with company fundamentals and focus instead on near-term *event-driven* catalysts likely to drive prices strongly up or down.

Negotiated pricing: The traditional process used by underwriters to price IPOs. Underwriters solicit and receive *indications of interest* from their large institutional clients. The underwriter then makes a subjective appraisal of aggregate demand by looking at the *order book* and speaking with large clients. The underwriter sets the price, in consultation with the issuer, at a level that balances the conflicting need to raise capital for the issuer and to compensate their *buy-side* clients for the risk of investing in companies without trading histories.

Net offerings: The SEC for years has allowed small companies to bypass the expensive system of using an underwriter through the Small Company Offering Registration process. Because many of the companies doing direct public offerings use the Internet to attract buyers by posting their prospectuses on the Internet these offerings are called Net offerings.

Net road show: An online version of the *road show*. The Internet (Net) has opened up a new way for companies to sell their deals to the public. Underwriters are starting to post on their Web sites the presentation that management makes to institutional investors. These Net road shows range from the video of an actual road show presentation, complete with questions from investors, to slides accompanied by audio. Regrettably, underwriters limit access to Net road shows to institutional investors by requiring passwords and changing them frequently.

Offering price: The price at which the IPO is first sold to the public. It is set by the *lead manager*, usually after the close of stock market trading the night before the shares are distributed to IPO buyers. In the case of some foreign IPOs, the pricing occurs over the weekend.

Offering range: Indicated on the front page of the *preliminary prospectus*, the price range within which a company expects to sell stock. The range usually has a spread of $2. For example, $15 to $17. However, the ultimate price to the public may be above the range, below the range, or within the range, depending on demand and market conditions.

One-on-ones: Private meetings between the most powerful institutional investors and the management of the IPO. As with the group *road show* presentations, management is limited in its discussion to what is contained in the *preliminary prospectus.*

Order book: The listing of buy orders from investors. It indicates how well orders are building for an IPO or a *secondary* deal. The book for a deal can be many times *oversubscribed.* In fact, an oversubscribed deal is desired by both underwriters and investors because it means that there will be an initial pop in the stock when it begins trading. Also referred to as "the book."

Overallotment: The fancy name for the *green shoe*, the underwriting agreement that allows the underwriters to buy up to an additional 15 percent of shares at the *offering price* for a period of several weeks after the offering.

Oversubscribed: The term used to describe a deal that has more orders than there are shares available. Many underwriters like to see a book several times oversubscribed because they know that investors inflate the size of their *indications of interest*. When a book is grossly oversubscribed, it is said to be a *hot deal*.

Penalty bid: A fee imposed by some brokerage firms on an individual broker whose client sells an IPO within a certain period of time. This is done to discourage individual investors from quickly selling IPOs. Thus, a broker who would incur a financial penalty if a client wants to quickly sell an IPO has a built-in conflict of interest. Long a little-publicized practice, penalty bids are now receiving greater scrutiny by the SEC and some state regulatory agencies. In any case, individual investors should find out before buying an IPO whether the brokerage firm imposes penalty bids. However, if your broker fails to return telephone calls or fails to sell securities as you direct, you should seriously—and immediately—consider changing brokers.

Pinks: A form of a *preliminary prospectus* containing no price range or number of shares; sometimes used by foreign companies doing an IPO in the United States. The *offering price* and number of shares are eventually set and published in the *final prospectus*.

Pipeline: The number of IPOs scheduled to offer their shares. Once a company files its registration statement (or S-1) with the SEC, it becomes part of the expected pipeline of IPOs expected to be priced over the next few months. It usually takes an IPO eight weeks to emerge from SEC review to its offering.

Postponed: The deferment of an IPO to a later time, if ever. This is what happens when an IPO fails to attract sufficient buyers. Sometimes the *lead manager* will lower the price to entice buyers. When a deal is postponed, it usually takes at least six months for an IPO to hit the comeback trail. Examples of big name IPOs that had successful debuts the second time around after being postponed were Donna Karan and Goldman Sachs.

Preliminary prospectus: The offering document printed by the company containing a description of the business, discussion of strategy, presentation of historical financial statements, explanation of recent financial results, management and their backgrounds, and ownership. The preliminary prospectus has red lettering down the left-hand side of the front cover of the prospectus and is called the *red herring*. It is the company's principal marketing document. Management, when touring on the *road show*, is limited to discussing only the information contained in the prospectus.

Premium: The difference between the IPO price and its opening price. In a perfect world, IPOs are designed to be priced at a discount to existing publicly traded companies. In theory, this is meant to reward early investors for buying an unseasoned company with no public track record. In reality, it is the *lead manager*'s educated estimate of the highest price at which there will be solid demand for the IPO, both on the offering and in the *aftermarket*. Some investors think the difference between the IPO price and the price at the first day's close is a better measurement of the IPO premium due to the confusion that normally surrounds balancing buy and sell orders at the opening.

Price action: Refers to the character of recent trading activity in a particular stock, usually within the context of price volatility and trend strength over a short span of time.

Public venture capital: A derogatory term used to describe a company in an early stage of development (i.e., lacking revenues, operating profits, and perhaps even products) that ordinarily would be financed with private capital trying to access the public markets by doing an IPO.

Quiet filing: An SEC filing lacking pertinent information. Sometimes a company has unresolved issues—choice of underwriter, number of shares to be offered, timing—or thinks it may have a lengthy SEC review. Such a company would make a quiet filing of its *registration statement*. The registration statement might lack an *offering range*, number of shares to be offered, and the total number of shares.

Quiet period: The further restrictions on the issuance of research faced by the underwriters after the IPO is priced. It lasts up to 25 days. However, under some circumstances the underwriters can issue a research recommendation more quickly. If the distribution is complete, meaning they have disbanded the *syndicate* and are not exercising the *overallotment*, the SEC allows a safe harbor for research.

Red herring: The term of art for the *preliminary prospectus*. It gets its name from the printed red disclaimer on the left side of the prospectus.

Registration statement: A document that a company must file with the SEC to go public. This document, the S-1, filed electronically via EDGAR, contains a description of the company, its management, and its financials. The material is reviewed by the SEC for its completeness, amount of disclosure, and its presentation of accounting information. The IPO cannot go forward until the SEC is satisfied with the document. In some cases, where the SEC takes issue with a company's accounting methodology, for example, the registration process can take months.

Renters: IPOs of the moment that are in demand more because of positive group momentum than underlying fundamentals. These are short-term holds. Often these stocks sell off once positive momentum tires and investors move on to the next hot area. Generally, these stocks lack the growth or tangible results that distinguish market leaders from me-too companies. They are prime candidates to become *fallen angels*.

Reverse Leveraged Buyout (LBO): The decision to go public by a company that took itself private through a *leveraged buyout*. A common investment strategy is for the management of a company or a financial group to acquire a company using debt. These buyouts are usually highly leveraged, hence the name LBO. When the owners decide to use the IPO market to reduce the company's debt load, the process is called a reverse LBO because they are replacing debt with equity. They are able to accomplish this only if they have improved the operations of the company sufficiently to attract public equity holders.

Road show: A series of breakfasts, lunches, and dinners during which management makes its pitch to institutional investors when a company launches its IPO. These presentations are organized by the *lead manager* and are held at hotel dining rooms in major cities. Usually, but not always, the road shows start on the West Coast and finish in New York or Boston, which have the highest concentrations of large institutional investors. For particularly hot IPOs, these presentations attract hundreds of investors who are jammed 10 or 12 to a table.

Roll-up: An IPO of independent companies in the same industry that merge into a single company at the time of the offering. Mostly used in fragmented industries, the approach has been applied to equipment rental firms, floral distributors, office products distributors, travel agencies, temporary staffing organizations, dental practices, and car dealerships. The financier most associated with the concept is Jay Ledecky, who took public U.S. Office Product, U.S. Floral Products, and Consolidated Capital, which invests in roll-ups.

Secondary: The selling of additional stock to the public via an offering underwritten by investment banks by a company that is already publicly traded. Companies conduct secondary offerings to raise more capital for the firm and to increase the liquidity of the stock to attract additional holders and trading activity.

Selling shareholders: The shareholders of the IPO who are selling shares at the time of the offering. The front cover of the prospectus indicates the total amount of shares being offered. The identities and breakdown of shares sold are detailed within the prospectus. The prospectus will also indicate whether shareholders will be selling on the *green shoe*. Investors should be skeptical of any IPO in which shareholders are selling large amounts of stock.

Sell-side: Term used to describe the investment banking, equity research, institutional sales, and retail brokerage divisions of securities firms. Referred to as the *sell-side* because of the sales functions these departments take on in the underwriting process and as trading-commission generators.

Short sale: A tactic used when an investor expects a company's shares to decline in price. The investor borrows shares from an entity that owns the shares and sells them on the market. In return, the lender is entitled to interest on the shares borrowed and a return of the shares. A position is considered closed out when the investor buys back the shares and returns them to the original owner. This is known as *covering*.

Short interest: The percentage of a company's publicly traded shares that have been sold short and have not been purchased and returned to the original owners. Sometimes seen as a proxy for positive or negative sentiment about a stock.

Short squeeze: A situation that occurs when those with *short interest* are forced to buy back their shares and close out their short positions because of strong buying pressure.

Shotgun investing: The tactic of making diversified investments within a young industry or sector in which market leadership is unclear. The idea is to identify and gain exposure to potential market leaders at reasonable prices. As a leadership hierarchy comes into focus, investors then peel off positions in marginal entities and consolidate their investments in the strongest players.

Smart money: Experienced and big investors that are well integrated into the Wall Street information flow and tend to be ahead of the market in anticipating budding trends.

Spinning: Giving important brokerage firm customers shares of an IPO. A little talked about subject until the *Wall Street Journal* published an article describing how some investment banks favored certain clients with IPO shares in the hope of getting future investment banking business. For example, the CEO of a privately held Silicon Valley software firm who has an account with XYZ Securities might find that he or she was the recipient of a tidy profit from several thousand shares of a particularly hot issue that was bought and sold on the same day.

Spin-off: The selling by a company of a portion or all of a division to the public in the form of an IPO. The parent company would do a spin-off for several reasons. First, to raise capital; the parent may be highly leveraged. Second, to rationalize its operations by selling off a noncore business. In this type of spin-off the managers of the newly public company are (or should be) motivated to perform well by getting stock in the new spin-off. Finally, a parent may decide to spin off a division to draw attention to it and perhaps to raise the stock price of the parent.

Stabilizing bid: The attempt by the *lead manager* to ensure a successful IPO. After the IPO begins trading, the lead manager may decide that the members of the *syndicate* need to provide a stabilizing bid to ensure that the IPO doesn't fall below its *offering price.*

Stuffed: Getting more shares of an IPO than you wanted. Institutional investors usually make indications of interest that are several times larger than what they really want, hoping to get a reasonable *allocation.* While this strategy works most of the time, sometimes the *order book* doesn't build the way the lead manager hopes. At this point, the *lead manager* can cut the price of the offering, which might increase demand, cut the size of the offering, or give the institutional investors all the stock they requested. This is called "getting stuffed." Institutional investors who get stuffed usually think there is something wrong with the stock and sell, putting pressure on the stock price and confirming that the deal was a dud.

Syndicate: The group of underwriters who have the responsibility for selling the IPO to the general public. A syndicate can consist of 2 managers for a small IPO or 10 managers for a large multi-*tranche* offering. A syndicate might include underwriters who specialize in institutional business as well as retail-oriented firms. Syndicates once had a legitimate selling function. Today, the *lead manager* usually does all of the selling. The co-managers just share in the risk of underwriting the IPO.

Teach-In: A presentation by the management of an IPO to stockbrokers. To educate the sales force about an upcoming IPO, the lead manager will sponsor a teach-in during which time the management of the IPO will make a presentation to the sales force and answer their questions. This event normally occurs at the launch of the road show.

Tombstone: The advertisement of an IPO in financial newspapers. When an IPO is completed, the *underwriting group* advertises their involvement by publishing a list of underwriters in the financial press. The underwriters are listed in descending order of importance. The lead manager's name appears on the uppermost left.

Tracking stocks: The carve-out of a business from a large company. When a parent company wants to recognize the underlying value of one of its businesses, it can either spin off a portion of the shares of the company to the public, thus establishing a value for the business, or it can issue tracking stock. Unlike the shares of a spin-off, which have claim to the assets and profits of the spun-off company, a tracking share has no such claim. As the term states, the shares are meant to "track" the performance of that particular business. A parent company may choose to issue tracking stock because it wants to retain full voting control over the business or because the assets of the division cannot be easily separated from the parent. Tracking stock is also called "letter stock." Examples of tracking stocks are GMH (GM's Hughes division), ZD Net (Ziff Davis's Internet division), and AT&T Wireless.

Tranche: A French word used to describe segments of the IPO being sold in different countries. A multi-tranche distribution is commonly used for large U.S. and foreign IPOs where there is demand both in the United States and in the home country.

Underwriter: A brokerage firm that agrees to buy shares of stock from a company and sells them to the public at an agreed-upon price. Underwriters assume the risk of selling the stock to the public. The underwriter controlling the sale is called the *lead manager.*

Underwriting group: The brokerage houses that team with the *lead manager* to underwrite an IPO. Members of the selling group are part of the syndicate, the group of underwriters formed to underwrite an IPO. The manager and co-managers reserve the actual selling of IPO shares (and the accompanying fees) to themselves. Underwriting group members are usually listed on the prospectus because they performed prior services to the company going public and get only a small portion of the fees from the offering. However, underwriting group members do share legal and financial risks of the underwriting.

Unseasoned: A new company that has just begun trading. One reason why IPOs are different from stocks in the broader market indexes is that they lack a trading history, have a limited float and have not developed long-term shareholders who are knowledgeable about the company. For these reasons the stock is said to be unseasoned.

Valuation multiple: An approach to valuing companies that relies on comparing a company's stock price to its income from operations, cash flow from operations, or earnings per share. The higher the multiple, the more richly valued the company is. Underwriters use valuation multiples of an IPO's peers, or *comparables*, to determine the appropriate level at which the IPO should be priced.

Vaporware: Derogatory term for IPO issuers peddling products that are not yet commercialized or that lack significant demand from potential customers. Often used when the investment community harbors suspicions that an issuer's growth targets are not supported by past sales uptake. Also a generic expression for companies with wildly optimistic hopes for speculative business models.

Venture capital: Firms that invest in private companies that need capital to develop and market their products. In return for this investment, the venture capitalists exact a price—significant ownership of the company and seats on the board of directors. For the most part, venture capitalists focus on companies in the technology, medical and retail sectors. Venture capitalists raise money from institutional investors, state pension funds, and high-net-worth individuals, usually in the form of partnerships. Investors should look at the venture capital firm's track record and expertise when evaluating an IPO.

Vultures: A somewhat unflattering term for investors who purchase the equity of companies whose stock prices are severely depressed. Vultures try to capitalize by purchasing what they consider to be assets underpriced by the market. After buying up stock on the cheap, vultures wait for a reversal of fortune in the stock price and then unwind their position. Vultures are most often associated with leveraged buyout firms looking for deeply discounted companies in need of restructuring. The LBO firms rarely choose to make a long-term ownership commitment and instead prefer to opportunistically liquidate. For this reason, vultures are sometimes called financial buyers. IPOs of companies that are concurrently doing a *reverse LBO* usually have the involvement of this type of investor.

Whisper numbers: Earnings estimates that are often circulated within the investment community but are different from estimates found in research reports written by Wall Street equity analysts. The discrepancy in official estimates and word-of-mouth estimates results from models that are not always up to date and the tendency of analyst models to be conservative. It is asserted by some that analyst estimates do not truly reflect the analysts' performance expectations since much of the information that filters down to Wall Street comes directly from the subject companies. Much of the controversy surrounding whisper numbers has to do with why Wall Street does not incorporate independent value judgments when formulating estimates, rather than blindly accepting information from companies eager to manage expectations.

Index